The African and Caribbean Historical Novel in French

Francophone Cultures and Literatures

Michael G. Paulson and Tamara Alvarez-Detrell
General Editors

Vol. 3

PETER LANG
New York • Washington, D.C./Baltimore
Bern • Frankfurt am Main • Berlin • Vienna • Paris

Paschal B. Kyiiripuo Kyoore

The African and Caribbean Historical Novel in French

A Quest for Identity

PETER LANG
New York • Washington, D.C./Baltimore
Bern • Frankfurt am Main • Berlin • Vienna • Paris

Library of Congress Cataloging-in-Publication Data

Kyoore, Paschal B. Kyiiripuo
The African and Caribbean historical novel in French: a quest for identity/
Paschal B. Kyiiripuo Kyoore.
p. cm. — (Francophone cultures and literatures; vol. 3)
Includes bibliographical references and index.
1. Historical fiction, African (French)—History and criticism.
2. Historical fiction, Caribbean (French)—History and criticism.
3. French-speaking countries—In Literature. 4. Caribbean Area—
in literature. 5. Africa—In literature. I. Title. II. Series.
PQ3984.K95   843'.08109—dc20   94-16864
ISBN 0-8204-2555-9
ISSN 1077-0186

Die Deutsche Bibliothek-CIP-Einheitsaufnahme

Kyoore, Paschal B. Kyiiripuo:
The African and Caribbean historical novel in French: a quest for identity/
Paschal B. Kyiiripuo Kyoore. – New York; Washington, D.C./Baltimore;
San Francisco; Bern; Frankfurt am Main; Berlin; Vienna; Paris: Lang.
(Francophone cultures and literatures; Vol. 3)
ISBN 0-8204-2555-9
NE: GT

Cover design by Nona Reuter.

The paper in this book meets the guidelines for permanence and durability
of the Committee on Production Guidelines for Book Longevity
of the Council of Library Resources.

© 1996 Peter Lang Publishing, Inc., New York

All rights reserved.
Reprint or reproduction, even partially, in all forms such as microfilm,
xerography, microfiche, microcard, and offset strictly prohibited.

Printed in the United States of America

To the memory of
my father Germano Kyoore Siekyoghrkure
my mother Monica Kyiiripuo
to my brothers and sisters;
you taught me wisdom and human dignity

Textual Note

The expression "pure-blooded African" used in reference to some characters in the chapter on Antillean writers means "slaves newly arrived from Africa". This clarification is to avoid misinterpretation of the intended meaning of the term.

We sometimes inadvertently use the pronouns "she" and "her" instead of "he" and "his" respectively when referring to O.R. Dathorne. We regret the typographical error.

Table of Contents

Acknowledgements	ix
Preface	xi
Introduction: *Notions of Historical Fiction and the Importance of the Negritude Movement*	1
1. Paul Hazoumé: *Doguicimi*	33
2. Nazi Boni: *Crépuscule des temps anciens*	57
3. Jean Malonga: *La Légende de M'Pfoumou Ma Mazono*	79
4. Ahmadou Kourouma: *Monnè, outrages et défis*	101
5. Léonard Sainville: *Dominique Nègre Esclave*	123
6. Edouard Glissant: *Le Quatrième Siècle*	149
Conclusion	167
Notes	191
Bibliography	199
Index	211

Acknowledgements

I am grateful to my former Professor, the late Dr. Richard Bjornson of The Ohio State University who was a mentor to me. The late Dr. Josaphat Kubayanda, my former Spanish Professor, both at the University of Ghana and The Ohio State University, as well as a brother in our Dagara clan system, was an inspiration to me.

I owe a word of gratitude to Professor Jack Corzani, Director of the Centre d'Etudes Littéraires Maghrébines, Africaines et Antillaises (C.E.L.M.A) of Université de Bordeaux III (France). He introduced me to post-graduate work on francophone African and Caribbean writers.

A Joyce Fellowship sabbatical leave from Gustavus Adolphus College during the Spring Semester of 1995, gave me time to edit the final version of my manuscript.

This book is my contribution under the African "palaver tree."

Preface

Critics of African and Caribbean literatures have examined the issue of hegemonic relationships between the colonizer and the colonized within the colonial context. Works such as those of Frantz Fanon, Aimé Césaire, Albert Memmi and Edward Said among others, have influenced in no small way the recent anti-colonialist school of critics.

In this book, I examine some of the early as well as more recent literary works, some of which were inspired by the Negritudist movement which sought to define the Black "being" by revalorizing what was perceived as black culture.

Post-colonial literary theories have something in common with the whole ideology behind the creation of the Negritude movement. Negritudists were reacting to their situation as colonial subjects. They found a need to redefine their identity in an attempt to reject the image imposed by the colonial predicament. Today, we find some of Senghor's theories narcissistic and essentialist. Nonetheless, the point being made here is that post-colonial literary theorists do in many ways adopt some of the tactics of Negritudist discourse. Why is there the need to redefine the way we read African, Caribbean and Afro-American literature? Because we realize that there is some re-appropriation of the discourse of the colonized and former colonized in Western literary criticism. Therefore, I believe Afro-centricity (we do not always agree on its definition!) is an alternative way of reading texts by Africans of the continent and the Caribbean diaspora.[1]

We need to examine the ideological motivations behind the tendency for scholars to neglect works such as those of Paul Hazoumé. Is it for purely literary reasons? For, after all, *Doguicimi* is not of a lesser literary value than some of the so-called classical European historical novels. Afro-centric reading offers an alternative way of looking at the texts examined in the present study.

My choice of some early writers such as Hazoumé was motivated by the desire to demonstrate how anthropology-inspired works of fiction in the colonial period were an attempt to redefine the history of African peoples. The factors that influenced the creation of historical fiction in francophone Africa and the Caribbean are closely examined. My study suggests that Glissant and Sainville are two Martiniquan writers at very different levels in terms of their literary sophistication. Their stance on Negritude is also quite divergent. All the writers examined here had something in common. They all wrote historical fiction, but they also brought their different personal experiences to bear upon their fictional creation. The choice of African writers is limited to the sub-Saharan region because that was the scope of my research. There are also other francophone Caribbean writers whose works could have been included in this study. It is not a study on Negritude, but we need to appreciate the tremendous impact that the concept had on some of the writers whose works are examined here.

The debates surrounding Negritude, Afro-centricity, and post-colonial literary theory are evidence that there is a constant challenge to redefine ourselves in the contemporary geo-political system where hegemonic forces continue to define other peoples through only their world-view. This book is a modest attempt to examine how some African and Caribbean writers redefine their societies through historical fiction.

Introduction:
Notions of Historical Fiction and the Importance of the Negritude Movement

Much has been written about the European historical novel. However, the African and Caribbean historical novel in French has not received the attention it deserves. Considerable research has been done on Negritude poetry, which shares many ideological concerns with the African and Caribbean historical novel, but until now, scholars have not devoted an equivalent effort to the study of the African and Caribbean historical novel as a genre and as a form of socially committed writing.

This study proposes to define the term "historical novel" and to focus on the type of historical novel that has emerged in Francophone Africa and the Caribbean. In general terms, the historical novel can be defined as a novel inspired by actual historical events. In such novels, the evocation of a genuine past is crucial to the act of fictional creation. As Alfred Sheppard says, "without the Past, the Historical Drama and the Historical Novel would have no interest, no use and no meaning" (Sheppard 10).[1] He goes on to argue that the definition of the term "historical novel" must recognize a past in which imagination plays an important role.

According to this definition, the historical novelist creates fiction from his or her imagination which, however, employs the facts of history as its essential raw material. It is this quality of imagination that guides the novelist in choosing what aspects of history to focus upon and what aspects to omit. This selection on the part of the novelist is dependent on where he or she places primary emphasis and upon the ideological stance that lies behind the fictional creation.

Critics like Arnold Bennet have argued that the author of a historical novel re-creates an age in which he did *not* live (quoted in Sheppard 15). This criterion does not provide a sufficient basis for defining the historical novel, because the authors of such works in many cases witnessed at least some of the events they recount in their narratives. As such cases demonstrate, history cannot be arbitrarily defined in terms of a distant time period; history continues to occur in the present. What distinguishes a historical novel from any other novel is therefore the fact that the historical novel is mainly inspired by actual historical events in a way that other forms of novels are not.

Jonathan Nield introduces another possibility for defining the historical novel when he argues that "a novel is rendered historical by the introduction of dates, personages or events, to which identification can be readily given" (Sheppard 15). In Sir Walter Scott's work for example, we encounter the most important personalities of English and, to a lesser extent, French history: Richard-the-Lion-Hearted, Louis XI, Elizabeth, Mary Stuart, Cromwell, and others.

As Sheppard points out, historical novelists are faced with the problem of selection. They must continually decide what to reject and what to select in terms of events, characters, and other markers of historical time (Sheppard 85). This selection process can have different sorts of impact on the reader. For example, it can draw attention to events or characters generally regarded as insignificant by historians. From this perspective, the selection process influences readers' perceptions of history. They are made to re-evaluate their own understanding of history because this selection questions certain commonly accepted interpretations of history as it is recorded within the context of a certain canon.

Authors of historical novels also frequently introduce minor characters and fill in gaps left by documentary history. For instance, Scott's "hero" is always a more or less average English gentleman. He generally possesses a certain, though never outstanding, degree of practical intelligence, as well as moral fortitude and a sense of decency. Ivanhoe is a "romantic" medieval knight who is a correct and decent but average representative of the English petty aristocracy. The choice of such a character therefore lends importance to characters who have little or no importance in the eyes of historians.

The choice of minor characters to "fill in the gaps" of history enables novelists to go beyond historians in making history "come alive" by enhancing the vividness of events and demonstrating how they affect real people—people with whom readers can empathize. In depicting an inarticulate mob for example, serious historians have little opportunity to document the responses of individuals, whereas historical novelists are free to invent individuals whose responses enable readers to experience what it must have been like to participate in such events (Sheppard 238).

According to Paul Veynes, history involves the narration of true events, whereas novels present imagined events as if they were true. In this context, history resembles a science, although it differs from scientific endeavors in the sense that it seeks not to acquire knowledge about the singularity of events, but about their specificity, about what is intelligible about them. Although he contends that history is impersonal, he also points out that it shares certain characteristics with historical fiction:

> L'histoire est un roman vrai et la conception que l'histoire se fait de la "causalité" historique est exactement la même que celle que se fait un romancier de la causalité, telle qu'il la met en œuvre dans son roman... (1970, 423-424)
>
> [History is a true novel and the conception that history makes of historic "causality" is exactly the same that a novelist makes of causality, as he uses it in his novel...]

Introduction

In his book *Comment on écrit l'histoire*, Veynes goes on to argue that historians must make choices to avoid narrating small details that would detract from the larger picture they are attempting to create. Choice is also necessary to avoid the indifference that readers would feel if all facts were treated as equally valuable. However, choice always introduces an arbitrary factor, for historians must always fill in the gaps with hypotheses—what Veynes calls "rétrodiction" (the historical synthesis that results from the process of "filling in"). Because this process occurs in the writing of history as well as in the writing of historical fiction, the authenticity of all historical narration is questionable. For, how can anyone measure the extent to which the author of a history has filled in the gaps of his narrative with the products of his own imagination? As long as the notion of history itself remains ambiguous, the concept of the historical novel will also be problematic.

In a more recent study than that of Sheppard and Veynes on historical representation, Hayden White argues that what distinguishes "historical" from "fictional" stories is first and foremost their content rather than their form. The content of historical stories is events that really happened, rather than imaginary events; events invented by the narrator (1987, 27). Yet some of the writers of historical fiction considered in this book, claim authenticity for their historical fiction.

This book discusses the problem implied in the claim to historical authenticity made by African and Caribbean writers, for such claims are by their nature based on an ideology that views "History" as an important ingredient in their quest for authentic cultural identity. The use of historical facts in these novels is problematic as well because we know that, in the final analysis, they are still works of fiction.

The writer most commonly associated with the development of the genre that has come to be known as the historical novel is Sir Walter Scott. Through his meticulous attention to minute details, Scott created a vivid sense of local color in novels such as *Ivanhoe* and *Waverly*. As suggested in Sheppard's definition of the historical novel, Scott enhances the vividness of events and seeks to evoke their impact on individual people. The attempt to convey an impression of this impact has in fact become a defining characteristic of the historical novel, often enabling writers to underline the moral and political lessons they would like readers to draw from their works.

The economic and ideological basis for Scott's historical novels derives in part from the transformation that occurred in people's existence and consciousness as a consequence of the French Revolution (Lukács 31). According to Georg Lukács, Scott's historical novel is the direct continuation of the great realistic social novel of the eighteenth century. The enormous social and political transformations of the past provoked a feeling for history, an awareness of historical development in England. Scott takes advantage of this sentiment by seeking to embody the most important stages of English history in his writing. As Lukács points out, he does so by portraying the struggles and antagonisms of his society by means of characters who, in their psychology and destiny, always represent social trends and historical forces. Lukács concludes that:

> Scott's greatness lies in his capacity to give living human embodiment to historical social types. The typically human terms in which great historical trends become tangible had never before been so superbly, straightforwardly and poignantly portrayed. And above all, never before had this kind of portrayal been consciously set at the center of the representation of reality. (45)

The principle of typicality described by Lukács can also be found in African and Caribbean historical novelists, as can Scott's awareness of the connectedness of past, present, and future. Elaine Jordan believes that a Romantic principle of piety and continuity lies at the heart of Scott's writing: a sense of the past that is necessary to a proper sense of the present and the future (in Baker 146). This same sense later became a driving force behind the writing of African and Caribbean historical novels. Lukács regards Scott as a patriot who was proud of his people and their history, and according to him, this cultural pride is essential for the creation of genuine historical novels. A similar pride in their people also characterizes the writing of African and Caribbean historical novelists.

Scott was not the only important European historical novelist who was inspired to write novels that expressed this sense of cultural pride. It has often been a driving force behind the historical novelist's search for an authentic identity. In France, Alfred de Vigny in his historical novels goes back to the time of Richelieu in order to reveal, in artistic form, the historical sources of what he considers as "errors"—the socio-political systems that have impeded a positive transformation of French society. Unlike Scott, Vigny makes the dominant figures of history the main characters in his novels. His portrayals of them are generally accompanied by moral reflections. Like Victor Hugo, he perceives history as a series of moral lessons for the present (Lukács 77). In fact, this tendency is nearly always evident in historical novels.

Lukács defends the view that "the great task of the historical novel is to *invent* popular figures to represent the people and their predominant trends" (317). He further argues that there are important similarities between the classical period of the historical novel and the historical novel of the twentieth century. Although both aim at presenting the historical movement of popular life in its living relation to the present, the twentieth-century historical novel is more closely linked with the great and urgent problems of the present. For

Lukács, this emphasis on the present contrasts sharply with the earlier historical novels of, for example, Gustave Flaubert.

Lukács also discusses the way in which a writer's political commitment achieves expression in the historical novel. For him, the writers of contemporary historical novels have the opportunity to promote a better understanding of the people's heroic struggles against imperialist exploitation, and oppression, for today's historical novelists depict the historical forerunners of these struggles (345). Lukács' concept of the European historical novelists is also applicable to African and Caribbean historical novelists, for they too are inspired by the forerunners of the present generation in their struggle against colonial hegemony, exploitation, and oppression—in this case the slavery and colonialist institutions that were imposed on them by Europeans.

We also endorse Dorothy Blair's definition of the African historical novel as "a serious and reverent attempt to recreate a chronicle of past times and the exploits of authentic or semi-legendary figures" (73). It is a valid criteria for both the African and Caribbean novels considered in this book.

To understand the ideological basis for the sort of historical novel that emerged in francophone Africa and the Caribbean, one must view the writing of its practitioners within the context of the Negritude movement. Negritude was a cultural and political awakening of black intellectuals in a world dominated by European hegemonic discourse that sought to impose on them a Euro-centric concept of the world. Black intellectuals were interested in going back to their roots to define their own authentic cultural identity in terms of its linkage to Africa. Indeed, historical factors had made it necessary for them to undertake the search for cultural identity in the first place, for such a quest involves their need to affirm a viable cultural identity in a world that had denied the very existence of their culture.

The idea of cultural authenticity was central to the development of the Negritude movement, the origins of which can be traced back to the American Negro-Renaissance movement (or Harlem Renaissance) at the beginning of this century. In 1903, W.E.B Dubois wrote *The Souls of Black Folk*. In it, he questioned the American racist system, and contended that black Americans had as much right to freedom as did any other citizens. Dubois' writing served as an inspiration for Negro-Renaissance works and later influenced African nationalists like Blaise Diagne, Kwame Nkrumah, and Jomo Kenyatta. Members of the Negro-Renaissance group in America not only denounced repression; they also re-asserted their pride in their Black African heritage. In their manifesto, for example, they declared that they wanted to express their personality without shame or fear.

Langston Hughes, Claude McKay, and other black poets of the Negro-Renaissance movement had a significant influence on black intellectuals from Africa and the Caribbean during the 1930s. In particular, they impressed the Negritude writers with the manner in which they asserted their African origins with pride (Kesteloot). Léopold Sédar Senghor of Senegal, Léon Damas of Guyana, and Aimé Césaire of Martinique were the three most important figures in the Negritude movement.

Senghor himself credits McKay with being the true initiator of the values he associated with the Negritude movement. In his writing, McKay had attacked Christianity and the whole system that had legitimized slavery, colonization, and the assumption of Black social inferiority. He recommended a return to the values of the people who had maintained their "instinctive personality." McKay and other black American poets expressed their return to their roots by adopting African rhythms in their works. This spirit of "retour aux sources" had a profound impact on Negritude writers. In his novel *Dominique Nègre Esclave*, for example, the Martiniquan historical writer Léonard Sainville attacks the hypocrisy of European Christian missionaries who contributed in their own way to the perpetuation of slavery.

According to Michel Fabre, of all the writing by Afro-Americans of the Harlem Renaissance available to French-speaking Blacks, the most influential was Claude McKay's novel *Banjo*. *Banjo* analyzes the solidarity within the black diaspora. It also rehabilitates the primitive versus so-called civilization. It provided a path to reflection for French West Indian and African students caught in the web of French assimilation (Fabre 153).

McKay dispelled the illusion that there was no French prejudice against Blacks, even though Africans intent on assimilation insisted it did not exist. McKay's attempted rehabilitation of the noble "savage" by stressing primitivism in a positive manner was, according to Fabre, a heralding of Senghor's definition of Negritude as "the sum of values of the black world" (Fabre 153). Before Senghor, McKay had thus ascribed to the black person the mythical qualities of dancing, feeling and soulfulness. French-speaking blacks saw *Banjo* as primarily an important contribution to the political, social, and ideological analysis of their own plight. According to Fabre, when in 1932 a group of Afro-Caribbean students breaking with the moderate tone of the *Revue du Monde Noir*, violently denounced cultural assimilation in the poetry of their elders, their reference and inspiration was the literature of the Harlem Renaissance (Fabre 154).

In essence, the American Negro-Renaissance paved the way for the Negritude movement. Black African and Caribbean intellectuals had direct contact with their American counterparts who were studying in Paris during the 1930s. Like the black Americans, African and Caribbean intellectuals experienced the racial prejudices that characterized the white-dominated social and political system in which they were obliged to live. To a certain extent, they faced the same realities as black Americans did. The recognition of this fact fostered a strong sense of solidarity between Blacks of the diaspora and Africans at that time. This sense of solidarity is manifest in their common quest for a viable cultural identity.

When Antillean intellectuals published the journal *Légitime Défense* (with a title borrowed from a poem by André Breton), they helped catalyze the awakening process in this quest for an authentic black cultural identity. They attacked racial prejudice. They affirmed a pride in their African origins. They denounced the literary mimetism characteristic of Antillean writings of the time, and they called for a revolutionary movement like that exemplified by the American Negro-Renaissance. Edward E. Jones, an American student who was studying in Paris at the time, describes the phenomenon this way:

> Ces étudiants voulaient faire cause commune avec leurs frères noirs dans leurs efforts pour faire face au monde soit indifférent soit hostile des blancs [...]. Cette ambiance a facilité la naissance de la prise de conscience raciale dont l'idée [...] de la Négritude est sortie. (68-69)

> [These students wanted to pursue the same cause with their black brothers in their effort to confront the white world which is either indifferent or hostile...This atmosphere facilitated the birth of racial awareness...from which the idea of Negritude was born].

Somewhat later, Senghor, Césaire, and Damas founded the journal *L'Etudiant Noir*, which served as a vehicle for the articulation of similar aspirations. At the same time, a movement called "Indigénisme" was developing in Haiti, and its avowed purpose was the assertion of Haitian pride in the African origins of the people.

Writing on Negritude and Black writers, O.R. Dathorne remarks in one of his works that it is no accident that the creative attempts to invent a past through Negritude was the product of Black French West Indians. It was the invention of people in alien lands who had created no indigenous culture (1974, 308). He also notes that Africa became a theme in Caribbean literature as a result of its development in Haiti, its influence in Cuba or Puerto Rico and also as a result of the interest that Europe developed in primitivism, especially in the African "primordial" (433).

In a more recent work on French Caribbean literature in which he traces the development of the Negritude movement, Roger Toumson comments that in the 1930s, what he calls the "conscience antillaise" expressed itself in a literature which had as its objective the affirmation of a collective Afro-Antillean identity (353). The abolition of slavery in 1848, he contends, had not definitively ended the exploitation of the mass of black workers. Young Antillean students who lived in Paris experienced the cynicism of the compradore bourgeoisie and feudal oligarchy of the first half of the twentieth century and solidarized with other exploited peoples like Africans or Black Americans. They saw a great contrast in terms of development between the metropole and their own islands:

> La littérature de la Négritude à laquelle allaient être désormais identifiées toutes les littératures noires, n'était qu'un aspect particulier d'une littérature anticolonialiste qui, dans un mouvement d'ensemble, vulgarisait, à l'échelle de trois continents, les préceptes théologiques ou anthropologiques de la libération nationale. La révolte nègre prenait place dans le courant d'une contestation élargie à l'ensemble du Tiers-Monde. (Toumson 370)

> [The literature of Negritude to which all black literatures would be associated from now on, was only a particular aspect of an anticolonialist literature which, in a movement as a whole, vulgarized at the level of three continents, the theological or anthropological precepts of the national liberation. The black revolt was registering its effect in the vogue of a bigger protest in the Third World].

Thus, Negritude was a response to colonialism and colonial exploitation and the literature it produced was one of protest and revolt. When it was protest writing, Toumson notes, it denounced racial and social inequalities. When it demanded political rights, it was for the status of full French citizenship for the colonized. It was inspired by the Shoelcherian tradition, the leftist ideology of the time that had been legitimized by the government of the Front Populaire. They saw a communality in Black pride and faithfulness to the France which proclaimed human rights (Toumson 323).

This movement which influenced to a large extent the writers whose works will be examined in this study, fed on concepts of the nineteenth and twentieth centuries:

> La Négritude s'est nourrie opportunément des divers courants criticistes du XIXe et du XXe siècles. Elle s'inspira, au coup par coup, au gré des circonstances, des débats contradictoires qui ponctuèrent sa marche en avant, emprunta aux uns et aux autres; scientifiques, philosophes, historiens ou ethnologues. Elle prolongea et approfondit le procès qu'avaient intenté à la société bourgeoise contemporaine et à sa civilisation, d'un bord comme de l'autre, spiritualiste et matérialiste. C'est au point d'intersection de ces deux axes de pensée que s'établit la Négritude. (Toumson 377)

> [Negritude opportunely fed on the different critical movements of the nineteenth and twentieth centuries. It was inspired directly, in spite of the circumstances, by the contradictory debates which characterized its

progress, borrowed from all sources: scientists, philosophers, historians or ethnologists. It prolonged and deepened the criticism that the spiritualists and materialists had lashed out at contemporary bourgeois society and its civilization. It is at the confluence of these two main currents of thought that Negritude was established].

It is this direct influence of European concepts on a movement that sought to define and theorize on black culture that made Negritude very unacceptable to certain critics Black and non-Black alike. At the same time, it was almost natural that Senghor in particular should be so much influenced by contemporary European ideas, given the type of assimilationist educational system the French set up in their colonies.

European ethnologists also played a significant role in the revalorization of black culture. For example, Leo Frobenius in *Histoire de la civilisation africaine*, Maurice Delafosse in *Les Noirs de l'Afrique*, and others helped discredit the prejudices that Europeans had developed over the centuries about Africans. The works of these European ethnologists served as an inspiration to Negritude writers, some of whom were the historical novelists whose works will be examined in the present study. These ethnologists were reacting against the Euro-centric view of Africa and Africans. In effect, they were challenging the perception of the African as a "bon sauvage" [good savage]. European racist theories such as those advanced by Lucien Lévy-Bruhl, who viewed Africans as living in a pre-logical state, could not be ignored. Indeed, the ethnological debates that took place during the 1920s and 1930s in France were crucial in the transformation of the attitudes that Africans and Caribbeans themselves had toward an Africa that had until then largely been regarded as the "Dark Continent." European intellectuals contributed in no small way to the awakening of the world with regard to European misperceptions of other peoples. Léon Fanoudh-Siefer in his study of the myth of the Black in French discourse, traces the origin of such discourse and demonstrates how it manifested itself in French literature as well as in French colonial language usage. He also stresses the important role played by French intellectuals in rejecting the stereotypes of black people in French discourse:

Après la seconde guerre mondiale [...] des intellectuels français de plus en plus nombreux dénoncent de plus en plus ouvertement les mythes relatifs à l'Afrique noire qui meublaient confortablement les esprits. (194)

[After the second world war...more and more French intellectuals denounce more and more openly the myths about black Africa which comfortably fed people's minds].

Jean-Paul Sartre, Gaston Bachelard, and Marcel Griaule were among these European intellectuals, and they supported the founding of the journal *Présence Africaine* as well as of the publishing house of the same name. Fanouhd-Siefer remarks that the articles in the first issue of *Présence Africaine* of 1947 represented an attempt to rehabilitate the black person within the concept of Euro-centric hegemonic discourse of the "Other."[2]

Founded by Alioune Diop in 1947, *Présence Africaine* published its first issue concurrently in Paris and Dakar and soon became the principal organ of black activism at the time. According to Kesteloot, *Présence Africaine* was also supported by other important French intellectuals such as André Breton, Albert Camus, Théodore Monod, Michel Leiris, and Georges Balandier as well as by black intellectuals like Senghor, Césaire, Richard Wright, and Paul Hazoumé—one of the historical novelists whose work will be considered in this book. (254)

Although the journal was not created solely for political purposes, it inevitably served as a forum for black intellectuals and for Europeans sympathetic to their cause, for all those, in fact, who desired to question the colonization process and its consequences for black people everywhere. The publication of the proceedings of the First Congress of Black Writers and Artists is an excellent example of the role the journal played in awakening people to the injustices inherent in colonialism. The articles published in the journal at this time reveal the intense awareness of black intellectuals about their situation vis-à-vis the colonial master.

In his address at a conference at the "Centre International" of Bruxelles in March 1958, Alioune Diop emphasized the link between political engagement and the cultural independence for which Black peoples were fighting. He argued that: "les hommes de culture, en Afrique, ne peuvent plus se désinteresser du politique, qui est une condition nécessaire de la résistance culturelle" [men of culture in Africa can no longer be disinterested in politics, which is a necessary condition for cultural resistance]. (Kesteloot 264)

During the late nineteenth and early twentieth centuries, French colonial writers had sought to justify the claim of the so-called "mission civilisatrice" [civilizing mission]. Their works constituted a literature that claimed to present the truth about an Africa that Europeans tended to see only in exotic terms, but this perception of their culture was precisely what prompted African and Caribbean historical novelists to propose alternative visions of the past as well as of the present.

To understand the historical backdrop against which Blacks from Africa and the diaspora found it necessary to re-evaluate their identity in the contemporary world, one needs to understand the nature of Euro-centric perceptions of Black people in general. Lord Lugard, a

British Governor of West Africa during the colonial era, might be considered a representative spokesman for this point of view. In 1922, for example, he defended European rule over Africa in the following terms:

> As Roman imperialism laid the foundations of a modern civilisation, and led the wild barbarians of these islands along the path to progress, so in Africa to-day we are repaying the debt, and bringing to the dark places of the earth, the abode of barbarism and cruelty, the torch of culture and progress, while administering to the material needs of our own civilisation. (618)

Lugard's own declaration makes it clear that the ultimate purpose of colonization was economic gain for Europe and not the desire to attain some abstract humanitarian ideal of sharing European "civilization" with Africans. In his work, Léon Fanoudh-Siefer describes how European perceptions of black people emerge in their writing and in turn contribute to the oppression of the supposedly inferior "Other," whose image they themselves have created:

> Ces stéréotypes, qui simplifient et déforment la réalité jusqu'à la caricature, et dont la littérature est largement responsable, sont des sources de malentendus et d'incompréhension, souvent génératrices de conflits et de guerres. L'histoire de l'Europe en est pleine. Mais ces malentendus regrettables ou tragiques tournent au scandale lorsqu'ils aident à créer et à entretenir une inégalité de fait entre peuples oppresseurs et peuples opprimés. (9)

> [These stereotypes which simplify and deform reality to the extent of caricature, and of which literature is greatly responsible, are sources of misunderstandings and incomprehension, often provoking conflicts and wars. The history of Europe is replete with this. But these regrettable or tragic misunderstandings become scandalous when they help to create and to maintain an inequality of fact between oppressor peoples and oppressed peoples].

European literature was therefore one medium through which stereotypes about other peoples were created. Black intellectuals reacted to this situation by using the same weapon. They used fiction to subvert widely held negative images of black peoples.

Negritude discourse and the historical fiction inspired by it represent attempts not only to correct the misconceptions and myths of the European "Other"; they also subvert this discourse in a concrete fashion, as Fanoudh-Siefer explains:

> Un des traits principaux du nègre—tel qu'il est présenté dans le mythe—est son indolence, sa paresse congénitale. En mettant l'accent sur l'inaptitude

> du nègre au travail et sur son aptitude remarquable à la flânerie, les coloniaux croient saisir ainsi la dimension majeure de l'âme nègre: presque tous déplorent ce qu'ils considèrent comme une inclination du nègre pour la vie facile, et s'insurgent contre le droit du nègre à la paresse. Pour eux, indolence, paresse et flânerie se confondent. (161)
>
> [One of the main characteristics of the black person—as painted in myths—is his indolence, his congenital laziness. By putting the emphasis on the inaptitude of the black person toward work, and his remarkable aptitude for idleness, the colonists think they have in this way touched upon the main aspect of the black soul. Almost all deplore what they consider to be a tendency for the black person to like an easy life, and rise against the right of the black person to be lazy. For them, indolence, laziness, and idleness go together].

The crucial issue here is the emphasis on what Europeans considered to be the laziness of black people, for this image of laziness served as an effective way of creating "otherness" in the minds of colonized peoples. It also served as a justification for the so-called "mission civilisatrice." European perceptions of black people were necessarily conditioned by such stereotypes. Slavery and colonization had been rationalized by Europeans on the basis of their conviction that the black race was an inherently inferior race. This discourse was subverted in the Negritude-influenced historical fiction that is the subject of this book. Others have discussed this relationship; for example, previous scholars of Glissant's works have studied his re-writing of history in fictional terms, but they have not examined in detail how Glissant textually subverts the Euro-centric discourse of the Other.

In European discourse, terms like "civilized" and "primitive" were often applied to Africans and to other colonized peoples in ways that assumed the universal applicability of European discourse. European scholars tended to interpret the African world view in terms of a mind that was supposedly "primitive" in comparison to that of "civilized" Europeans. Levy-Bruhl's "mentalité prélogique" [prelogical mentality] is a characteristic example of such thinking. As a Professor at the Sorbonne University in Paris, Lévy-Bruhl had a significant impact on French perceptions of Africa. Fanoudh-Siefer explains the influence of Lévy-Bruhl and his universalizing contemporaries in the following terms:

> [...] La littérature et la politique se sont rencontrées. Il fallait montrer au monde que les populations noires étaient arriérées, primitives, adonnées au fétichisme et à la superstition, embourbées dans une mentalité prélogique et irrationnelle. Après cela, on avait bonne conscience, d'autant plus qu'on avait la caution scientifique que constituaient les travaux de Lévy-Bruhl sur

la mentalité primitive (à la fin de sa vie, du reste, Lévy-Bruhl est revenu sur ses conclusions, avouant le mal qu'il a permis [...]). (171)

[Literature and politics merged. They had to show the world that Blacks were backward, primitive, addicted to fetishism and superstition, bogged down in a prelogical and irrational mentality. After that, they had a clear conscience, all the more so since they had the scientific warning which constituted the works of Lévy-Bruhl on the primitive mentality (moreover, at the end of his life, Lévy-Bruhl went back on his conclusions, acknowledging the harm he caused].

Colonial hegemony was therefore viewed as justifiable on the grounds that theories such as Lévy-Bruhl's supposedly provided a strong scientific basis for Europeans' right to colonize others. Lévy-Bruhl's renunciation of his earlier concept of the "primitive" is particularly significant because it demonstrates that colonialist discourse was less scientific than its proponents had claimed.

Fanoudh-Siefer goes on to show how the use of terms such as "fetish," "sorcerer," and "superstition" helped to perpetuate the European concept of the African as a primitive "Other" (171). He then remarks that people often used Lévy-Bruhl's theories in framing their interpretations of their relationship with colonized peoples: "Levy-Bruhl embrassait, à travers le mot de primitif, non seulement les vrais primitifs, mais aussi tous les colonisés en général et en particulier ceux qu'on appelle maintenant 'les hommes de couleur'" (171). [Through the word "primitive" Lévy-Bruhl included not only the real primitive, but also colonized peoples in general and particularly those that are now called "men of color"]. This statement illustrates how colonialist discourse implicitly claimed universal validity for its underlying assumptions. After all, it was in the colonialists' interests to see all colonized peoples in a way that, in their eyes, justified their destruction of other peoples' cultures.

Levy-Bruhl's confession is revealing in the sense that it graphically illustrates the type of "scientific" theories that were used to justify colonial enterprises. In his *Carnets,* he confesses:

J'avais déjà mis beaucoup d'eau dans mon vin depuis vingt-cinq ans [...]. J'abandonne une hypothèse mal fondée [...]. Je ne parle plus d'un caractère prélogique de la mentalité primitive [...]. Du point de vue strictement logique, aucune différence essentielle entre la mentalité primitive et la nôtre [...]. J'affirmerai, une fois de plus, que la structure logique de l'esprit est la même chez tous les hommes et que par conséquent les "primitifs", tout comme nous, rejettent la contradiction quand ils l'aperçoivent [...]. (257-281)

> [I had already watered down my wine a lot for twenty-five years...I abandon a hypothesis without any good foundation...I do not speak any longer of a prelogical character of the primitive mentality...From the strictly logical point of view, there is no essential difference between the primitive mentality and ours...I will assert one more time that the logical structure of the mind is the same thing in all men and that consequently the "primitives" just like us, reject contradiction when they notice it].

In these terms, Lévy-Bruhl dismisses the scientificity of his own previous theories. Nevertheless, these non-scientific theories exercised an enormous influence on the perceived relationship between Europeans and their colonized "Other." One of the major goals of the historical novelists considered in this study was to create a counter-discourse that would subvert the commonly held, stereotyped images based on these non-scientific theories.

The stereotyped image of black people as infantile is evident in the remarks of Frenchmen such as Reverend Maurice Briault, who compares Africans to big children. In fact, he was convinced that "la meilleure définition du Noir est que c'est un grand enfant, un enfant qui reste tel jusque sous les cheveux blancs" (quoted in Fanoudh-Siefer 174) . [The best definition of the black person is that he is a big child, a child who stays in his state till he grows gray hair]. In colonialist discourse, the image of Africans as children served to justify European theories of African dependency. They argued that Africans needed Europeans because they were incapable of developing on their own. By means of such arguments, colonial conquest and its attendant consequences could be presented as justifiable.[3]

In twentieth-century Africa, colonialists thought they discerned features that could be identified with people who had lived in medieval France or in other parts of the world during previous centuries. Some writers equated black people with characters such as those ridiculed by La Bruyère, La Fontaine, and Rabelais in their writings (Fanoudh-Siefer 180).

While paying tribute to Maurice Delafosse and other European ethnologists who had demonstrated intellectual honesty and scientific prudence in their attacks upon the Euro-centric discourse of the "Other," Fanoudh-Siefer laments the fact that most of them continued to interpret African culture through the grid of their own European world view. Roland Barthes also denounces the Euro-centrism of the official colonial language after the Second World War. He argues that such a language was not meant simply to communicate, but to intimidate. Thus, official colonialist language perpetuated the myth of the primitive "Other." As Barthes points out:

> Le vocabulaire officiel des affaires africaines est, on s'en doute, purement axiomatique. C'est dire qu'il n'a aucune valeur de communication, mais seulement d'intimidation. Il constitue donc une "écriture", c'est-à-dire un langage chargé d'opérer une conscience entre les normes et les faits, et de donner à un réel cynique la caution d'une morale noble. D'une manière générale, c'est un langage qui fonctionne essentiellement comme un code, c'est-à-dire que les mots y ont un rapport nul ou contraire à leur contenu. C'est une écriture que l'on pourrait appeler cosmétique parce qu'elle vise à recouvrir les faits d'un bruit de langage, ou si l'on préfère, du signe du langage. (1957, 155-161)
>
> [The official vocabulary of African affairs is, one imagines, purely axiomatic. That is to say that it has no intention of communication, but only intimidation. It thus constitutes a "writing," that is to say a language meant to create a conscience between norms and facts, and to give to a cynical reality the warning of a noble moral. In a general manner, it is a language which works essentially as a code. That is to say that the words have either no relationship with or an opposite one to their content. It is a writing that one could call cosmetic because it tries to recover the facts from a noise of language, or if one prefers, from the sign of the language].

Barthes thus underscores how colonial language itself revealed the mechanisms of European exercise of power. Europeans were not interested in genuine communication with the colonial "subject." For this reason, the language they used was filled with messages that were meant to intimidate and thereby to facilitate the control of colonized peoples. Confronted with the myths that had been perpetuated by the sort of language described by Fanoudh-Siefer and Barthes, African and Caribbean writers, including the historical novelists under discussion in the present study, transformed these negative images into positive ones—a process that was developed by the early adherents of the Negritude movement.

The theme of a "retour aux sources" was a central preoccupation of Negritude writers, and in their quest for a viable cultural identity, they espoused traditional African values and motifs. For example, Senghor glorifies the African woman, the black woman, and evokes childhood memories of his native Senegal in his poetry. His basic impulse was to create a literary work based on a knowledge of his own people's history and culture. Similarly, some of the historical novelists treated in this study adopted the Negritude concept of "retour aux sources" as a center of focus in their own work. In fact, it is for this very reason that they chose to create fiction inspired by the "true history" of their own people. When they wrote novels inspired by the history of slavery or the history of the colonial period, they were drawing upon the same ideological backdrop as the one that had been utilized by Negritude writers.

For most of the writers treated in the present study—Nazi Boni, Paul Hazoumé, Jean Malonga, Ahmadou Kourouma, Léonard Sainville, and Edouard Glissant—the impulse to write historical novels can only be understood within the context of the Negritude movement. Boni was an active participant in it. He even dedicated his historical novel, *Crépuscule des temps anciens,* to Senghor. Hazoumé was also involved with the Negritude movement, and his *Doguicimi* reflects the Negritude rejection of the idea that Africa was a "tabula rasa" before the arrival of Europeans on the continent. Sainville too was an active participant in the Negritude movement. He worked all his life for the affirmation of black cultural identity, and his commitment to the Negritude cause is clearly reflected in his historical novel *Dominique Nègre Esclave.* Glissant is more of a progressive Negritudist, for he believes in going beyond what the early Negritude writers sought to achieve, as he intimates in his novel *Le Quatrième Siècle.* In Glissant's view, black people from the Caribbean need to look toward the future instead of remaining stultified in an ostensibly glorious past. His concept of "Antilleanité" is a variation of the Negritude concept; it represents an attempt to find a way out of the present predicament and to create a better future.

The first chapter of this study focuses on the ambivalent situation of Hazoumé as an "évolué" writer. The ideological basis behind the portrayal of traditional power structures in *Doguicimi* will be examined closely to illustrate how Hazoumé creates an anti-colonial discourse while portraying the Dahomeyan kingdom on the eve of European colonial rule. At the same time, this study will discuss the pro-colonial dimension of *Doguicimi* in order to explore the problematic nature of the "dialectic" between history and fiction. In historical fiction, the direction in which this dialectic moves will always be determined by the ideological position of the writer, and Hazoumé's ambivalence toward French colonialism is a dominant shaping influence in his novel.

In the novel, Doguicimi is the wife of a Prince, Toffa, who has left the city to participate in a war waged against the neighboring Mahi. The Dahomeyans are defeated, and it is not known whether or not Toffa is still alive. Toffa's rival, the designated heir to the throne, tries to seduce Doguicimi during her husband's absence, but Doguicimi resists all his advances. During a second war against the Mahi, the Dahomeyans are victorious, but at that time, they discover that Toffa has already been killed. Doguicimi decides she will be buried with the skull of her beloved husband. She cannot be dissuaded from her resolve, not even by the "Vidaho," the man who has been trying to seduce her ever since her husband went off to war. At the end of the novel, Doguicimi insists upon being buried alive with her husband's skull, exemplifying an extraordinary courage, fidelity, and love. The theme of extreme fidelity to a dead spouse is also a typically

European one, for example in Madame de LaFayette's *La Princesse de Clèves*. Yet, it is difficult to say whether or not in his creation of *Doguicimi*, Hazoumé was directly influenced by this type of European writing, although he must have been familiar with this work.

One important theme that will be explored in this first chapter is the use of a heroine as an indication of the writer's ideological position. Hazoumé glorifies the heroine in a way that is characteristic of Negritudist discourse. Although the novel is hardly feminist in the modern sense of the word, it is significant that Hazoumé portrays a female character who has the courage to challenge the traditional male superiority complex. Doguicimi herself delivers an extended diatribe against male dominance. The use of a heroine is also important in this historical novel because it conveys a positive image of the African woman. The truth about the history of the Dahomeyans is that women played a crucial role in their society. Amazons were an important force in the Dahomeyan army, for they actively engaged in combat at wartime, a fact which is often downplayed by historians and novelists alike. Hazoumé's idealistic portrayal of his heroine also serves as a symbol of pride for the present generation of African women in a male-dominated society. Molara Ogundipe-Leslie in her collection of essays on African feminism emphasizes the need to challenge certain traditions which tend to keep the African woman in a rather subordinate situation in terms of power (Ogundipe-Leslie, 1994). Yet, this gender relationship should only be seen in its African cultural context and not through the prism of Euro-centric theories.

His depiction of the power structure of the Dahomeyan kingdom is particularly significant because it clearly demonstrates the falsity of the Euro-centric view that Africa was a continent without culture in pre-colonial times. What Hazoumé demonstrates is that the Dahomeyan kingdom had a highly developed culture with an elaborate power structure. The establishment of this fact alone is a major step toward the definition of a viable cultural identity that was not wholly dependent upon European universalist conceptions of "civilization."

In *Doguicimi*, therefore, readers are confronted not with a "civilizing" process implemented by superior Europeans, but rather by a conflict of civilizations. This conflict is reflected in Toffa's long speech at the beginning of the novel. In this speech, he tries to persuade the Council of Elders that the Europeans are no true friends of the Dahomeyans. He points out their selfish political and economic interests, as evidenced by their introduction of slave trade. The idea to stress here is that the anti-colonial discourse is placed in the mouth of Hazoumé's exemplary hero, Toffa, who seeks to explore the truth about the relationship between the indigenous Africans and the European invaders. This truth is characteristic of nearly all colonial encounters, and Hazoumé underscores it in his attempt to re-write the history of his people in his own quest for an authentic cultural identity.

Inspired by true history, the fictional *Doguicimi* demonstrates that Africans had their own socio-political systems before the advent of colonialism and that the history of African peoples did not begin with colonialism. By extension, the novel also suggests how colonialism destroyed indigenous institutions and imposed European systems of government on the people.

However, there is an underlying internal tension in Hazoumé's anti-colonial discourse because he himself was ambivalent toward French colonialism. The position he adopts at the end of the novel actually undercuts the ideological stance implicit in the novel itself. George Hardy's preface to *Doguicimi* and Hazoumé's own epilogue to the novel defend the overall impact of the French colonial presence in the area and thereby deconstruct the anti-colonial thrust of the narrative.

The ambivalent position of the African and Caribbean novelist in his anti-colonial stance is dramatically reflected in the case of Hazoumé, who wanted to see the end of many aspects of the civilization he portrays in *Doguicimi*. For example, he was opposed to slavery and human sacrifice. At the same time, he wanted his readers to recognize the nobility of characters like Toffa, Guézo, and Doguicimi. In a sense, this tension is an integral part of Hazoumé's psyche. As an "évolué, he sought to be French, but as an African, he was attempting to assert his independence and his cultural identity in the face of a civilization that denied it. Part of this ambivalence is explained by the fact that Hazoumé himself did not come from the Dahomeyan kingdom, but from the area of Porto Novo, which had frequently been menaced by Dahomey.

This tension is apparent not only on the thematic level of the novel, but also in its narrative style. The long arguments between Toffa and other members of the Council of Elders (about whether or not to go to war against the Mahi) take up several pages in the novel. On the thematic level, Toffa and other Elders are debating an issue that is crucial to the African-Caribbean historical novelist. How does one assert one's identity when one is an "évolué" in the French system? On the narrative level, the debate between the Elders enables Hazoumé to portray direct exchanges between the characters—to portray the palaver that is such an important element of African culture. Issues are settled among the Elders.

On the thematic level, the debate among the Elders also reflects the ambivalent position of Hazoumé himself. What role does European education play in his search for and his assertion of cultural identity? In *Doguicimi*, there is a dialectic between his own traditional African heritage and the European cultural values inculcated in him during his formal education. In novels about colonial and post-colonial periods in Africa, the culture conflict is often reflected on the level of the characters. In Hazoumé's historical novel about pre-colonial Africa and the beginning of colonialism, however, this conflict is reflected primarily in the writer's own position as a French "évolué."[4]

The second chapter in this book deals with Nazi Boni's *Crépuscule des temps anciens*. In re-writing the history of his people, Boni presents the heroic struggles of his ancestors against French invasion as an inspiration to African nationalists who were struggling at that time for independence. In effect, the writing of *Crépuscule des temps anciens* was an overt rejection of the Euro-centric image of Africa as a "Dark Continent." Like Hazoumé, Boni sets out to demonstrate that African history did not begin with the advent of colonialism. In the pre-colonial era, there were highly developed socio-political institutions among African peoples such as the Bwa, whom he depicts in the novel. From this perspective, his re-writing of African history also constitutes an assertion of pride in the African cultural heritage.

European writing about Africa constitutes what has often been called "colonial discourse." In his *Colonial Encounters*, Peter Hulme argues that the basic idea behind colonial discourse was the need to produce something for Europe, to articulate procedures, modes of analysis, kinds of writing, and clusters of imagery that suited the European view of the Other (56). In his novel, Boni depicts how Europeans, more specifically the French, encountered the Bwamus and imposed colonial rule on them by force, but he also shows how the Bwamus resisted the European idea of producing something for themselves. The Bwamu civilization portrayed in *Crépuscule des temps anciens* reflects not the perspective of an outsider, but the vantage point of a writer who is part of the culture he is describing. Inspired by the true history of the Bwa, *Crépuscule des temps anciens* sustains the argument that Africans had their own civilization before the advent of colonization. The corollary of this argument is the contention that the European colonial enterprise destroyed civilizations such as that of the Bwamu. Boni's account of the senseless destruction wrought by colonial rule in Upper Volta re-inforces the ideological thrust of the novel as an example of anti-colonial discourse.

The thesis in this chapter is that Boni re-wrote the history of his people in order to establish the truth about colonial encounters in general. Re-writing the history of his people implies a questioning of European concepts of pre-history. As Hulme has pointed out, Europeans defined history as the presence of written records. The premise is that we know what happened in historical societies because there are written records that preserve the truth about them. Pre-history is always seen by Europeans as having ended with the colonial encounter. But Hulme argues that written records, like archeology, are texts that must be read and interpreted. In writing *Crépuscule des temps anciens*, Boni redefines such terms as "history," "civilization" and "culture." The definition of these terms cannot, he argues, be the sole preserve of the West. Boni's discourse therefore serves as a counter-discourse that undercuts European discourse about the Other—the Other in this case being the African.

As Edward Said asserts in his book *Orientalism*, the relationship between the West and the Other has been a relationship based on power, domination, and a complex hegemony. According to him, Europeans' conviction that they are superior to other peoples defined their concept of the Other. Imperialism, Said declares, was posited upon the binary typology of advanced and backward races, cultures, and societies. Said further argues that the Oriental was assumed to be the member of a subject race and therefore had to be subjugated (40). This argument also obtains in the case of the European scramble for and partition of Africa. The image of the Other promulgated by colonialist discourse is precisely the image that the African and Caribbean historical novelist seeks to correct.

By presenting colonial hegemony against the backdrop of Bwa civilization, Boni draws attention to the way in which European hegemony had destroyed African civilizations such as that of the Bwa. His treatment of history clearly undermines the colonialist argument that Europeans had brought civilization to Africa. As Aimé Césaire argues in *Discours sur le colonialisme*, colonization de-humanizes the colonizer himself. This argument is strikingly illustrated by Boni's historical novel in which the French senselessly massacre the Bwas because they resist invasion. One of the reasons for this dehumanizing action is, as Senghor argues somewhere else, that colonialism was not based on the mutual exchange of cultural values. This lack of mutuality is a key aspect in Boni's portrayal of the situation in *Crépuscule des temps anciens*. The French brutality in their first encounter with the natives offers an example of this colonial hegemony. The political and economic interests of France superseded any idea of a possible exchange of cultures in the colonial enterprise.

In the writer's attempt to re-establish the truth about his people, history is crucial, and that is the point emphasized by Manessy in his preface to the novel:

> Le *Crépuscule des temps anciens* est une œuvre attachante à plus d'un titre par la sincérité de l'auteur, anxieux de ne point trahir son peuple, par la vivacité et l'exactitude de ses descriptions, par la matière même du récit qui commence par une évocation de l'âge d'or pour s'achever dans le sang et les ruines de la grande révolte de 1916. De cette révolte et de sa repression, le Bwamu porte encore les stigmates: son indépendance y a péri, son équilibre

démographique en a été pour longtemps rompu, son térritoire s'est ouvert aux entreprises étrangères. Ce n'est pas cependant l'image d'une civilisation disparue qui nous est offerte. (11)

[*Crépuscule des temps anciens* is a captivating work in more ways than one because of the sincerity of the author, anxious to not betray his people at all, the liveliness and the preciseness of his descriptions, the style itself of the story which begins with the evoking of the golden age to end in the blood and the ruins of the big revolt of 1916. The Bwamu still have the scars of this revolt and of its repression. Her independence was lost in the process, her demographic equilibrium was as a result broken for a long time. Her land opened to foreign businesses. Nonetheless, it is not the picture of a lost civilization which is offered us].

In terms of its influence on the writer's ideology, the traumatic experience recalled here is significant. Manessy is emphasizing the fact that the advent of colonialism also had a profound effect on African civilization. As he rightly points out, Boni is not portraying a civilization that has been completely wiped out. The culture of the indigenous people has, to a large extent, survived the shock of colonial encounters, and that is why Boni himself calls on African researchers to help safeguard their cultural heritage, as he did in writing a historical novel about his own people.

Boni's rejection of the Euro-centric view of Africa, calls into question some of the major assumptions behind the usual distinctions between center and periphery. In colonialist discourse, the West is perceived as the center. The "Other," or the African, is relegated to the periphery. Boni's novel rejects this interpretation of African civilization. According to him, European culture was being imposed on people who already had a well-developed culture of their own. For the Bwas, as for most other peoples in Africa, the first confrontation with Europeans was the beginning of a cultural contact that was never based on mutual exchange, but rather on the forcible imposition of European culture on the Other.

Cheikh Anta Diop's theories in his *L'Unité culturelle de l'Afrique Noire* are relevant to Boni's chronicle of the Bwa people and to Hazoumé's chronicle of the Dahomeyan people, in the sense that they too were attempting to re-establish the origins of African history. Anta Diop's study unequivocally rejects the Euro-centric view of African history. Like Diop, Boni believes that Africans should study the past not just for the sake of learning about their own history but to assimilate the lessons that are embedded in it.

These historical novelists tried to do in their own way what African historians like Diop and Adu Boahen accomplished in their writing; in other words, they reinterpreted the history of Africa in a way that purged it of the inaccuracies, myths, and misconceptions which were characteristic of Euro-centric history. As Boahen argues in his James Schouler lecture, most of what has been written about colonialism in Africa has been written primarily from a Euro-centric point of view. The principal preoccupation of those who wrote such histories has been the origin, structure, operation, and impact of colonialism, but as he points out, one aspect of the situation has been consistently overlooked:

> The crucial questions of how *Africans* perceived colonialism, what initiatives and responses they displayed in the face of this colonial challenge, and above all how they reacted after the forcible imposition of colonialism [...]. (vii)

The stories that Hazoumé and Boni recount are an example of how Africans reacted to colonial conquests recounted from the point of view of insiders who had been the victims of these encounters. African peoples were not passive victims of colonialism, and African historical novelists were inspired by this fact in their rejection of the Euro-centric interpretation of History.

Some European historians have even argued that the benefits of colonialism far outweighed the negative consequences of colonial encounters in Africa. According to these historians, European colonialism was beneficial to Africans themselves. In contrast to such ethnocentric representations of history, Boni portrays the Bwa kingdom as an example of what colonialism destroyed in African socio-political systems. To subvert the Euro-centric discourse of the "Other," African and Caribbean historical novelists used the same history that had served as the source of European myths and prejudices about Africans, but they presented it from the African perspective.

One important aspect of the cultural heritage portrayed in *Crépuscule des temps anciens* is religion as practiced by the Bwa people. This religion is depicted as part of what Africans must know in order to appreciate their origins, their history. In *Crépuscule des temps anciens* (as in Hazoumé's *Doguicimi*), readers learn that religion permeates the whole life of an African people. Persuading readers to recognize the importance of this religious sentiment is one goal of Boni's affirmation of pride in his African cultural heritage.

Like the earlier proponents of Negritude discourse, Boni demonstrates how religion serves as an important aspect of the culture of the people he is portraying in his fiction. His narrative emphasizes the fact that Africans did not need a "mission civilisatrice" to bring them knowledge about the existence of a Supreme Being. In Bwa society, order is maintained by people's fear of invoking the wrath of the Ancestors.

In chapter three, we will examine Jean Malonga's *La Légende de M'Pfoumou Ma Mazono* as legend and as historical fiction. Malonga is interested in oral tradition and his legend is the re-writing of the history of his people. The chapter looks closely at the legend as a love story which portrays the customs of his people through the interaction of the main characters in the novel.

Ahmadou Kourouma is also a writer well versed in oral tradition as we witness in his second novel *Monnè, outrages et défis*. The fourth chapter of this study focuses on this novel. It attempts to underscore the fact that Kourouma's novel represents a new type of historical fiction from francophone Africa which has evolved from its precedents.

The fifth chapter of this book will examine the question of the Other in Léonard Sainville's historical novel *Dominique Nègre Esclave*. In this novel, Sainville subverts the discourse of the center through his revalorization of the image of the maroon (revolted slaves who lived in the mountains and occasionally descended to the plantations to raid their masters' farms).[5] For Sainville, the maroon is not a primitive savage who can be bought and sold like an object, as he had been depicted in Euro-centric discourse. On the contrary, Sainville's maroon subverts the discourse of the master by persistently rejecting the image imposed on him by the white béké (French slave owner).[6] He in effect established a counter-discourse of his own. Homi Bhabha perceptively argues that, in the colonial situation, one should not talk only about the discourse of the colonizer (as seems to be the case in Said's theory), but also about the counter-discourse of the colonized. His point is particularly relevant to a discussion of Sainville, for the Martiniquan writer successfully reproduces this counter-discourse in his historical fiction about slavery.

Sainville was a professional historian. He even taught history at the Sorbonne for several years. He worked all his life to foster the recognition of black cultural identity. Like Boni, he was inspired to write a historical novel as a result of his own research into the history of his people. The documentation that provided him with the raw material for the writing of *Dominique Nègre Esclave* was later used in a chapter of his "La Condition des Noirs dans les Antilles Françaises de 1800 à 1850"—a "Doctorat d'État" thesis that he presented at the Sorbonne in 1970 after twenty years of research.

Dominique Nègre Esclave was published in 1951 in commemoration of the centenary of the abolition of slavery. The novel is about the history of maroon revolt in the French Caribbean during the first half of the nineteenth century. The main character is the picaresque-like hero Dominique. By comprehending the nature of Dominique's "adventures" with different slave masters, readers achieve a remarkable insight into the real nature of slavery in the

French Caribbean. Dominique repeatedly changes masters, revolting and marooning at every opportunity and becoming more hardened and more witty after each experience with a new master.

Sainville believes that the maroon revolt was a crucial factor in the history of Antilleans, who are seeking to define an authentic cultural identity; therefore, he presents his major character Dominique as an important element in his own articulation of an anti-colonial discourse. Like the maroons in Glissant's *Le Quatrième Siècle*, Dominique is a symbol of the victimization inflicted on black people within the sado-masochistic system implemented by those who benefited from slavery. In the context of this shameful past, the Antillean needs to re-assert himself in his quest for an authentic identity. In his famous poem *Cahier d'un retour au pays natal*, Aimé Césaire touched upon the need for the Antillean to proudly assert his cultural identity by going back to his roots and by fully accepting the history represented by the maroons. Sainville adopts the same ideological stance.

Like Glissant, Sainville is a committed writer. In *Dominique Nègre Esclave*, his concern is to revalorize the image of the maroon in Antillean history, for he contends that the abolition of slavery did not come about solely through the efforts of people like Victor Schoelcher, as some European historians have argued. In contrast to European works that have depicted maroons as "happy savages," Sainville's anti-colonial historical novel rejects this false image by demonstrating that the maroon was neither "happy" nor "savage."

The revalorization of the image of the maroon is crucial to the historical novelist from the Caribbean because of the significance of the maroon in the history of Antillean people, and Peter Hulme's theories in *Colonial Encounter* can help us redefine this image as we look more closely at the slave-master relationship that Sainville portrays in *Dominique Nègre Esclave*. Upon their arrival in the Antilles, slaves were baptized and given names by their masters. Branding the backs of slaves with a hot iron symbolized the master's power of life and death over them as well as his power to impose a new identity on them. This process of forced acculturation inevitably influenced the way contemporary Antilleans regard themselves. Within this context, maroons developed their counter-discourse by revolting against the sub-human treatment that was imposed on them. This counter-discourse is what Glissant and Sainville emphasize in their historical novels. From their perspective, the maroons were heroes.

The relationship between contemporary Antilleans and the French has been shaped for centuries by the Euro-centric perception of the Other during the era of slavery. This relationship has permeated the consciousness of Antilleans to the point that many of them internalized an inferiority complex vis-à-vis Europeans. One of

Sainville's major goals in writing *Dominique Nègre Esclave* was to demonstrate the falsity of this image of Antillean identity, for he is concerned with inculcating his people with a new sense of pride in their own past, in their own history. Frantz Fanon (in *Peau Noire, Masques Blancs*) outlined a similar project when he touched upon Antilleans' perceptions of themselves as French citizens; he clearly demonstrated how living among the French makes the Antillean realize the illusory nature of this perception.

Fanon was a psychiatrist who studied the mentality of Antilleans vis-à-vis whites. He underscores the schizophrenic nature of the Antilleans' lack of pride in their origins, their race. The Antillean grows up in his society and is conditioned to feel a sense of inferiority towards other peoples. The following quotation summarizes Fanon's analysis of the predicament of the Antillean black:

> Quand on m'aime, on me dit que c'est malgré ma couleur. Quand on me déteste, on ajoute que ce n'est pas à cause de ma couleur [...]. Ici et là, je suis prisonnier du cercle infernal. (1952, 94)
>
> [When they like me, they say that it is in spite of my color. When they hate me, they add that it is not because of my color... Everywhere, I am a prisoner of the infernal circle].

The Antillean, according to Fanon, is thus caught in a vicious circle where he finds it difficult to grow up with a sense of pride in his own cultural heritage. He becomes a victim of what is propounded in the so-called canon. Historical novelists such as Sainville and Glissant responded to this predicament with a revalorization of the image of the maroon.

In *Dominique Nègre Esclave,* Sainville not only highlights the Manichean relationship between Whites and Backs in a way that graphically illustrates Fanon's theories; he also underlines the ideological basis for questioning the colonial enterprise and the supposedly humanitarian Western philosophies that were used to support it. After all, even French "philosophes" such as Voltaire and Montesquieu, recognized the evils of slavery on humanitarian grounds but continued to argue that it was necessary for the economic well-being of France. The Antillean historical novelist developed a counter-discourse to oppose the dominance of such ideas. Sainville's Dominique—the revolted maroon—exemplifies this counter-discourse and its implicit challenge to the supposedly universal validity of the slave master's discourse.

The sixth chapter of the book will deal with the discourse of Antilleanity in Glissant's *Le Quatrième Siècle*. One of the most well-known contemporary francophone writers, a militant political activist, Glissant has published (and continues to publish) novels, poetry, and essays. He is the francophone Caribbean writer most intimately associated with the concept of "Antillanité." Briefly stated, Antilleanity is the search for an identity that would enable the people of the Antilles to reconcile their African, their Amerindian, and their European heritages. Glissant (like the other novelists discussed in this study) views writing as a form of political engagement. His commitment to a search for authentic identity implies a rejection of the stereotyped Euro-centric view of Antilleans and their history. In this quest for identity, he uses the maroon as a mythic symbol of Caribbean history. As Barbara Webb has observed, "Glissant reclaims the mythic function of the maroon as cultural symbol of rebellion and possibility in Caribbean history" (48). Yet, the maroon is only one paradigm in the concept of Antilleanity.

In fact, Glissant's writing emphasizes the symbiotic nature of Antillean culture. Like the African historical novelist, he desires to rewrite the history of his people to correct commonly accepted inaccuracies and to establish a legitimate basis for them to feel pride in their Caribbean cultural identity. For Glissant, as for Sainville, writing signifies an act of engagement with the world as well as a search for inner fulfillment (Silenieks 5-15).

As Silenieks reminds us, Glissant believes that the Afro-Caribbean writer should commit himself to a decisive act which, in the domain of literature, signals his participation in the building of a nation (*L'Intention poétique*, 185). Nation-building is predicated on the recovery of the past. For the Caribbean, the trauma of the past is ever present, reaching back to the genocide inflicted upon the original Amerindian inhabitants of the islands, extending through slavery and colonial exploitation, and persisting into the social injustice of the present (Silenieks 5-15). It is a history that, in Glissant's words, prevents the people of the Caribbean from "possessing the land." For him, this history entails a "prophetic vision of the past" because it rectifies the inaccuracies and falsifications that have been imposed on Black history by Europeans. Frederic Jameson offers a convenient explanatory model for this phenomenon when he contends that, as far as the archetypal figures of the Other are concerned, the essential point is not that the Other is feared because he is evil; on the contrary, he argues, the Other is evil *because* he is Other, alien, different, strange, unclean, and unfamiliar (Jameson 115). Colonial power was created around this type of discourse; indeed, the society of slavery functioned on the basis of this perception of the European Other, and Glissant's *Le Quatrième Siècle* develops a counter-discourse to this perception.

In his recent work on Antillean literature from the eighteenth to the twentieth century cited earlier, Toumson commented on how Victor Schoelcher's writing is in a way at the origin of the concept of Antilleanity that Glissant was later to develop in his writing in the twentieth century. Schoelcher, Toumson argues, had the merit of fighting against anti-black racism but also developed the idea of "Antilleanity" by demonstrating the unity of the histories and cultures of the different peoples of the Caribbean: "Ainsi les idéologues de la Négritude pourront-ils répondre, à leur compte l'essentiel du message qu'apportait l'humanisme schoelchérien" (370). [Thus the ideologues of Negritude will be able to respond in their own way to the essential message that Schoelcherian humanism carried]. Toumson's perceptive study allows us to make the link between Antilleanity and the Negritude movement. Through historical fiction, Glissant articulates this notion of Antilleanity which is the uniqueness of Caribbean culture.

The concluding chapter will be a survey of the applicability of the term "historical novel" to other works from Africa and the Caribbean. A part of the objective will be to define the relationship that exists between Western models of historical writing and African-Caribbean historical fiction.

One difference between the African/Caribbean historical novel and its European counterpart as defined by Lukács is that of narrative form. African and Caribbean writers have different preoccupations from those that inspired nineteenth-century European historical novelists. For ideological reasons, they tend to have been inspired by oral traditions. These traditions are crucial in the quest for an authentic cultural identity because they constitute the primary source for African and Caribbean history as perceived from the perspective of insiders. African and Caribbean historical novelists are generally committed writers in the Sartrean sense, although they confront an entirely different predicament from the one encountered by twentieth-century European historical novelists. This predicament derives from the fact that they belong to a people that has been colonized. The history of colonialism has an importance for them that it cannot have for European historical novelists. Even the act of writing means something different for them than it does for European writers.

Oral tradition gives the work of African and Caribbean historical novelists a sense of authenticity and underscores their rejection of the Euro-centric view of the Other. Using oral tradition also reflects these writers' desire to return to their origins. For instance, the history of the Bwamu in *Crépuscule des temps anciens* is based largely on oral traditions. Knowledge is passed on to the younger generation through legends, proverbs, and songs which serve as sources of entertainment as well as a mode of instruction. As Chinua Achebe says in his novel *Things Fall Apart*, proverbs are the palm oil with which words are eaten. African writers therefore attach much importance to the use of proverbs in fiction written in European languages, for this technique reinforces their pride in their cultural heritage. The use of proverbs also displays the writers' knowledge of the traditions of their own people.

In the African context, the use of proverbs is associated with the art of speech making and identified with wisdom. In *Doguicimi*, *Crépuscule des temps anciens* and *Monnè, outrages et défis*, the authors have frequent recourse to proverbs. The creation of an oral register through the use of proverbs authenticates the historical fiction which, for them, has an ideological function.

Another important question that this book will address in the concluding chapter is the extent to which the African/Caribbean historical novelist has succeeded in marrying the European narrative style with traditional modes of folktale narration. Boni, Hazoumé, Malonga, and Kourouma did develop effective styles that reflect the tone of the "anciens" while employing French narrative conventions. Caribbean historical novelists were perhaps more influenced by European precedents; yet they also differ from African writers in the sense that they live in a society where creole is the mother tongue of many, although it has officially been relegated to a secondary position. Glissant, for example, was familiar with Walter Scott and Balzac, but he had also been inspired, even during his early childhood, to write after having listened to the stories of a "quimboiseur" (a type of traditional healer who is often the source of oral history). As a consequence, his narrative style clearly reflects many traditional Martiniquan creole story-telling techniques.[7]

Much has been written about the realism of the European historical novel and about the problem of recreating reality in a fictional context. Citing the names of existing places and actual people has been said to create an illusion of verisimilitude in the European historical novel. African and Caribbean historical novelists create a similar impression by insisting on the authenticity of the historical sources that serve as a backdrop to their novels. For example, Boni writes in his preface:

> J'ai voulu, intentionnellement, que l'originalité de *Crépuscule des temps anciens*, résidât, au moins en partie, dans sa sincérité, pour ne pas dire, son pragmatisme. (19)

> [I intentionally wanted the originality of *Crépuscule des temps anciens* to be at least in part, in its sincerity, not to mention its pragmatism].

As far as Sainville is concerned, he affirms:

> Authentique [...] le cadre où se meut l'action, et pas un instant, les nécessités de la création romanesque ne viennent bousculer la réalité intrinsèque des principaux faits à travers lesquels se déroule l'intrigue. (11)

Introduction

[The context in which the action takes place is authentic, and not for an instant do the necessities of novelistic creation jostle the intrinsic reality of the main events through which the plot develops].

The purpose of such statements in the prefaces to their respective novels is to influence readers to approach their narratives with the assumption that what they are about to read is historically authentic. In constructing their fictional worlds, African and Caribbean historical novelists also use specific facts and details to create the impression of verisimilitude.

Just as for their European counterparts, the facts of history are the essential raw materials for African and Caribbean historical novelists. They choose what aspects of history to focus upon and what aspects to omit. For this reason, readers are continually confronted with several basic questions: what is real and what is acquired in the historical novel? Do references to verifiable events and personalities guarantee that historical novels have successfully communicated the essence of actual history? In this respect, the African and Caribbean historical novel poses the same problems of interpretation as its European counterpart does. Whether in Europe or in the former colonies, the ideological motivation behind the writing of historical novels always has a dual reference—to the historical period in which it is set and to the contemporary period in which it is being written.

To test the validity of the conclusions drawn on the basis of my analyses of *Doguicimi, Crépuscule des temps anciens, La Légende de M'Pfoumou Ma Mazono, Monnè, outrages et défis, Le Quatrième Siècle,* and *Dominique Nègre Esclave,* the study will examine more briefly a series of other novels by African and Caribbean writers. The Martiniquan writer Roland Brival's *Montagne d'Ebène* is particularly interesting in this respect because it was inspired by the same historical events as Sainville's *Dominique Nègre Esclave.* However, it is a much more recent publication. Why did Brival develop a renewed interest in historical fiction during the 1980s after the Negritude concept had been repeatedly called into question by a younger generation of African and Caribbean writers. Like Sainville, Brival attempts to demystify the abolition of slavery. He adopts the same ideological stance as Sainville. However, Brival's anti-colonial discourse is communicated as a function of the authentically African hero he creates.

In his search for an authentic cultural identity, Brival believes in the necessity of a return to Africa; for this reason, he makes his hero a pure-blooded African. In contrast, Sainville had focused on a creole hero because he was convinced that such a hero would make his story more authentic. According to him, the mixed-blood slave encapsulated in his character the ambivalent history of the Antilles. In

Brival's novel, the locus of critical consciousness is embedded in the point of view of the Black, the hero. In contrast, critical consciousness in Sainville's novel is represented by the voice of the author himself. Although Sainville and Brival adopt different approaches to the identity problem, they both address the crucial task of using history in the quest for an Antillean identity.

Jean Ikellé-Matiba's *Cette Afrique-là!* (published in 1963) will be examined briefly. This historical novel is an indictment of German and French colonial rule in Equatorial Africa. It is the autobiography of the narrator himself, Franz Mômha. He is educated under German colonial rule in very harsh conditions and becomes a civil servant. Subsequently, he is a victim of German defeat in the First World War. He returns to marry and work in his village, but the French colonists have also introduced forced labor. As Richard Bjornson has succinctly put it, in writing this novel, Ikellé-Matiba has "reaffirmed an African sense of dignity and discredited the clichés upon which European justifications of the colonialist enterprise had often been based" (1991, 63). The narrator is a true historical personality. In recounting his experiences living under German and subsequently French colonial rule, he creates a *mise-en-abyme* of an autobiography within the author's story. The narrator's account is a re-writing of the history of his people. In spite of his traumatic experiences under colonial rule, Mômha believes in reconciliation with the former colonizers. As Bjornson has argued, he is a mouthpiece for Senghorian Negritude of "civilization of the universal" (1991, 66).

Felix Couchoro's *L'Esclave* will also serve as a test case for my conclusions about the African/Caribbean historical novel. Like Hazoumé and Boni, Couchoro used traditional oral story-telling techniques to reinforce the idea of Négritude and African cultural identity, but he was less successful than they were in terms of overcoming the stereotyped images inculcated in him by his Western education. In his historical novel, he seems to be propounding a progressive Negritude that eschews outmoded traditions. But if an African's traditional values are at the heart of his quest for a viable cultural identity, how can he import foreign values without losing his own cultural authenticity? Although Couchoro attempts to answer this question, his attachment to European cultural models is too great, and unlike Glissant, Sainville, Malonga, or Boni, he never develops a convincing counter-discourse to undercut the colonial discourse that denied the cultural identity of his people.

Lucien Goldmann's structuralist theory offers us a useful tool in an attempt to grasp the nature of the literary project undertaken by historical novelists from Africa and the Caribbean. Goldmann believes that literary works arise out of social consciousness and behavior, and he seeks to establish the ways in which they are linked to society. He sought to correlate the structure of a literary work with what he came to call the "mental structure" of its author or of the social group to which its author belongs. By mental structure, Goldmann means patterns of ideas and concepts. He also sees a correspondence between the personal experiences of writers and what they write. Although this study sometimes draws upon Goldmann's methodology, the present approach to the historical novel is far more concerned with minority discourse as a rejection of the subjective interpretation of history in Euro-centric discourse. The point is that European documentary history that ignores or distorts the experience of non-European societies cannot legitimately claim to be the only valid history. African and Caribbean historians and historical novelists have, in fact, amply demonstrated the falsity of this claim.

For all the writers who are the subject of this study, writing was an act of political engagement which has its own moral and ideological responsibilities. Like traditional African story-telling, the African and Caribbean historical novel is not "art for art's sake." Trapped in the ambiguous situation of colonized or formerly colonized individuals, the authors of these novels probe the history that shaped their destiny in a way that transforms writing into an act of revolt against the identity that the West sought to impose upon them. The reading of the African and Caribbean historical novel in this study is inspired by the belief that no society has a monopoly on the interpretation of history, for as Alex Haley wrote in the last paragraph of his much acclaimed novel *Roots*:

> So Dad has joined the others up there. I feel that they *do* watch and guide, and I also feel that they join me in the hope that this story of our people can help alleviate the legacies of the fact that preponderantly the histories have been written by the winners. (729)

This book therefore does a reading of African and Caribbean historical novels which is posited on the assumption that they constitute a re-writing of history—a rejection of Euro-centric historical accounts that have pretentiously claimed universal validity. At the same time, it also questions socio-political discourse in contemporary Africa and suggests that more recent historical novelists like Ahmadou Kourouma go beyond a mere diatribe against colonialism to cast a sharp critique at their society.

1

Paul Hazoumé: *Doguicimi*

The focus of this chapter will be on the ambivalence of Paul Hazoumé's discourse in his novel *Doguicimi*. We will explore the conflict between two sorts of discourse in this historical novel. The ambivalent nature of Hazoumé's approach emerges in his attempt to offer a positive fictional account of the kingdom of Dahomey of the early nineteenth century while at the same time creating a generally positive image of the impact of French colonialism in Africa. This ambivalence can also be seen in Hazoumé's depiction of the heroine Doguicimi, whom he uses as a mouthpiece to criticize nineteenth-century Dahomeyan customary practices and also to argue in favor of French colonialism.

Doguicimi is a work which until recently when it was translated by the late Richard Bjornson was relatively little known by the anglophone world. In fact, according to Adrien Huannou writing in 1980, Paul Hazoumé's *Doguicimi* was not studied much in Hazoumé's own native country, Benin (Huannou 1980, 207). The republication of *Doguicimi* has made this neglected classic more accessible to the literary world. Robert July has written that as a literary form and social expression, the novel was a late arrival in Africa and that its appearance was not noteworthy until after the Second World War (107-108). Negritude writing was mainly in the form of poetry and this was the case of the writing of the three people considered as fathers of the movement—Senghor, Césaire, and Damas. July has observed that written tracts in the nineteenth century were produced of necessity by westernized Africans and were written in European languages partly for the convenience of communication among the literate few. Through literary treatise, scientific study, political argument, journey essay, or published correspondence, African writers commented upon their concern with the impact of the West on traditional African organizations (July 107). *Doguicimi* is one of such testimonies of an African writer's concern with the impact of the West on African culture.

Paul Hazoumé's historical fiction *Doguicimi* is about the impact of colonization on indigenous African socio-political systems. Though Hazoumé was an adept of the Negritude movement, very little has been said about his personal contribution, even in a work like that of Lylian Kesteloot which has become a major reference text for the history of the Negritide movement. This lack of information on Hazoumé's contribution to the movement does not help us in our attempt to assess how it influenced his fictional creation, and more specifically why he is so ambivalent in the position he takes in the novel. Nonetheless, we know that Hazoumé had an important role in the founding of the journal *Présence Africaine* and that he took part in the first Congress of Black Intellectuals and Artists at the Sorbonne University (Paris) in 1956 along with prominent personalities from Africa and the diaspora like Dr. Price-Mars, Senghor, Césaire, Richard Wright, and Jacques Rabemananjara to mention a few (Adande 199).

Claude Wauthier has also observed that the works of African historians and anthropologists were marked with a certain nationalist ardor and cites the example of the works of Cheikh Anta Diop of the Senegal and the Ghanaian Charles de Graft Johnson as examples. He goes on to point out, however, that not all of these works were marked by this fervor, for there were works like Hazoumé's *Doguicimi* which actually paid homage to the colonial power (Wauthier 101). This chapter examines why Hazoumé took this position. Wauthier observes further that nationalists used the works of people like de Graft Johnson as a direct source of inspiration for their nationalist zeal. In 1937, the Nigerian Nnamdi Azikiwe emphasized the need to teach Africans to be proud of their history, and J.E. Caseley Hayford of Ghana demanded specifically in 1911 in his *Ethiopia Unbound*, the creation of a Gold Coast (as Ghana was then called) university with a chair of African history (Wauthier 101).

Paul Hazoumé lent his support to the Negritude movement which had some of the fervor exemplified by these African nationalists. According to Philipe Decraene, several French publishing houses refused to publish *Doguicimi* (12). Though he does not explain this lack of interest, we can conjecture that it was partly because of the anti-colonialist stance in the novel.

An adept of the Negritude movement, Hazoumé finds himself in quest of a viable cultural identity in the face of French colonial hegemonic discourse in Africa. But this quest for an identity reveals the impact of French colonialism on him and the ambivalent position he adopts in his attitude vis-à-vis the history of what used to be called the Dahomeyan empire. The focus of this chapter is to examine the ambivalent nature of Hazoumé's discourse in *Doguicimi* and to underscore how his concern for historicity is a quest for a viable cultural identity in a colonial context. The intention is to explore two sorts of discourse in his historical novel. The ambivalent nature of Hazoumé's discourse emerges in his attempt to offer a positive fictional account of the kingdom of Dahomey of the early nineteenth century while at the same time creating a generally positive image of the impact of colonialism in Africa. This ambivalence can also be seen in Hazoumé's depiction of the heroine Doguicimi, whom he uses as a mouthpiece to criticize nineteenth-century Dahomeyan customary practices and also to argue in favor of French colonialism.

As Christopher Miller has contended, the processes of projection, by means of which the colonizer's identity is replicated and his desires satisfied, are directly related to colonial policy. Translated into political terms, these projections become what Miller calls the colonial "inscription"—the imposition unto Africa of French systems of thought, the making "French" of Africa (14). Edward Said, as Miller points out, has referred to the same phenomenon in another part of the world as "manifest Orientalism" (Said 206). Miller argues that the fact of colonialism and its impact on African cultural systems broke down any absolute barrier between Africa and the West. Hazoumé specifically deals with this type of relationship between the French and the "colonial subject." To understand the nature of Hazoumé's ambivalence in his attempt to assert pride in his African culture through historical fiction, one must read his novel against the historical backdrop of his participation in the discursive system that Said and Miller have described. French colonial policy and its stereotypical images of reality were "inscribed" in the minds of educated Africans such as Hazoumé. The problematic nature of Hazoumé's writing is therefore a reflection of the influence that French colonial policies had on him. Hazoumé specifically deals with the antagonistic relationship between the colonizer and the colonized. The argument here is that we can appreciate the dichotomy between colonizer and colonized that Hazoumé portrays in the relationship between the Europeans and the Danhomenou in *Doguicimi* by drawing upon Albert Memmi's analysis of this type of hegemonic relationship in his works (*Portrait du Colonisé*). Memmi postulates that the colonized person was never characterized in an individual manner. He or she was drowned in an anonymous collectivity. Negritude was a response to this concept of the colonized in modes that emphasized "otherness" and "difference" in the same way that Europeans saw Africans in universalist and essentialist modes. Hazoumé's historical fiction is characterized by this Negritudist attempt to recuperate the dignity in African identity denied by European anthropology. Hazoumé writes about the Dahomey kingdom, but the entire discourse of his fiction is characterized by the Negritudist concept of an African culture and the problematic nature of his writing is a reflection of the influence that French culture had on him.

As Guy Ossito Midiohouan has demonstrated, the francophone tradition in Africa dates back to the time when Hazoumé and other early African writers were receiving their education in French-administered schools. Involvement or collaboration with the French was the rule rather than the exception with the elites of his generation. The primary objective of formal education in the French colonies was to create just such an elite by granting them access to the French language. Writers like Hazoumé served as bridges between the colonizer and the colonized (Miller 15). He and others such as Bakary Diallo were therefore profoundly indebted to the colonial system for their education, among other things, and for the language in which they wrote (Midiohouan 1986). Alexandre Adandé has also observed in an interview with Adrien Huannou that Hazoumé belonged to that generation of francophone African intellectuals who understood the need to create for themselves a conscience of ethnicity in order to fight the assimilationist policies of the colonizers. He further remarks that colonization was based on the Europeans' theory of their so-called civilization vis-à-vis an Africa that was considered a *tabula rasa*. Though Hazoumé was never ambiguous about his love for France, he manifested a religious zeal in his fight against the injustices in colonial rule in his attempt to safeguard his African culture (Huannou 1982, 39). The crucial question is whether this acculturation provides a sufficient explanation for the ambivalent nature of his discourse in *Doguicimi*.

We can discover a clue to this ambivalence by examining Georges Hardy's preface to the novel. It is significant that Hardy, a representative of French colonial power in Africa, should write a preface in which he proudly claims Hazoumé as a product of French assimilationist policies in its colonies. He was the Director of the "École Coloniale" and therefore an administrator of the colonial regime. Hazoumé could not be too critical of the colonial administration represented by people such as Hardy, who regarded him as a faithful exponent of the "raison d'être" of what the French called their "mission civilisatrice" in Africa. Furthermore, Hazoumé would never have been able to publish his novel if he had not enjoyed the endorsement of colonial administrators such as Hardy. The point is that Hardy's preface helps us understand Hazoumé's position as an "évolué" writer in the French colonial context. The fact that Hardy claims him as a product of French assimilationist policies undercuts Hazoumé's own attempt to assert a pride in his culture. The preface to *Doguicimi* is therefore an integral part of the overall discourse of the novel, and we need to explore it in order to understand Hazoumé's own ambivalent stance in the novel.

From the beginning of this preface, Hardy presents Hazoumé as an example of the "good work" that has been done by French colonialism in Africa. Describing the Dahomeyan writer as a prototype of the educated elite that French colonial administrators were seeking to produce in Africa, he explicitly declares:

C'est pour la France, bien entendu, un singulier mérite que d'avoir, au lendemain même de l'installation coloniale, opéré de telles conquêtes intellectuelles et morales. (9)

[It is for France, of course, a remarkable achievement to have, soon after the institution of colonial rule, made such intellectual and moral conquests].[1]

What Hardy suggests here is that *Doguicimi* is a testimony to the success of France's attempt to "civilize" Africans. Hardy's presentation of the novel thus introduces *Doguicimi* as a justification for the entire colonial enterprise in Africa. In fact, his comment is a typical example of colonialist discourse, for it defends European imperialism on the grounds that it brought education to the indigenous people of the continent.

There is a certain irony in Hardy's paternalist undertone, however, because, although he recognizes the value of recording the history of African civilizations, he remains adamant in insisting upon the beneficence of the French colonial enterprise that destroyed this civilization. He clearly reveals this attitude when he describes Hazoumé as:

> [...] un curieux mélange de modernisation européenne et de traditionalisme africain. Si son teint ne trahissait pas son origine, vous le prendriez pour un Français de France; tout dans sa façon libre et gaie de s'exprimer, dans son allure courtoise, dans ses gestes aisés, et mésurés, dans l'aimable ardeur qui émane de sa personne, est d'un homme de chez nous. (10)
>
> [...] a curious blend of European modernization and African traditionalism. If his complexion did not betray his origin, you would take him for a French of France; everything in his free and gay way of expressing himself, in his courteous look, in his graceful and moderate behavior, is of somebody from our society].

According to colonial standards, therefore, Hazoumé qualifies as a "citoyen français" [French citizen] (to use Hardy's own words) by virtue of what the French consider to be his successful acculturation.

In the novel itself, Hazoumé's account of the Dahomeyan kingdom is ambivalent in the sense that it is both anti-colonial and pro-colonial. In the epilogue for example, Hazoumé not only renders homage to the heroine Doguicimi, he also glorifies French colonialism by suggesting that the French deserved credit for having brought an end to the wars between indigenous ethnic groups. He concludes:

> Le drapeau français devait, un démi-siècle plus tard, réussir pleinement, c'est-à-dire, faire regner au Dahomey la paix, la liberté, et l'humanité. (510)
>
> [The French flag was to fully succeed half a century later, that is to say in bringing a reign of peace, liberty and humanity to Dahomey].

In this passage, Hazoumé is suggesting that French colonialism benefited Africans because it supposedly conferred peace and liberty upon them. Yet, throughout his narrative account of the Dahomeyan kingdom, he repeatedly acknowledges the fact that Europeans encouraged the slave trade which brought dissension and suffering to the peoples of the West African coast.

This insight into the true nature of the European impact on African society is clearly expressed before the first Hounjroto War in the novel, for Doguicimi's husband Toffa argues against the waging of a campaign that was presented by the King as a revenge upon the neighboring Mahi, who had killed four European "allies" of the Dahomey. During a long diatribe in which he seeks to convince the other princes that the French are no true friends of his people, Toffa argues:

> Il est temps que nous nous libérions du préjugé qui nous fait considérer les Troncs-Blancs comme des amis. Nous avons beau les traiter comme tels, ils méprisent foncièrement toutes nos démonstrations d'amitié. Ils ne sont pas non plus disposés à reconnaître le dévouement des Danhomênous pour eux [...]. Quand, à force de protestations, nous finissons par obtenir leur amitié, elle n'est jamais profonde ni sincère. Il n'y a rien d'étonnant à cela. La différence entre les Blancs et nous est grande. (40-41)

> [It is time to free ourselves from the prejudice that makes us regard the White Bellies as friends. In spite of treating them this way, they profoundly despise all our manifestations of friendship. Nor do they want to acknowledge the affection of the Danhomênous for them (...) Even when through protest we succeed in gaining their friendship, it is never a deep or sincere one. There is nothing surprising in that. The difference between the white men and ourselves is great].

Toffa's arguments are crucial for our understanding of the ambivalent discourse in Hazoumé's novel. He recalls the historical circumstances in which colonial encounters occurred. His argument also dismisses the idea that colonialism was good for the colonized since, as he contends, it was based on a disrespect for the Africans' own world view. What Toffa's diatribe suggests is that colonialism involved a conflict of cultures in which Europeans made no attempt to understand the cultures of those they were seeking to dominate. Such passages suggest that Hazoumé's narrative has anti-colonial undertones.

Here we can take into account Abdul JanMohammed's analysis of Homi Bhabha's reading of Edward Said. JanMohammed takes Homi Bhabha to task for implying that the native (in the colonial context) is somehow in "possession" of colonial power. He charges that Bhabha asserts the unity of the "colonial subject" and so "repressess the political history of colonialism" (JanMohammed 59-87). What Bhabha's reading of the colonial discourse suggests is that the colonized was not a passive "other." Hazoumé underscores this point in what is anti-colonial discourse in his portrayal of Toffa. This depiction does not suggest a repression of political history of colonialism. It rather re-emphasizes the fact that the colonized is aware of how he or she is perceived by the colonizer in that hegemonic relationship in which Europeans' economic interest in slave trade is paramount in their relation with the "Other."

Toffa also criticizes the Europeans' hypocritical attitude vis-à-vis the Dahomeyans. According to him, there can be no sincere friendship with Europeans because they instituted slave trade and encouraged wars among African ethnic groups who supplied them with the human "commodity" that they bought and sold. Toffa's attack on colonialism remains, however, highly ambivalent within the context of the novel because, while criticizing Europeans for introducing the slave trade, the author at the same time portrays the Dahomeyans as a people who antagonized their neighbors and Europeans as a result of their belligerent activities.

Yet this belligerence itself must be placed into its historical context. As Toffa points out in his speech to the Elders, Europeans have been enriching themselves at the expense of Dahomeyans who naively believed in the possibility of engaging in a sincere friendship with them:

> Les Blancs nos amis! Les Blancs nos amis! répétait Toffa en hochant la tête [...] Drôle d'amis que des gens qu'on entoure d'affection et qui n'en rendent jamais la réciproque, mais qui pour s'enrichir encouragent les Danhomênous à se faire tuer dans d'incéssantes guerres et à s'empoisonner par l'alcool! (40)

> ["The whites our friends! The whites our friends!" Toffa repeated, shaking his head (...) "Strange friends on whom we lavish affection but who never reciprocate; who, to enrich themselves, encourage the Danhomênous to kill themselves in endless wars and to poison themselves with alcohol"].

What Toffa says here is significant for our understanding of the ambivalent nature of Hazoumé's attitude towards colonialism. Within the novel, Hazoumé emphasizes the fact that the Dahomeyans did gain from their relationships with Europeans. They traded with them at the expense of their neighbors, who often became the victims of incessant Dahomeyan wars and slave raids. Thus, even if Toffa's speech is anti-colonial, Hazoumé himself clearly did not approve of the role the Dahomeyans were playing in terms of their relationship to the European presence in Africa.

Toffa goes on to argue that even the gods have manifested their disapproval of the European presence in the Dahomeyan kingdom. He explains that "Agbé" (the god of the sea, equivalent to Neptune in the European classical tradition) shows his anger by causing white people's boats to capsize at sea. After having accused Europeans of failing to understand Dahomeyan culture, he thus proceeds to judge them according to the standards of his own culture. Within this context, they appear to be effeminate and undeserving of the respect of people like the Dahomeyans, who believe in force as an important factor in their relationship with their neighbors. In the following quotation, we can admire the nobility which, Toffa argues, is important in Dahomeyan culture, but this nobility must be understood within the context of Hazoumé's own opposition to the way that Dahomey terrorized its neighbors by using force to subordinate them to Dahomeyan rule. Talking about the Europeans, Toffa argues:

> Comment les Danhomênous, qui n'adorent que la force, peuvent-ils se lier d'amitié avec des gens qui sont la faiblesse même? [...] Le farniente des Blancs a contaminé déjà les Noirs qui vivent à leur mode à Gléhoué; ceux-ci ne se rendent dans la capitale que portés dans un hamac où on les voit mollement assis. C'est sans doute pour préserver les Danhomênous de la souillure qui résultent de leur contact avec ces immondes bêtes de mer qu'Agbé se fait furieux, trouble la mer, suscite d'impétueuses lames qui engloutissent parfois leurs canots ou les brisent quand ils veulent aborder notre côte. (41)

> [How can Danhomênous, who respect only strength, make friends with people who personify weakness? (...) The white people's false paradise has already corrupted the black men who live like them at Gléhoué; they never enter the capital unless they are carried in hammocks, in which they can be seen sitting indolently. Certainly it is to save the Danhomênous from being contaminated through their contact with these foul beasts from the sea that Agbé becomes furious, roils the waters of the sea, and whips up a violent surf that sometimes swallows their boats or breaks them into pieces when they try to land on our shores].

In this passage, Toffa presents a certain ideal in Dahomeyan culture, but although Hazoumé admired nobility, he could not accept the excesses carried out by the Dahomeyans in the name of preserving their customary practices.

What Hazoumé admires in Toffa is his sense of duty towards his society. He sacrifices his life in the war against the Mahis, even though he knows that this war has been unjustly forced on his people by their Sovereign King—Guézo. Toffa obviously respects the traditions of his people, but the war against the Mahis was primarily a slave-trade raid. So, if Toffa represents the ideal sense of force for the Dahomeyans, he is also a symbol, for Hazoumé, of what the Dahomeyan kingdom came to stand for in the history of the nineteenth century as recorded in written form by Europeans—a society infamous for its brutal and inhuman activities. Toffa therefore represents an anti-colonial discourse, for he unequivocally criticizes Europeans; at the same time, Hazoumé's portrayal of Toffa serves as an overt criticism of the political ambitions of nineteenth-century Dahomey.

Doguicimi, the title character in the novel, also exemplifies Hazoumé's ambivalent attitude toward colonialism, for although she respects the customs of the ancestors, she publicly questions the Sovereign's totalitarian rule. She is portrayed as a loving, caring mother, for even though she does not have any children of her own, she treats all the children of her co-wives with such kindness that they flock to her house until they are forbidden to do so. Doguicimi's goal is not to overturn the system; in fact, her own speeches reveal a complete willingness to accept the idea that the male should be the head of the family. She herself never questions the fact that Toffa is her master. Thus, in one sense, Doguicimi is an exemplary noble female character.

Nonetheless, her attitude represents a threat to the commonly accepted Dahomeyan assumption that the woman is the "property" of her husband and her Sovereign. For example, she challenges the king's abuse of power in several ways. She attacks him verbally, calling him "le monstre" [the monster] and describing him as somebody who has "la folie des grandeurs" after he has insisted upon going to war against the advice of Toffa and others. Her behavior is even more disrespectful in her gestures. Standing with her hands on her waist, one foot in front of the other, and spitting on the ground in disgust, she defies the customs of her people. She has, in fact, adopted the "attitude d'une personne prête à la lutte" [attitude of someone ready to fight]. The king's anger and nervousness show that her defiance of the status quo has had its desired impact. Doguicimi's questioning of the king's absolute power is thus, from one perspective, a questioning of traditional African values.

As John Erickson rightly points out, there is conflict between Guézo and Doguicimi because the two are in opposition to each other. Guézo personifies the act of kingship, embodies the function of governing, and assumes the maintenance of a social order linked with sacred rituals that have been passed down to him from his venerable ancestors. In contrast, Doguicimi places fidelity to her husband and a respect for the sacredness of her marriage vow above all else. Erickson suggests further that Doguicimi acts as a mirror for Guézo, causing him to recognize himself and his role as a humanizer of Dahomeyan cultural tradition (484).

If Erickson's interpretation is valid, Hazoumé is using Doguicimi to criticize the way the Dahomeyan king exercises absolute power over his people. Partly because he exercises absolute power, Guézo can declare an unjustifiable war against his neighbors in order to capture slaves for the Europeans. And Guézo can exercise absolute power because society accords him the role of spokesperson for the ancestors. The same society passes an unfavorable judgment on Doguicimi because her behavior is considered to be contrary to its norms. According to them, the Sovereign has the power of life and death over his subjects, and Doguicimi deserves to die after having challenged this absolute power and called the king's infallibility into question. Mockingly, she asks him:

> Tu veux que les Danhomenôus citent ton nom après celui d'Agonglo, qu'ils t'appellent Guézo le Puissant, qu'ils célèbrent tes louanges? Rien plus ne te distingue du tyran. (107)
>
> [You want the Danhomênous to cite your name after that of Agonglo, to call you Guézo the Powerful, to sing your praises? Nothing distinguishes you from the tyrant any more!]

According to Doguicimi therefore, Guézo would like to be recognized in history as a powerful king; he would like to be compared to the great kings who came before him. But in her judgment, his abuse of power disqualifies him from such recognition.

Doguicimi's stance vis-à-vis the Dahomeyan sovereign's exercise of power reflects Hazoumé's own attitude toward the Dahomeyan kingdom. In his quest for an authentic cultural identity, Hazoumé seeks to present pre-colonial Dahomey as the example of a well-structured society with a well-established socio-political system; at the same time, he attacks the way the Dahomeyan king wields absolute power at the expense of both the Dahomeyan people and their neighbors. This double purpose in his narrative creates a paradox. But Guézo himself is in an ambivalent situation. The crowd is easily swayed by the decision of an all-powerful sovereign, and when he condemns the royal wife who dares attack Doguicimi, the people in the crowd turn on her because she has offended the norms of society by touching a profane individual:

> C'est juste! C'est juste! Une épouse de Panther ne doit jamais se souiller au contact des demons! La coutume est intransigeante sur ce point. Doguicimi est plus digne de pardon que cette reine sacrilège. (112)
>
> ["That's right! That's right! A Panther's Wife must never pollute herself through contact with demons! Tradition is inflexible on this point. Doguicimi is more worthy of pardon than this profane queen"].

In this way, the crowd seems to endorse the power handed down to the king by tradition, but Hazoumé's portrayal of Guézo's might reveals another aspect of the ambivalence that characterizes his historical fiction. In fact, Guézo's power is limited by the customs of his people.

Placed in its historical perspective, Guézo's declaration of war against his neighbors and his orders to carry out the traditional human sacrifices are merely actions that represent what is expected of him by his own people—the people who bestowed power on him in the first place. In other words, he is keeping alive a tradition of royal behavior.

But Hazoumé does not depict Guézo only as a tyrannical ruler, as was often the case in European accounts of the Dahomeyan kingdom. Guézo himself admits that he is only the custodian of a power that has been handed down to him by the ancestors. His decisions are dictated by what is expected of him by custom:

> Je n'ai pourtant pas, dans ce royaume, toute l'autorité qu'on me suppose. Enfermé dans la tradition, obsédé par la coutume dont je ne dois pas m'écarter d'un pas, sollicité par mon entourage, je ne suis le plus souvent qu'un instrument entre de multiples mains invisibles pour le peuple qui m'impute à tort les actes dits royaux, mais en réalité, connus et exécutés par mes Maîtres secrets. (218)

> [Yet, in this kingdom, I do not have all the authority that people associate with me. Imprisoned in tradition, obsessed with customs from which I must not stray in the least, solicited by people in my entourage, I am, most often, only an instrument in a multitude of hands that are invisible to the people, who wrongly attribute many so-called royal acts to me, which in reality have been conceived and executed by my secret Masters].

Guézo (a tyrant in the eyes of European chroniclers as well as in those of Hazoumé himself) cannot be properly judged unless one understands the social norms within which he exercised his power as sovereign.

Some African historians' accounts of Guézo have been far more generous to him than have been those of Europeans. An example is Joseph Djivo, who describes the historical Guézo as a generous, noble individual:

> C'est un homme affable, aux manières dignes. Réaliste, il sait concilier au besoin les obligations de la tradition avec les exigences de la politique. Ni les ordres des ancêtres ni les oracles du "fa" ne sont pour lui plus fort que l'état. C'est la raison pour laquelle, contre la désapprobation générale des morts et des princes, il entrepend la première guerre contre Hounjroto en 1822. (60-61).

> [He is an affable man with dignified manners. A realistic person, he knows how to reconcile, when the need arises, the obligations of tradition with the demands of politics. Neither the orders of the ancestors nor the oracles of "fa" are for him more powerful than the state. It is the reason why, against

the general disapproval of the dead and the princes, he undertakes the first war against Hounjroto in 1822].

The war that Djivo refers to here is the war Hazoumé recounts in his novel. In Guézo's view, his declaration of an unpopular war against Hounjroto actually lies in the interest of his own people. This stance demonstrates the ambivalence of Guézo's position, for he feels constrained to exercise excessive power over his neighbors because tradition demands that he do so.

Although Hazoumé's pride in African culture is reflected in his depiction of Dahomeyan society as a well-structured kingdom, he also describes in minute detail the religious practices of the Dahomeyans in a way that justifies his attack upon them. In his account of human sacrifices in the Dahomeyan kingdom, for example, he actually reinforces Western stereotypes about the supposedly barbaric and exotic nature of African societies. The following description shocks the reader's sensibilities to the breaking point:

> Les "chevaux" [victimes humaines du sacrifice] tombaient, tombaient toujours. Mêwou, dont le regard ne quittait pas le bas de l'autel, ordonnait, d'un geste du bras qui s'élevait puis s'abaissait, l'envoi des victimes au sacrificateur. Inlassablement, Migan les achevait d'un geste large et sûr. Le sang coulait, coulait abondamment, la terre gorgée n'en voulant plus boire. Les aides du victimaire pataugeaient dans la boue de sang, de pâte d'igname vomie et de la terre, et enlevaient activement les têtes et les cadavres. Les gémissements des "chevaux" tombés face contre terre, leurs efforts pour redresser la tête que le cou rompu refusait de porter, la diligence des serviteurs du victimaire qui nettoyaient la place [...]. (165)

> [The "horses" (human victims of the sacrifice) fell continuously. Mêwou, who fixed his gaze on the base of the altar, ordered with a gesture of the arm moving up and down that the next victim should be sent to the sacrificial priest. Tirelessly, Migan finished them off with an unerring, sweeping motion. Blood flowed, flowed so abundantly that the soaked earth did not want any more of it. The executioner's assistants wallowed in mud soaked with blood, regurgitated yam puree and dirt as they busily removed the heads and the bodies. The moans of the "horses" that had fallen head first to the ground, their efforts to lift up heads that broken necks refused to support, the diligence of the servants who cleaned the site...].

This passage speaks for itself. The human "chevaux" [horses] are the unfortunate captives of wars that were waged against the Dahomeyans' neighbors. The cruelty with which the act is carried out by Mêwou justifies Hazoumé's own resentment of Dahomeyan customary practices. His interest in a detailed description of the act deconstructs the possible positive image that could come out of his assertion of pride in his African heritage. The passage is significant because Mêwou and Migan are Ministers to the court and therefore represent the power of the King. Their abominable acts are clearly carried out with the blessing of the King, and Hazoumé wishes to underscore the fact that this was an essential aspect of Dahomeyan history.

Hazoumé would like his reader to gain an insight into the Dahomeyan belief system. The sacrificed slave is believed to carry a message to the ancestors about how well the living are maintaining the customs of the kingdom. These customary practices are part of the history of Dahomey, and Hazoumé is obviously concerned to provide a historically accurate account of it, but his perception of Dahomeyan customary practices also has an ideological underpinning. The description of the horror of the situation is not gratuitous because Hazoumé's ultimate aim is to justify his support for the French colonial enterprise in one particular region of the continent.

Hazoumé's vivid descriptions of human sacrifice imply his opposition to customary practices that made the Dahomeyans unpopular in the eyes of Europeans as well as in those of their fellow Africans:

> Migan immola devant le seuil de chaque sépulcre l'esclave qui assistait à genoux, entre deux aides du victimaire, aux réparations de la case. La victime irait rendre compte, au roi intéressé, des travaux faits sur sa tombe et de l'ornement de sa dépouille. (124)

> [Before the threshold of each sepulchre, Migan sacrificed the slave who was kneeling between two of the executioner's assistants as the hut was being repaired. The victim would go to inform the king in question about the work done on his tomb and about the adornment of his remains].

The living maintain the link with the dead by sacrificing the slaves. In making sure that the tradition is carried out, Guézo is appeasing the dead kings because he knows that at his own death, the living will be expected to sacrifice slaves for his sake. Hazoumé uses his vivid descriptions and the role played by Guézo to underscore his opposition to Dahomeyan customary practices. He arranges his narrative in such a way as to justify his ideological stance vis-à-vis the Dahomeyans.

An ardent Catholic, Hazoumé could not in any way ignore the ignominies committed by Guézo and other Dahomeyan kings in the name of the Ancestors. Yet he did not see any contradiction between his admiration for the ideals of the Dahomeyan kingdom and his support for the "civilizing mission" of French colonialism (Bjornson xvii). But how can Hazoumé reconcile this position with his pride in his cultural identity?

His ambivalent position vis-à-vis the Dahomeyans is partly due to the fact that he himself did not come from Dahomey but rather from Porto Novo, which had been a bitter rival of the Dahomeyans since the early nineteenth century. Coupled with his Western Catholic education, this background made it difficult for him to sympathize with the more inhumane aspects of Dahomeyan customary practices. The fact that Hazoumé became a French citizen after the First World War is another expression of the pro-colonialist stance he adopts in his fictional writing.[2] In fact, *Doguicimi* does not portray an unequivocally positive image of Africans, as was the case in most Negritude writing of the period. Although he does offer a generally positive image of Guézo, Toffa, and Doguicimi, he undermines it by focusing long detailed descriptions upon scenes of human sacrifice. In other words, Hazoumé subverts the anti-colonialist potential of his discourse by dwelling upon descriptions that tend to distract the readers' attention from the "raison d'être" behind his assertion of pride in his African heritage. Hazoumé's pro-colonialist stance is also evident in the way he uses Doguicimi at the end of the novel to serve as a mouthpiece for his own views. During the course of the novel, she becomes a symbol of nobility, but her imagined concluding remarks constitute a clear justification of French colonialism in Dahomey. If Doguicimi were still alive, Hazoumé conjectures, she would welcome the French administration of the country, even though there is nothing in his earlier portrayal of her to suggest that she would have had any opinions on the subject at all. Nonetheless, according to Hazoumé, Doguicimi would have wished for the French to intervene and to stop the expansionist activities of the Dahomeyans and their inhuman sacrifices:

> Doguicimi, j'ai imaginé aussi qu'à la réception de cette mission d'Europe à la cour de Guézo tu avais souhaité plutôt l'avènement des Zojagués—Français—qui te paraissaient réunir les qualités nécessaires pour pouvoir mettre fin aux incéssantes guerres des rois dahoméens, à la traite des Noirs et au sacrifice humain qui ruinaient le pays plus qu'ils ne l'enrichissaient. (509-510)

> [Doguicimi, I also imagined that, when this mission from Europe was received at the court of Guézo, you had rather preferred the coming of the Zojagués—the French—who, you thought, seemed to have the essential qualities that would enable them to stop the endless wars of the Dahomeyan kings, the slave trade, and the human sacrifices that were ruining the country more than they were enriching it].

As Huannou rightly remarked; "ce discours est tout entier une justification anticipée de la colonisation du Dahomey par la

France...Par sa bouche, c'est le citoyen français Paul Hazoumé, c'est le futur conseiller à l'Assemblée de l'Union Française qui parle" (1978, 210). [Through his words, it is the French citizen Paul Hazoumé, it is the future representative at the Assembly of the French Union who is speaking]. Yet even if Doguicimi is opposed to the inhuman customary practices of her people, she does not necessarily have to advocate the French "civilizing mission" as the only possible alternative to them. In fact, Hazoumé's narrative itself hardly constitutes a justification for this contrived ending. Earlier in the novel, Doguicimi herself expressed concern about the impact of colonial rule on the culture of her people, arguing that:

> Avant l'arrivée des Blancs dans ce pays, le désir de nos ancêtres était, comme leur besoin, très modeste. Votre société a imposé à nos grands-pères une nouvelle vie et placé la puissance de l'argent et la supériorité de la civilisation matérielle au-dessus de leurs préoccupations qui étaient exclusivement d'ordre moral [...]. Leur goût de lucre ne devait plus connaître de bornes; il introduisait bientôt dans leurs cœurs ces bas instincts: le faste, la cupidité, l'envie, la jalousie et l'égoisme qui eurent pour conséquences les incéssantes guerres, l'esclavage et le sacrifice humain contre lesquels les hommes de votre race s'élèvent aujourd'hui. Luttez contre la conception matérialiste que votre venue à vous, les Blancs, a introduite dans l'esprit de ce peuple. (398)

> [Before the arrival of the white people in this country, our ancestors' desire, like their need, was very modest. Your society imposed a new sort of life on our grandfathers, and put the power of money and the superiority of material well-being at the top of their preoccupations, which had been exclusively moral in nature....Their taste for lucre had no more limits; it soon introduced the basest instincts into their hearts: ostentatiousness, greed, covetousness, jealousy, and selfishness, which all resulted in the endless wars, slavery, and human sacrifice against which the men of your race have risen today. Fight against the materialistic attitude that your coming, the white people's coming, introduced into the minds of these people].

Doguicimi clearly did not see the advent of colonialism as a blessing. On the contrary, she attacks French hypocrisy in criticizing the slave trade that they themselves introduced into the area. Although she does not condone slave trade and human sacrifice, she does point out that Europeans are as reponsible as the Dahomeyans for the evil they represent. From this perspective, Hazoumé obviously fails to provide a narrative justification for the role he assigns to his heroine at the end of the novel.

Hazoumé's ambivalence toward French colonialism is compounded by his attempt to reconcile his historical account of the Dahomeyan kingdom with a fictionalized love story involving both

Doguicimi and the king who regrets not having kept her in his own harem. Part of Doguicimi's nobility is manifested in her faithfulness to Toffa, who, ironically, expresses little respect for women and their trustworthiness. When Toffa goes off to war, Doguicimi sends him the amulettes he needs for his protection, and at the end, she asks to be buried with his skull, which had been retrieved during the Dahomeyans' second war against the Mahis. In both instances, she is clearly depicted as a noble individual who is worthy of the utmost trust. But in this ambiguous portrayal of his heroine, Hazoumé employs various narrative techniques which clearly reveal his own ideological stance in the novel.

The ambivalence of *Doguicimi* reflects the ambivalence of Hazoumé's attitude toward history—an ambivalence that emerges in his manipulative use of an omniscient narrator, whose interventions bridge the gap between the past and the present by interpreting comparisons between contemporary Dahomeyan society and the society of the historical period that inspired his fictional creation. In this way, for example, he can make an ideological statement about the African woman. He regrets that traditional values which guided women like Doguicimi are losing their force in society:

> Mais elles sont légion aussi nos mères, c'est-à-dire des femmes qui ont été élevées, dans leur famille, avec l'idée de ne se jamais prostituer, celles qui savent qu'une telle inconduite est déshonneur tant pour elles-mêmes que pour leur famille et celle de leur époux. A la pudeur native de nos mères était ajoutée, reconnaissons-le, la crainte d'un châtiment de la part des fétiches et des ancêtres [...]. Cette crainte, puissant frein, maintient les mœurs dans leur intégrité chez les fétiches du Dahomey et fait que, par leur grand nombre, les femmes vertueuses consolent de la faute des autres qui sont encore une infime minorité, mais dont le nombre s'accroît depuis que, sous prétexte d'émanciper la femme noire, on lui facilite le divorce. (509)

> [But our mothers are also legions, that is to say, women who were raised by their families with an abhorrence of ever prostituting themselves, those who recognize that such immoral behavior is a disgrace as much for themselves as for their family and that of their husband. The natural modesty of our mothers was, we have to admit, strengthened by the fear of a punishment by the ancestors and the fetishes...This fear, a powerful restraint, sustains an integrity of morals among the fetishists of Dahomey, and as a result the large number of virtuous women compensates for the deviance of the others, who are still only an insignificant minority, although their numbers have been growing ever since divorce was made easier under the pretext of emancipating the black woman].

Through this authorial intervention, Hazoumé takes a stand on a contemporary issue—the problem of marriage and divorce. If he regrets the impact of the Dahomeyan kingdom's imperial ambitions on its neighbors, he also regrets the influence of European culture on traditional African moral systems.

This direct authorial intervention to moralize about social issues reflects the influence of oral story-telling techniques on Hazoumé. The narrator of an oral tale often moralizes at the end of his or her story, for the story itself always has a moral in it. Similarly, Hazoumé's fiction contains moral lessons. For example, he moralizes about the ambitions of Dahomey in the nineteenth century and about its inhuman customary practices. He also moralizes about the influence of colonialism on indigenous African customs and traditions. But it is important to note that Hazoumé's moral lessons derive both from his African upbringing and his Western Catholic education. Drawing his morality from these two different cultures sometimes leads to ambivalence, as evidenced in the position he adopts in the novel vis-à-vis French colonialism.

Another oral technique in *Doguicimi* is the theatrical nature of the narrative itself. At the beginning of the novel, Hazoumé uses the crier Panlingan to create a theatrical atmosphere and to give the reader the impression that he or she is about to see a theatrical representation. As Panlingan performs his daily ceremony, singing the history of the Dahomeyan kingdom, we get an insight into the way in which oral history is passed from generation to generation. Oral story-telling often involves call-and-response patterns. By going around the whole palace and by evoking the names of all the kings and their accomplishments, Panlingan is inviting the people in the palace to take part in his daily ritual for the awakening of the king. In this way, they will be participating indirectly in re-creating the history of the kingdom. Their presence and their participation is essential for the ceremony. They are part of a play that initiates readers into the intricacies of Dahomeyan customs:

> Sur les lèvres des Danhomênous qui l'entendaient, se pressaient ferventes des prières à l'adresse des ancêtres dont ils imploraient les bénédictions pour le Danhomê qu'ils avaient fondé, agrandi, rendu puissant et prospère et qu'ils devaient continuer à protéger. (15)

> [Upon the lips of the Danhomênous who heard him, fervent prayers were addressed to the ancestors, imploring their blessings for the Danhomê which they had founded, enlarged, and made powerful as well as prosperous and which they should continue to protect].

This passage suggests the communal participation of the people in a ritual performed on their behalf by Panlingan. The reader sees how this communal spirit is acted out by both the person on stage (Panlingan) and the audience (the people in the palace).

Hazoumé also introduces oral story-telling techniques through the use of songs. In those sung after Dahomey has gone to war with her neighbors, the singer involves the crowd as he recounts the history of the great kings of Dahomey. For example, one song relates the tribulations of the Dahomeyans as they fought one kingdom after another. At this particular moment in the story, the singer's desire is to console the people after their recent defeat in the first war against the Mahinous. The words of the song thus serve as an encouragement to the people in the face of defeat and humiliation.

For example, the first stanza ends with the words: "Nous sommes petits par le nombre! Mais grands par la vaillance" (172). [We are small in number but great in valliance]. By evoking the valor of the Dahomeyan people in the past, the singer seeks to counter the psychological impact of their defeat in the present. For the singer, the Dahomeyans will become victorious again, like their ancestors, and they will avenge their defeat. Throughout the song, the singer inspires a sense of solidarity among the people. Hazoumé uses him to reinforce a sense of the novel's historicity.

Another oral technique adopted by Hazoumé is the frequent use of proverbs. These proverbs are translated literally from the vernacular, and even though they sometimes lose part of their original meaning, they add considerable local color to the novel. They also enhance the sense of historicity that is central to the idea of the historical novel. Adrien Huannou has commented on the influence of orality on Hazoumé's writing, and he affirms that, although Hazoumé must have consulted written documents in his anthropological research, his primary sources were undoubtedly oral ones:

> [...] La matière première de son ouvrage provient principalement de la tradition orale à laquelle il est redevable à plus d'un titre. Hazoumé tient son art de conter moins des romanciers français que des hérauts et chroniqueurs des rois d'Abomey et des conteurs traditionnels. (1987, 90).

> [...] The raw material of his work comes mainly from oral tradition to which he owes much. Hazoumé gets his art of narrating less from French novelists than from the heralds and chroniclers of Abomey kings and from traditional story tellers].

Huannou remarks further that Hazoumé embellishes his novel with other oral materials borrowed from his own Fon language (1987, 90). Through the use of songs and proverbs, Hazoumé gives us some insight into Dahomeyan belief systems, for these oral materials reflect how the Dahomeyans relate with one another and with their deities. For example, referring to a king as a lion or as a tiger suggests the type of valor that is expected of that king by his own society. By incorporating such elements into his narrative, therefore, Hazoumé authenticates his historical fiction and makes Dahomeyan customs comprehensible to his readers.

Furthermore, Hazoumé employs footnotes to clarify points in the narrative and to reinforce the sense that his fictional creation is historically accurate. Footnoting is a common practice in historical novels, for it is often used to enhance the illusion of verisimilitude. By resorting to footnotes, he also adds local color to his narrative. For example, he explains that in the Dahomeyan kingdom, measurement was done with a bamboo rod and that this practice was introduced by King Agaja. But this detail does more than add local color. It also serves to authenticate Hazoumé's fictional narrative:

> Mèsure de longueur créée par Agaja et qui valait environ cinq mètres. Elle lui avait servi pour mésurer la distance d'Abomey à la côte, après la conquête du royaume houéda. (41)

> [Unit of measurement, about five metres long, invented by Agaja. He had used it to measure the distance from Abomey to the coast after the conquest of the Houéda kingdom].

In this instance, he is referring to a verifiable historical fact by invoking the name of an authentic King and an authentic period in the history of the Dahomeyan kingdom, thereby lending a greater sense of authenticity to his narrative.

Hazoumé also evokes the slave-trade era in a footnote that explains the meaning of the word "zojagué"— "mot indigène désignant les Français, et dont l'origine remonte aux premiers temps de la traite des Noirs" (43). [Indigenous word meaning the French, and of which the origins date back to the first days of the slave trade]. By referring to the word that was used to mean the French people, he is not only heightening the verisimilitude of his narrative; he is also alluding to an important factor in the history of Dahomey—the slave trade—and bringing it into relation with the arrival of the French.

In another footnote, Hazoumé explains the customary practices that had made the Dahomeyans unpopular with Europeans and with their own neighbors:

> Jého: littéralement Chambre de perles. C'est un autel élevé à la manière d'un roi et au pied duquel on lui sacrifiait. La terre en était pétrie, dit-on, avec de l'huile de palme, le sang des victimes humaines et mélangée de pièces d'or et de perles, d'où son nom de Chambre de perles. (24)

> [Jêho: literally Room of Jewels. It is an altar which has been raised in the memory of a king and at the foot of which sacrifices are made to him. It is said that the soil was kneaded with palm oil and the blood of human

sacrifices and mixed with gold coins and perles, hence its name "Room of Jewels"].

This footnote suggests that the description of human sacrifice in the main body of the text is inspired by verifiable historical documentation. From both written and oral sources, Hazoumé wishes to justify his ideological stance towards Dahomeyan customary practices. All these footnotes contribute to the novel's universe of discourse in the sense that his use of historically verifiable people, places, events, and customs enhances the real-seemingness of his fiction. Like nineteenth-century European historical novelists, Hazoumé employs minutely detailed descriptions of places and events, often to the extent that he seems to have digressed from the main subject matter of his narrative. Such detailed descriptions can also evoke strong emotional responses in the reader. Thus, for example, Hazoumé's long and detailed descriptions of human sacrifice constitute one way of expressing his opposition to inhuman Dahomeyan customary practices. They also establish a basis for the reader's condemnation of these practices. Without intervening directly to moralize about the evils of such customs, Hazoumé manipulates the reader's emotions by creating a vivid picture of the cruel way in which the sacrifices were carried out.

What is most striking in *Doguicimi* is Hazoumé's concern for historicity. But precisely this concern lies behind the ambivalent discourse that characterizes the novel. Hazoumé's apparent anti-colonialist stance is not altogether different from that of the Negritude writers, but it is undermined by the pro-colonialist tone that he adopts, particularly in the epilogue to his novel. In this epilogue, he expresses his belief that a pro-colonialist attitude was justified by what he viewed as a need for the French "civilizing mission" to put an end to the expansionist ambitions of the Dahomeyan kingdom. Although Erickson does not regard the novel as an apology for colonialism, he overlooks the importance of this epilogue for any overall interpretation of the novel. Besides, a text sometimes has more far-reaching ramifications than those intended by the writer himself.

Erickson suggests that Hazoumé, mindful of the potential reaction of his French readers, included the epilogue as a "mild bit of self-serving flattery" (127). Commenting on the use of Doguicimi as a mouthpiece in the epilogue, Blair also suggests that Hazoumé's intention was to end the novel on a moralizing note and that the date of publication of the novel is relevant:

> This is a period when an African intellectual who has had success in France would be prepared to whitewash the image of the colonists and present them as having brought a measure of salvation to a primitive people. (77)

because he did not believe that his people should continue to be subjugated to foreign rule.

In a sense, Boni came to consider himself as a spokesperson for the collective consciousness of his people. The writing of historical fiction enabled him to speak in their name and against the European colonial enterprise that had sought to annihilate their culture. A committed writer in the Sartrean sense, Boni clearly announces his intention in the preface to his novel, and this purpose is strikingly similar to that of Sartre's "engagé" writer. As Sartre explains:

> L'écrivain "engagé" sait que la parole est action: il sait que dévoiler c'est changer et qu'on ne peut dévoiler qu'en projettant de changer. Il a abandonné le rêve impossible de faire une peinture impartiale de la société et de la condition humaine. (781)

> [The "committed" writer knows that speech is action: he knows that to reveal is to change and that one cannot reveal except by planning to change. He has abandoned the impossible dream of painting an impartial picture of society and the human condition].

Boni takes a stand in his historical fiction. He writes about the human condition, about the colonized subject, in the hope that he can help correct misconceptions that Europeans have disseminated about the history of his own people. His act of engagement is expressed through fictions in which he restates the position he adopted in declaring his political engagement.

Like Hazoumé, Boni seeks to create a discourse capable of questioning Euro-centric misconceptions about pre-colonial Africa. One way in which he does so is by recording the true facts about the powerful and well-structured socio-political systems of the Bwa people.

To assert a pride in his Bwa culture, Boni recounts how the Bwa people had developed their own political institutions before the advent of colonialism. Further, to subvert Euro-centric myths about Africa and Africans, he provides a detailed portrayal of the power-structure in traditional Bwa society. In *La Vie des Noirs d'Afrique*, André Démaison argues that before the advent of colonialism, African peoples only recognized an allegiance to the family, to the ethnic group with its chiefs, and to the ancestral totems. According to him, such allegiances held people together as a community in a situation where there was no sense of belonging to a nation comprised of different ethnic groups. Démaison was one of the French intellectuals who sought in good faith to make Africa better known to a world in which everything was still perceived and understood in relation to European standards of value. Nevertheless, even he fails to grasp a crucial aspect of African history—an aspect to which both Hazoumé and Boni draw attention by means of their historical fiction. For example, Boni's depiction of the Bwa kingdom demonstrates how a well-structured African system was destroyed by its encounter with the West. Within this system, there was an idea of nation. European colonization introduced this concept only in the limited sense that Europeans created arbitrary borders between their colonies after engaging in what has come to be known as the "scramble for Africa."

Like Hazoumé, Boni demonstrates that European political domination of the continent had devastating effects on the institutions of Africans. Unlike Hazoumé, he portrays how the Bwas were governed according to the norms of the ancestors and how they related with their neighbors. Boni is not critical of the traditional institutions that he describes in his historical fiction, but he does not have to deal with the political ambitions of the Bwa people as Hazoumé did in depicting the Dahomeyans, many of whose traditional systems he clearly condemned. Unlike Hazoumé, Boni is an insider passionately concerned with the historical reality of a people from whom he descended. The fact that Boni himself was a Bwa provides a political incentive that Hazoumé (who was not a Dahomeyan) did not have. This incentive certainly helps to account for his more positive stance toward the people he is depicting in his novel.

In *Crépuscule des temps anciens*, readers learn that Bwa sociopolitical institutions are governed by the "Conseil des anciens" of Wakara, a body which oversees the political stability of the society. Unlike Hazoumé in *Doguicimi*, the focal point for Boni is not a royal family represented by a king and those who help to sustain his power. On the contrary, his militancy expresses itself through the political power he ascribes to ordinary people.

To subvert the Euro-centric notion that colonialism was for the good of the colonized, Boni underscores the importance of what actually took place during the French colonial invasion of the region and how these events were perceived by the Africans living there. As Homi Bhabha points out, there was not just the discourse of the colonizer during the colonial era. There was also the counter-discourse of the colonized. Hence, the Bwa people were not merely passive observers of the colonial conquests which were to shape the destiny of their region. They actively resisted the incursions of the French. In an important footnote, Boni recounts how the French themselves reacted to Bwa resistance. Like his fellow historian Adu Boahen, Boni focuses on an aspect of colonial history that has often been neglected or distorted—the reaction of the native peoples themselves to the brutality of colonial conquests.

Nazi Boni: *Crépuscule des temps anciens*

Boni emphasizes the usual European blindness toward this aspect of history when he describes how the French Chief Administrator Vidal perceived the war with the Bwa:

> Pour en comprendre l'exacte signification, il est nécessaire de dire le fanatisme violent, le mépris absolu de la mort, l'audace et le courage tranquilles dont ont fait preuve les rebelles au cours des combats les plus meurtriers. Il faut dire aussi l'étroite cohésion, la discipline merveilleuse, l'esprit de solidarité et de sacrifices qui les animait et les portait aux actes d'héroisme les plus troublants. Des hommes, en grand nombre des vieillards, des femmes, des enfants, en groupes ou isolément, préféraient se faire tuer ou se laisser enfumer et griller dans les cases incendiées, plutôt que de se rendre, malgré la promesse de vie sauve qui leur était faite, ne voulant même pas profiter des facilités d'évasion que leur offraient les ténèbres de la nuit ou le retrait momentané de nos tirailleurs, pour échapper à la mort certaine qui les attendait. (233)

> [In order to understand the exact significance of it, it is necessary to admit the violent fanaticism, the absolute contempt of death, the calm audacity and courage that the rebels showed during the most deadly combats. One should also mention the close unity, the marvelous discipline, the spirit of solidarity and sacrifice which prompted them and moved them to the most disturbing heroic acts. People, most of them old men, women, children, in groups or alone, preferred to get killed or be smoked or burned in the huts on fire rather than surrender, in spite of the safe life which was promised them, not even wanting to seize the opportunities of the easy escape that was made possible by the darkness of the night or the temporary retreat of our soldiers, to escape the certain death that awaited them].

This footnote clearly reveals the inhumanity that was inflicted on Africans during the process of conquest and colonization. But Boni is also interested in the heroic counter-discourse of the Bwa people, for even the reaction of the French administration cannot conceal the fact that the Bwa fiercely resisted colonization.

As Homi Bhabha contends, the goal of colonial discourse is the creation of a space in which a "subject people" can produce a knowledge that is not controlled by the surveillance of the colonizer. Boni's fiction provides an excellent example of this process. According to Bhabha, colonial discourse seeks authorization for its strategies by producing a stereotypical knowledge that is antithetically evaluated. This sort of discourse is illustrated in the above quotation, for despite his admiration for the courage of the Bwa in resisting the incursions of the French army, Vidal does not expect a supposedly "inferior" people to prevail against the military might of a supposedly "superior" European power.

Bhabha also contends that a primary objective of colonial discourse is to construe the colonized as a racially defined population of degenerate types in order to justify conquest and to establish systems of administration and instruction (154). Against this backdrop, Boni's interest in historicity enables him to depict accurately the consequences of French colonial rule and to reject the notion that colonialism was good for those who were subjected to it.

In pursuing this goal, Boni portrays a Bwa society that was knit together by a strong sense of communality. Relationships between people in this society were governed by their shared faith in the conviction that they all descended from the same ancestors. In this sense, Boni's narrative is again characteristic of Negritude writing that confronts the West with the assertion that there are fundamental differences between African and European ways of life. In Bwa society, as can be seen in Boni's *Crépuscule des temps anciens*, the responsibility of the individual extends to the society at large because each family is considered to be a microcosm within the larger unit, the extended family.

For example, during the festival of the Ancestor Diyiou, relatives from distant places are welcomed not as guests but as members of the same family. For Boni, this spirit of belonging constitutes part of his pride in his own cultural heritage. It is also an integral component of the African religious sentiment, which he, like Hazoumé, refuses to idealize. In his preface, Boni states that he does not agree with those who demand that African writers should present an idyllic image of society. Unlike Hazoumé, however, Boni's narrative refuses to pander to a European taste for the exotic. As he himself explains:

> D'aucuns seront tentés de me reprocher de n'avoir pas estompé certaines réalités d'apparence primitive. Cette attitude procèderait d'un complexe. Je répugne au vide du clinquant. J'ai voulu intentionnellement, que l'originalité de "Crépuscule des Temps Anciens" résidât, au moins en partie, dans sa sincérité pour ne pas dire son pragmatisme. (19)

> [Some people will be tempted to reproach me for not having concealed some realities which seem primitive. That attitude would come from a complex. I find the emptiness of flashy language repugnant. I wanted intentionally that the originality of *Crépuscule des temps anciens* lie at least partially, in its sincerity, not to mention its pragmatism].

Yet Boni's attitude is different from that of Hazoumé, who resented the Dahomeyan people (an ethnic group to which he did not belong) for their political ambitions and on account of their inhuman religious practices. In contrast, Boni posits his discourse upon an acceptance of the perceptions on which Bwa religious practices were based. A Bwa himself, he had a more profound sense of commitment to the people he was depicting than did Hazoumé.

Boni's depiction of his main characters Kya and Térhé demonstrates his detailed knowledge of the Bwa belief system. Anthropology and fiction are well married in Boni's portrayal of the relationship between the two men, on the one hand, and between them and the rest of society, on the other. The political rivalry between them reveals a manichean tension between good and evil in Bwa society, for according to the Bwa perception of the world, the supernatural (or unexplainable) manifests itself in the daily life of the people. For example, in Boni's description of the yearly festival during which relatives come from long distances to Bwa land, the real-seeming physical world fuses with the world of the unknown in a way that resembles the "magical realism" or "marvelous realism" of Latin American writers:

> Ils pilent des enfants dans les mortiers, les réduisent en marmelade, les roulant en boules à la manière des scarabées. Puis, il leur suffit de souffler dessus pour les réssusciter! Il faut absolument voir ces choses. (72)

> [They pound children in mortars, turn them into marmalade, rolling them into balls like beetles. Then, they only have to breathe on them to bring them back to life! You absolutely have to see these things].

Magical realism here means the ability to manipulate the supernatural by resurrecting the children after pounding them in the mortar. The supernatural is described as an integral part of the reality of the Bwas, although the last sentence in this passage suggests that Boni is conscious of his Western readers, for whom the African supernatural world would be unfamiliar. At the same time, he uses the traditional African oral narrative technique when he addresses his audience, the reader, directly.

Boni's sense of historicity also becomes apparent in the way he describes how the Bwas live in fear of the wrath of the gods. The spirits of the ancestors protect good people like Térhé but castigate evil ones like Kya. Térhé is protected by the ancestors because he never cheats in a game or during a war. He is a loyal warrior who kills to defend his land and to deliver it from the enemy. He kills to redeem people from oppression and to preserve the honor of his family and his society. Yet when he engages in such behavior, he is merely carrying out his duty to the ancestors. In contrast, Kya kills for pleasure and against the laws of the land. When he undertakes an unjustifiable expedition against the neighbors of the Bwa, he violates the laws of the ancestors and dies tragically. Society considers his fate to be a sort of retributive justice because his actions did not enjoy the blessing of the ancestors. Punished by the gods, he does not have the sympathy of his own people:

> On reconnut que la victime avait tous les torts. Les deux villes n'étaient pas en état de guerre. L'expédition de Kya ne se justifiait pas et ne pouvait en aucune façon bénéficier du soutien des Ancêtres et des divinités. (211)

> [It was accepted that the victim was very wrong. The two towns were not at war with each other. Kya's expedition was not justified and could not in any way win the support of the Ancestors and the deities].

In this passage, Boni demonstrates how religion governs the life of the people. At the same time, he is dismissing European claims that Africans needed to be colonized because they were innately belligerent people. Unlike the Dahomeyans in Hazoumé's *Doguicimi*, the Bwa wanted to live peacefully with their neighbors—an attitude that was generally overlooked or distorted in Euro-centric historical writings.

When Kya is punished by the gods for his actions, his fate serves as an example for the rest of society, and Boni's description of him reveals a profound understanding of the psychological impact of guilt within the Bwa cultural context. Because Kya has killed and desecrated the land against the laws of the ancestors, he is haunted by evil spirits:

> [...] Ses nuits, affirmait-on, étaient hantées des fantômes de ceux qu'il abattait. Ils entraient, ressortaient, revenaient, tournoyaient, chuchotaient, remplissaient jusqu'au matin sa maison d'un piétinement indéfinissable. Ils froufroulaient derrière les greniers, dans le plafond, faisaient voler en éclats maintes objets. Kya ne trouvait pas le repos dans son sommeil infesté de cauchemars. Il voyait toutes sortes de figures grimaçantes, de squelettes mouvants qui exécutaient une ronde dégingandée. (64)

> [...His nights, it was affirmed, were haunted by the ghosts of those he killed. They entered, went out, came back, swirled, whispered, filled his house with an indefinable stamping. They rustled behind the granaries, in the ceiling, broke a lot of things into pieces. Kya could not get any rest in his sleep full of nightmares. He saw all sorts of grimacing objects, moving skeletons which made gangling rounds].

Here again, readers are confronted with a marvelous realism. What happens to Kya is beyond rational explanation. For the Bwa people, it is possible to explain why Kya sees spirits that others cannot see, for not everyone becomes the target of evil spirits. Yet the supernatural events that happen to Kya are accepted by society as the normal way the gods express their anger towards an individual.

As John Mbiti has written, African religion underlines the humanness of man vis-à-vis the other reality from which he derives his origin as well as his continuing well-being; that reality is God. Kya might be regarded as powerful by his human victims, but he and society are constantly being reminded of the omniscience and omnipresence of the Supreme Being. Man cannot have his way if his actions are not endorsed by the ancestors. For example, Kya's father Lowan, cannot invoke the evil spirits on Térhé because the latter is under the protection of the gods:

> Toutes ses démarches aboutirent à des résultats troublants. Il apprit que Térhé était né sous le signe du succès et du bonheur, que son avenir était faste, que ceux qui tenteraient de jeter un sort sur lui, subiraient l'effet du boomerang, car il jouissait de la protection des dieux. (168)

> [All his attempts ended in troubling results. He learned that Térhé was born under the sign of success and happiness, that his future was good, that those who would try to cast a spell on him would suffer the effect of the boomerang, for he was under the protection of the gods].

Like an anthropologist or a historian, Boni explains how Bwa society interprets the reaction of the gods, yet readers cannot help but realize that Boni's fictional rendering of the Bwa also reflects his profound personal knowledge of their spiritual reality.

This knowledge is enhanced by his skillful use of Bwa legends and myths to subvert Euro-centric notions about the Africans' lack of religion before the advent of colonialism. For example, Boni incorporates into his narrative an account of Bwa creation myths and a description of the relationship that existed, according to Bwa legend, between humans and God at the beginning of time:

> Un incontestable mimétisme existait entre la Nature et l'homme. Celui ci et celui-là vivaient en symbiose unis par une invisible force centrique. L'univers multiple semblait tenir d'une seule âme, tant l'harmonie, ne fut-ce qu'en apparence, était parfaite entre les êtres et les choses... (22)

> [An unquestionable mimetism existed between Nature and man. The latter and the former lived in harmony, united by an invisible central force. The multiple universe seemed to hold in a single soul; harmony, be it in appearance, was so perfect between beings and things].

Boni's description of Bwa society during the precolonial period is characteristic of Negritude writing, for it conveys the impression that Bwa society resulted from a perfect harmony between God and his creatures and that this idyllic society lost its stability when it came into contact with the hegemonic cultures responsible for colonial conquest.

Just as European fiction sometimes draws upon Greek and Roman mythology or the Christian Bible to lend dignity to more commonplace scientific representations, Boni exploits the mythology of his people to provide a profoundly human, spiritual dimension to his story and to counter the impact of Euro-centric discourse about Africa. By placing the creation story at the beginning of the novel, he is employing a stylistic device that enables him to situate the Bwa people in the global perspective that characterized their own view of the world. As Mbiti has argued, creation stories in Africa may vary, but there is nearly always a general belief in God as the Creator of all things (Mbiti 58).

In Boni's account of creation in Bwa mythology, some of the symbols would be familiar to European readers. According to the Christian Bible, for example, Adam and Eve were expelled from the Garden of Eden because they disobeyed God. Boni alludes to this story in recounting the Bwa version of creation:

> Il semble en effet, qu'à l'époque, le Grand-Maître-de-l'Univers eût conservé à cette fraction de l'Humanité une portion du paradis terrestre jadis légué à Adam et Eve. (23)

> [It seemed in effect that at that time, the Big-Master-of-the-Universe had reserved for this part of Humanity a portion of the earthly paradise given to Adam and Eve long ago].

In this version of creation myth, a woman first ate the forbidden fruit and broke the bonds of trust that had existed between God and man at the beginning.

> Il fallut la négligence d'une femme, il fallut ô malheur! qu'une femme transgressât les recommandations de *Dombéni* pour que, furieux, le ciel s'envolât haut, très haut, très très haut, encore plus haut, emportât et ses richesses et ce qui alimentait le genre humain. (23)

> [Through the negligence of a woman, what misfortune! through a woman's transgression of the recommendations of *Dombeni*, the sky, furious, flew away high, very high, very very high, higher still, carrying away its riches and what fed the human species].

Like the Christian version of the creation myth, Bwa creation stories tend to portray women in negative terms, although Boni himself glorifies the heroine of his novel just as Hazoumé had done with Doguicimi. As in the Christian Bible, the bond between human beings and the divine are broken after a woman betrays the trust that had been placed in them. Furthermore, in both stories, man must toil for his survival after the woman ate the forbidden fruit.[2]

Boni's idyllic account of the Bwa belief system accords with his Negritudist objective of confronting the West with a more positive image of Africa than the one that Europeans had promulgated to justify Christian proselytism as well as their "civilizing mission." He clearly ascribes the destruction of Bwa institutions to the arrival of European colonialism. In a footnote, he himself decries the negative impact of colonialism on Bwa religious practices, pointing out how some of them, such as the *Do*, had disappeared entirely as a consequence of Christian influence in the area:

> Le culte du *Do* régresse avec l'évolution et les progrès du christianisme. A Bwan, il a cessé d'exister depuis 1958. (203)

> [With the evolution and progress of Christianity, the *Do* cult is less practised. At Bwan, it has ceased to exist since 1958].

Such footnotes reinforce the sense that Boni's account of Bwa religious rites is historically accurate, but they also underscore the impact of French colonialism on the culture of the people who had become the victims of it. The era in which these changes were taking place was truly the "crépuscule des temps anciens" because it was the time when indigenous institutions were collapsing. Under these circumstances, Boni's plea for African researchers to help preserve their rich cultural heritage takes on a tone of urgency. Like Hazoumé, Boni emphasizes the fact that Africans did not need a European "mission civilisatrice" to believe in God. In fact, that "mission civilisatrice" actually destroyed the belief system that held the Bwas together and rendered coherent their belief in a single God.

Like other early African writers who incorporated historical and sociological dimensions in their fiction, Boni links his account of the Bwa belief system with a strong sense of community. As in much of the Negritude writing of the period, Boni's *Crépuscule des temps anciens* presents African society as embued with a communal spirit that was lost as a consequence of contact with Western culture. In describing this communal spirit, Boni clearly understands it from the vantage point of an insider. Using the myths and legends of the Bwa people, he shows how the extended family system enabled people to live in a spirit of communality—a spirit reinforced by belief in the family's totem (an animal regarded as sacred because it represents the spirit of the ancestors). It is Gin'le the "ancien," well versed in the traditions of the land, who explains the significance of the totem to the younger people.

The communal spirit is clearly expressed in the way the Bwa celebrate the "Yumbeni" festival of the ancestor Diyioua. For example, it becomes apparent in the property concept behind the treatment of domestic animals during the festival:

> [...] les *Nimisis* ou "Neveux", les "enfants des sœurs" c'est-à-dire tous ceux dont les familles maternelles sont originaires de Bwan, ont plein droit de se les approprier. Ils ne peuvent prétendre à l'héritage de leurs oncles, mais en revanche, sont autorisés à rafler leurs biens dans certaines circonstances. En l'occurence, cette pratique prescrite par la coutume dure aussi longtemps que la fête. (74)

> [...the *Nimisis* or "Nephews," "the sisters' children," that is to say, all those whose maternal families are from Bwan, have full right to it. They cannot claim inheritance of their uncles, but on the contrary, they are allowed to grab their property in certain circumstances. In this case, this practice prescribed by custom lasts as long as the celebration].

To give readers an insight into the Bwa concept of family relationships, Boni explains the unfamiliar and emphasizes the fact that the term "nephew" is understood in a wider sense than it is in Western societies. Once again, he is resorting to a Negritude discourse that presents African institutions and belief systems as fundamentally different from those of Europe. Negritude discourse thrived on "difference," and although Boni does not specifically mention this difference, it is constantly being suggested throughout his narrative. In the above passage, he is not only interested in describing how the "Yumbeni" festival was performed; he is also interested in showing how different it is from Western practices.

Like Hazoumé, Boni owes his knowledge of Bwa culture to his long contact with the "anciens." In societies profoundly shaken by the impact of colonialism, the "anciens" remained the guardians of a vanishing tradition. Only through them can ethnologists and historians like Hazoumé and Boni discover the oral sources of the history of their people. The contribution of the "anciens" was crucial for Hazoumé and Boni because they had been heavily influenced by Western culture as a consequence of the French formal education they had imbibed. In fact, Boni's narrative reinforces the oft-quoted saying by the Malian Amadou Hampaté Bâ who declared that, when an old man (or an old woman) dies in Africa, a whole library has burned down. In *Crépuscule des temps anciens*, the "anciens" are the unifying force in Bwa society. They remind their society what is acceptable and what is unacceptable according to the customs of the ancestors. The "anciens" are therefore the guarantors of tradition and those who maintain the communal spirit.

Boni also reinforces his portrayal of the communal spirit in Bwa society by his account of marriage customs. Indeed, Negritude writers often dwelt on such customs to justify their rejection of European value systems. In Boni's novel, the marriage between Térhé and Hadounfi is a societal affair that concerns more than two individuals. It concerns the entire community and requires that the august "Conseil des Anciens de Wakara" give it their blessing. As Nicolas Atangana has affirmed, marriage in traditional African society is an initiation into adulthood, allowing the couple to take their rightful place of responsibility in society (136). What Boni does is to present Térhé and Hakanni as an ideal couple. Hakanni respects the customs, breaking her pot as a manifestation of her love for Térhé when she hears the latter's name mentioned by somebody. Furthermore, Boni underscores the communal dimension in the polygamous marriage that unites Térhé with Hakanni and Hadounfi.

Although Boni is far from being a feminist writer, the legends and myths of Bwa society inspired him to glorify the African woman in a characteristically Negritude manner. In fact, there are many similarities between the ways in which Hazoumé and Boni close their novels. Boni does not use his heroine to support French colonialism as Hazoumé had done, but his heroine in *Crépuscule des temps anciens* does show her absolute love for her husband by refusing to withdraw from the blood pact she had signed, thereby accepting, like Doguicimi, the fate of a woman willing to die with her husband.

Having signed a blood pact with Térhé, Hakanni refuses to renounce that pact after Térhé dies as a result of having been poisoned by Lowan, who has never abandoned his desire to kill his son's rival. Hakanni refuses to accept her mother's advice to cancel the blood pact and to save her own life. When her request to be buried with Térhé's corpse is refused, she shocks everybody by revealing the secret of the blood pact she had signed with Térhé:

> Au moment de l'inhumation, Hakanni demanda à partager la tombe de Térhé. On la repoussa, la coutume ne le permettait pas. Elle insista et finit par révéler le pacte de sang qu'elle avait conclu avec son amant. On resta interloqué. (254)
>
> [At the time of burial, Hakanni asked to be buried in Térhé's tomb. She was not allowed. Custom did not permit it. She insisted and finally revealed the blood pact she had made with her lover. People were taken aback].

Even though Hakanni does not succeed in having herself buried with her husband (as Doguicimi did), she dies shortly after her husband's funeral.

Her stance is particularly noble in the sense that she refuses to commit suicide, as some members of the society had feared, because she respects the customs of her society and does not want to be given the dishonorable burial that awaits those who kill themselves. Among the Bwa, the corpse of a suicide victim is dragged to the burial ground and thrown into a hole. As Boni reports, "Elle [Hakanni] mourrait normalement, aurait des funérailles régulières et s'en irait en beauté" (255). [She (Hakanni) would die a normal death, would have a regular funeral and would depart in beauty]. What is underscored here is her dignity in wanting to be remembered as a woman who had died honorably.

Although such an ending has melodramatic overtones, readers cannot help but admire Hakanni's nobility. Like Toffa in Hazoumé's *Doguicimi*, Térhé is portrayed as an exemplary man who deserves the honor of having a wife who remains faithful to him even in death. Boni's dirge at the end of the novel is reminiscent of Hazoumé's epilogue about Doguicimi:

> La paix soit avec vous, Térhé et Hakanni. Vous avez mérité du *Bwamu* et de l'Humanité. *Pâti-Bââ* et *Pâti-Han*, partez unis et heureux vers les paradisiaques rivages et l'Au-délà où ne sévissent ni la haine ni le poison. Symbole de gloire, d'honneur et d'amour, partez, tournez sans regret le dos à l'aurore des temps nouveaux, et abandonnez à son triste sort l'étrange monde des m'as-tu vu. (256)

> [Peace be with you, Térhé and Hakanni. You deserve *Bwamu* and Humanity. *Pâti-Bââ* and *Pâti-Han*, leave, united and happy towards the heavenly shores and the Beyond where neither hatred nor poison is rampant. Symbol of glory, of honor and love, leave, without regret turn your back on the dawn of new times, and abandon the strange world of show-offs to its sad destiny].

Allowing them to enter a realm in which there is no hatred, Hakanni's and Térhé's departure symbolizes the end of the ideal world represented by pre-colonial Bwa society. Boni regrets the "crépuscule des temps anciens" and imagines Hakanni in a world where she will not regret having left behind a society that had fallen under the influence of an invading foreign culture. His use of a heroine to evoke the image of an ideal society is itself an ideological statement that reasserts his pride in his own cultural identity and rejects ethnocentric European claims to superiority.

Despite similarities with *Doguicimi*, however, the narrative form of *Crépuscule des temps anciens* is more efficient than that of the earlier historical novel because, although Boni draws on the same oral narrative techniques as Hazoumé, he does not indulge himself in the long ethnographic digressions that characterize *Doguicimi*.

Everything that occurs in *Crépuscule des temps anciens* revolves around the same theme: the destruction of Bwa socio-political institutions and the collapse of a well-structured belief system as the result of French colonialism. The influence of oral tradition on Boni's narrative manifests itself in many ways. For example, Chantal Zabus has commented on how he uses semantic shifts or extensions with words like "finir" and "soleil" (130). When some young men tease Hakanni about Térhé's love for her, she does the customary gesture of appreciation by breaking her pot. The mother cannot be upset with her because she too has done that in her youth before marriage: "'La vieille! n'avait-elle pas fait son soleil' et cassé des dizaines d'amphores?" (67). [Had the old lady not done her sun and broken ten or so pots?]. Thus the narrator translates Hakanni's mother's thoughts directly from the vernacular into French, playing with the expression "to do one's sun" which means she has spent her youth.

The guardians of the oral tradition are the "anciens," with whom Boni "traded" for a long time. The Crier in *Crépuscule des temps anciens* (as in *Doguicimi*) serves as a catalyst, symbolically reminding the members of society every night that they belong to the same family. In this sense, he represents the knowledge and wisdom of the "anciens." Yet the Crier is not the only one who symbolizes this sense of historicity in the narrative, for the griot also plays a significant role in Boni's textual quest for a viable cultural identity. In fact, the griot in *Crépuscule des temps anciens* serves as the eyes and ears of Bwa society. What he sings about individuals such as Térhé reflects the value system that is operative in his society. The Crier himself resembles the griot, convoking the villagers to listen to the message that Gnassan, the Chief of the land, has for them. The Crier also assures the approval of the griot, who testifies: "Kin! kin! kin! Grand'père ta parole sonne comme l'or..." (43). [Kin! kin! kin! Grandfather, your word sounds like gold]. A unifying force in Bwa society, the griot has an ideological function in the sense that he preserves the sense of unity and harmony that characterized pre-colonial Bwa society.

He encourages a respect for individual values and an aspiration to make positive contributions to society. He sings the honor of the individual, the family, the clan. For example, he praises Térhé in the following terms:

> Térhé! tu es un guerrier invincible, l'incarnation de la puissance humaine, le bouclier des opprimés, le porte-drapeau de toutes les causes de justice, le symbole de la vertu et de l'honneur. (147)

> [Térhé! You are an invincible warrior, the embodiment of human power, the shield of the oppressed, the flag-bearer of all causes of justice, the symbol of virtue and of honor].

Such praises reflect the norms of society and give expression to the cultural values of the Bwa people. He exclaims: "Le lion s'est remué! Son panache et ses grelots se sont envolés!" (147). [The lion has stirred. Its gallantry and its bells have vanished]. Térhé thus becomes a symbol of what masculine strength and courage stand for in society. Because the lion is a symbol of strength and endurance, the audience understands why the griot refers to Térhé in such terms. When he describes Térhé as the prototype of the Ancestor Djokandjo who had been invincible in war, the griot becomes a mouthpiece for Boni's own opinion about the role of people like Térhé in the history of the Bwa people. Boni's use of the griot in this fashion clearly demonstrates the importance of oral tradition in his re-writing of the history of his people.

To enhance the sense of historical verisimilitude in *Crépuscule des temps anciens*, Boni also creates a feeling of local color by including literal translations of words taken directly from the Bwa language. For example, the white Catholic missionaries are called "mon père-wa," and Protestant pastors are called "nansawuni wa." In fact, throughout the novel, Boni uses Bwa words such as "Nansarawa" for white people, "Dombeni" for God-the-Great, "Mb'woa" for Ancestor or Grand father, "Kanni-nipoa" for cave dwellers, "Yenissa" for elderly people and "Brawa" for young people. Boni provides translations of such words to facilitate comprehension by those unfamiliar with the Bwa language, but his use of them is a significant narrative device that serves to authenticate his historical fiction.

A related device is his use of Bwa legends and folktales to create a sense of local color, which in turn reinforces the impression of historical authenticity. For example, at one point he relates:

> Il y a, dit "Ancêtre", de cela environ *trois cents ans moins vingt*, le Bwamu jouissait d'un riche trésor de mystère et de magies, d'ineffables délices qui déteignirent sur les aïeux des grands-pères des pères de nos pères. (21)

> [Says the "Ancestor," about *three hundred minus twenty years* ago, the Bwamus enjoyed a rich treasure of mystery and magic, ineffable delights which influenced the great-grand-parents of the parents of the fathers of our fathers].

In this passage, Boni is acknowledging the source of his knowledge about Bwa history by referring to the "anciens" as the "Ancêtre." The "anciens" are the guardians of the traditions of the people, so by recalling what he has learned about the history and legends of his people, Boni is re-asserting his pride in the past when Bwa kingdom was rich and powerful. By doing so, he rejects the false Euro-centric notion that the history of his people began with colonialism.

In other legends that Boni invokes, animals and natural phenomena such as thunder and lightning take on anthropological forms. For example, in the legend about creation, thunder and lightning are presented as if they were human beings:

> Deux enfants divins: Karanvanni, le fils terrible et Hahovanni sa sœur débonnaire. Le premier ne décolère jamais, pique des crises de nerfs, tempête: *Pran! Pran! Pranan! pan! pan*! Les éclats de sa voix font trembler la terre, alors que le flamboiement de son épée aveugle les hommes. L'autre intervient chaque fois et lui conseille la douceur en ces termes: *Yêrêdê-dêdêdêdêdê*. (27)

> [Two divine children: Karanvanni, the terrible son and Hahovanni her good-natured sister. The former is always in a temper, gets a fit of nerves, rages: *Pran! Pran! Pranan! pan! pan*! The roar of his voice makes the earth shake, whilst the blaze of his sword blinds people. The other intervenes each time and advises him in the following terms to be calm: *Yêrêdê-dêdêdêdêdê*].

Lightning and thunder have a significance in Bwa mythology. They are represented as brother and sister who need each other's advice; suggesting that humans too can learn the moral of Karanvanni, who listens to the sister Hahovanni's advice all the time. The legend is therefore recognized as the source of a moral lesson for society. For Boni, this relationship is important because it is part of the history of his people, and he is interested in historicity.

The wisdom behind such legends is also transmitted to the younger generation by means of riddles such as those posed by the xylophonist: "J'ai rencontré un excellent couturier vêtu d'une blouse d'aiguilles. Qui dévine?" (38). [I met an excellent tailor wearing a smock made of needles. Who can guess?]. He gives another riddle about sexual attraction between males and females: "Mon grand'père faisait allusion à un sanctuaire broussailleux qui exerce sur le serpent un attrait irrésistible" (39). [My grandfather always made allusion to a bushy sanctuary which has an irresistible attraction on the snake]. What this riddle means is that the Bwas believe there is a natural attraction between men and women. Moral lessons on sex are often referred to in indirect terms because it is taboo to express them in plain language. Like the legends, these riddles have the effect of moralizing because, apart from being a source of entertainment to the audience, they teach the group's moral values, especially to the young. By drawing on them, Boni recognizes their importance as a force of cohesion in the socio-political systems of his people.

Boni also uses songs to invoke a sense of historical and cultural authenticity. For example, he cites war songs that inspire the Bwa to defend their land against foreign invaders. Often, the record of past experience contained in these songs serves as an inspiration to African nationalists who were fighting for the independence of their countries at the time that Boni was collecting his material and writing his book. For example, one of the war songs exhorts Bwa warriors in the following terms:

> Allez! allez! allez!
> Bwan! à Bwan! à Bwan!
> Allez au grand *Yumu*
> Au grand *Yumu*
> Au grand *Yumu* de l'Ancêtre Digioua
> Allez à Bwan
> Vaillants guerriers,
> La danse des braves. (71)

> [Go! Go! Go!
> Bwan! to Bwan! to Bwan!
> Go to the great *Yumu*
> To the great *Yumu*
> To the great *Yumu*
> To the great *Yumu* of the Ancestor Digioua
> Go to Bwan
> Gallant warriors,
> The danse of the brave].

By recalling songs that reflect the valiant attitudes of the Bwa in the past, Boni is not only asserting pride in the ancestors who resisted colonial occupation; he is also, like a griot, singing the praises of the militant nationalists of his own generation.

As already suggested above, Boni's use of footnotes to explain unfamiliar words and expressions or to relate the episodes in the story to verifiable historical events or personalities also serves to lend an aura of historical accuracy to his fictional narrative. For example, Boni devotes a page-long footnote to the historical evidence for his version of the events that transpired between the Bwa and the invading French army. In this footnote, he cites specific dates and the names of actual historical personages such as Colonel Motard, the Administrator Maubert, and the late Chief of the Karé district, Dambio Coulibaly, who betrayed his own people by fighting on the side of the invading French forces in the battle of May 1916 (234). The point is that Boni, the historical novelist, is also an archivist who substantiates his account by citing the fruits of his research in footnotes. In this sense, his historical fiction is clearly motivated by interests similar to those that inspired nineteenth-century European historical novelists before him. However, his use of footnotes also has another purpose that would have been quite foreign to his European predecessors, for Boni was intent upon rejecting everything that European colonialism represented.

From the above analysis, the significance of the subtitle to the novel therefore becomes clear: "Chronique du Bwamu". [Chronicle of the Bwamu]. Boni has done a fictional recreation of the chronicle of the Bwa people.

From an ideological point of view, Boni had much in common with Hazoumé. The major difference between them is that, whereas Hazoumé's *Doguicimi* reflects the author's ambiguous situation as an "évolué" writer, *Crépuscule des temps anciens* is an unambiguous anti-colonial statement. By weaving Bwa legends and myths into a true historical account, Boni communicates a sense of how the Bwa themselves perceive life and interact with each other and with the spirits described in their legends.

As Ngugi Wa Thiongo has said, a writer tries to make readers view not only a certain kind of reality, but also to view that reality from a certain angle of vision that is generally, although perhaps unconsciously, structured around the interests of a certain class, race, or nation (1981, 6). The validity of Ngugi's argument is clearly apparent in the case of Boni's historical novel. His portrayal of the Bwa belief system is itself an ideological statement, and his discourse falls under the general rubric of Negritude discourse. But unlike some adepts of that movement, he does not present an idyllic image of the Bwa or of African society in general, although he does seek to restore an appreciation for the value of African culture in a world where discourse is related to power.

Amilcar Cabral has also said that the value of culture as an element of resistance to foreign domination lies in the fact that culture is a vigorous manifestation on the ideological or idealist plane of the physical and historical reality of the society that is subject to domination (41). Boni's historical fiction reinforces this idea by showing how the revalorization of African culture can serve as an instrument of resistance to the European colonialism that seeks to subjugate other cultures to its own interests. Motivated by the same ideology that inspired his historical research, *Crépuscule des temps anciens* re-creates a Bwa world view that defies the stereotyped notions of Euro-centric discourse and implicitly exhorts readers to repudiate it. Although it has some characteristics of the classical European historical novel, it is above all a novel that is fundamentally African in its underlying ideology as well as in the narrative forms that Boni adopted from oral story-telling techniques.

3

Jean Malonga: *La Légende de M'Pfoumou Ma Mazono*

This chapter attempts to examine Malonga's novel as historical fiction within the backdrop of how the genre developed in French-speaking Africa. The novel was published at a time when the Negritude movement had a strong impact on French-speaking intellectuals from the continent. African writers (still under colonial rule) were obsessed about revalorizing their culture in the face of Euro-centric perceptions of the continent. It is significant for the development of this sensibility to acknowledge that the assimilationist policies of France had an enormous impact on how francophone Africans saw themselves and the rest of the world, especially in their relation with the metropole. This chapter proposes a reading of Malonga's novel as legend and as historical fiction. The novel deals with some common themes of everyday life that the reader could identify in any culture; love, war, exile, revolt and so forth, but all these themes are used to create a peculiarly African ambience.

Isidore Okpewo in his work on oral tradition in Africa defines legend as a subclass of historical tales. Legends, he says, are used in connection with the experiences of historical figures or events of a notable or memorable character (182). He identifies what he calls origin tales which, when they relate the origins of people, are legends. Legends normally deal with personalities and events that are considered so memorable that they deserve to be talked about or recounted again and again. According to his classification, Malonga's *La Légende de M'Pfoumou Ma Mazono* would be a romantic or mythical legend, which recounts events so remote to the present that the story-teller can engage in flight of imagination without fear of being challenged by the audience on the authenticity of his or her story. There is more difficulty for contemporary audiences to believe in the supernatural powers of some of the characters. Thus, when Malonga transforms his legend into a written form the supernatural events are even more difficult for the non-African reader to grasp.

Writing at a time when his country was still under the domination of colonial rule, Malonga has an ideological inclination to portray an image of Africa that his European reader was not necessarily familiar with. The major theme of the novel is the portrayal of a well-organized social system. There is no kingdom or empire as we come across in certain historical novels of the period like Hazoumé's *Doguicimi*. Nonetheless, there are political rivalries between neighbouring communities which struggle for power. There is also a class system which operates in such a way that slaves are maintained in a subordinate position in society. Malonga makes a cursory reference to slave trade with the Europeans at the end of the novel, but it does not become a major motif in the narration. This is what the narrator says in a footnote:

> Bissi-M'Poutou. Ceux de l'Occcident, c'est-à-dire ceux de l'autre côté de l'Océan. Ainsi appelés à cause de leur alliance et leur commerce facile avec les Bakongo considérés comme des traîtres à la race par leurs relations trop spectaculaires avec les négriers occidentaux. (152)
>
> [Bissi-M'Poutou. Those of the West, that is to say those of the other side of the Ocean. Thus called because of their alliance and their easy trade with the Bakongo considered as traitors to the race because of their too spectacular relationships with the western slave traders].

The fact that the author refers to this important historical incident only in a footnote suggests that it is not of major relevance to the legend of M'Pfoumou Ma Mazono on which the novel is based. Nonetheless, the footnote compliments the narrator's comments about the socio-political system that Ma Mazono sets up after he destroys an old system of serfdom and re-establishes a new type of political discourse in the society. Ma Mazono symbolizes change in society. From a humble background as the son of a woman who runs away after being caught cheating on her husband, Ma Mazono effects revolutionary changes in his society. He abolishes the system whereby one could possess slaves, and replaces it with a very egalitarian and utopian society in which there are no masters or slaves.

Mazono's evolution as a character is linked to the radical change that he wants to effect in the customs of his people. He is endowed with natural and supernatural gifts, but to understand how this character evolves, we need to go back to the beginning of the legend before his birth. Malonga paints a fascinating picture of an African culture to his foreign reader, and one can sense the Negritudist tendency to explain African culture to the French reader. He introduces the reader to some of the intricacies involved in choosing a marriage partner. As Boni demonstrated in his novel on the Bwa of Burkina Faso, marriage in Africa is not an individual affair but a group affair. It involves several families in the community. In *La Légende de M'Pfoumou Ma Mazono* too, Malonga explains why M'Polo's father wants one of her daughters for his nephew. Custom encourages this kind of marriage because it keeps the children within the extended family system. M'Polo does not think her daughters are too young to marry, for as she says: "Ignores-tu que c'est l'éducation et le rang social qui font la femme et non l'âge" (13). [Do you not know that it is education and social class which makes the woman and not age]. This customary belief encourages the marriage of young girls, especially with the approval of the mother. It also makes it difficult for a young girl to revolt against the family and society if she thinks she is not ready for marriage yet. Significantly enough, after all the tragedy provoked by the daughter's infidelity with the husband's slave, M'Polo ackowledges her role in this fate. She encouraged the daughter to marry at an age when she was not mature enough to deal with the temptations of youth and beauty. It is also significant that this realization comes at the end of the first part of the novel. After all, if M'Polo had not encouraged the daughter to marry, the events in this part of the novel would have been different. However, Malonga does not explore in any profound way this change of attitude towards customary marriage on the part of M'Polo. There is no radical evolution of the characters in terms of gender relation as a result of M'Polo's apparent passive acknowledgement of her role in the daughter's tragedy.

The narrator invites us to appreciate the elaborate customary practice of courting and dowry paying. Mi N'Tsembo is accompanied by an impressive entourage made up of slaves who carry the wine and the gifts meant for the fiancée. Yet in this elaborate ritual of courting and exchange of gestures of respect, the narrator suggests that the women are given a rather marginal role in affairs that concern them directly:

> M'Polo rappelle enfin ses filles près d'elle, pour laisser aux hommes le temps de se dire ce que les femmes ne peuvent que deviner, parce qu'on les tient jalousement à l'écart de tous les problèmes sociaux, même quand il s'agit de leur sort, de leur avenir, de leur vie. (17)

> [M'Polo finally calls her daughter aside, to allow the men the time to say what the women can only guess, because they are jealously kept out of all social problems, even when it is about their fate, their future, their life].

The role of women in this society will be commented upon later in this chapter, but the point here is that, even though the women seem to be the center of attention in this scene, they are nevertheless excluded from taking part in the deliberations that will lead to the official acceptance of the marriage of the new couple. The narrator adds rather sarcastically that we should leave the women in the kitchen to do their cooking; a rather indirect way of suggesting what the men themselves are thinking the women should be doing. The narrator seems to be very conscious of the complexity of these customary rites and how for the outside reader, they would be incomprehensible. Note how he makes this comment himself: "Nous féliciterons le lecteur s'il a le bonheur de percer le mystère caché derrière cette longue et filandreuse tirade" (9). [I will congratulate the reader if he has the luck of penetrating the mystery hidden behind this long and stringy speech]. Like the child who listens to the parents explaining customary practices, the reader reads attentively in an attempt to grasp the complexity of these customs. At the same time, these complexities and the mysteries surrounding them, give authenticity to the whole narrative as legend. M'Polo understands the custom that now that her mother is deceased, it is her responsibility to marry one of her daughters to the family of the husband of her late mother. The Lari people have a way of communicating messages. M'polo's father announces his visit for the purpose of asking for the hand of her granddaughter for his cousin by sending them a knotted piece of robe. We are told in a footnote:

> Corde nouée. Moyen de communication télégraphique chez les lari pour s'annoncer la date d'une visite ou d'une grande manifestation. Autant il y a de nœuds à la ficelle, autant il y a de jours de la petite semaine ou de la grande à couper. (12)

> [Knotted rope. A means of telegraphic communication among the Lari people used to announce the date of a visit or of a big event. The number of knots on the string indicate the number of days of the small or big week to cut].

The messenger carries a bag of salt, a piece of cloth, a basket of kola nuts, and tobacco. Only the insider can decode the meaning of these gifts, and M'Polo knows that her father is asking her to marry away one of her daughters. Malonga touches upon an important institution, marriage, and how it functions within a specific ethnic group in African society; the Lari.

When Mi N'Tsembo wants to explain the purpose of his visit to his in-laws, he does not talk in direct terms. He uses metaphors and other symbols which his audience understands. He has lost his wife and has wept so much that his old eyes cannot take it any more. He would like a wife for his nephew so that she can replace his deceased wife. He tells his in-law he is a reputable man and that is why he has come to seek his advice. His speech is flattering, but in the custom it is a sign of respect that he pays to his in-laws. Like other elderly people in general who have the experience with such functions, Mi N'Tsembo has the gift of the art of speech. As we saw in the chapter on Boni, it is a proof of wisdom which is believed to come with age and experience. Mi N'Tsembo does not say things directly. He talks of how he has shed all his tears and how his cooking utensils are full of cobwebs and the pots are nesting homes for the birds. It is time to clean them (18-19). The speech is followed by a gunfire and that signifies that it is the first girl that they are seeking to marry. Bitouala is given a more active role to play in this marriage that is being arranged between him and Hakoula. He hits the sacred drum to signal his approval of the choice of wife. Yet, the other person in this negotiation between the two families is still kept out of the scene until much later.

Marriage is arranged between two people whom the families believe are mature enough to raise a family. The narrator interrupts the flow of the narration on the customary rite that is taking place to tell us about the physical qualities of Bitouala. Though it interrupts the natural flow of the story, the reader is made to appreciate the importance of Bitouala as a choice of husband. He is made to understand why society thinks he is a good choice of husband for Hakoula. His physical attractiveness matches the beauty of the young woman whom he is about to be given in marriage. Not only is he physically attractive, he is a gifted person. He is the best shooter in Kadi-Kadi, the best runner and the most ingenious when it comes to tilling the land in preparation for sowing. Thus, in a way, this potential husband has certain exceptional qualities, some of which have suggesting undertones of a typical character in a legend: "En un mot, il est le mari idéal pour la jeune fille la plus difficile: beau, sportif, excellent danseur doué d'une voix caressante et grave (21). [In a word, he is the ideal husband for the most difficult young girl: handsome, athletic, excellent dancer gifted with a tender and deep voice]. As in most legends, there is an evocation of the supernatural before an important event takes place. At a moment when Bitouala is supposed to officially ask Hakoula if she will marry him, the narrator bursts into some poetic incantation, as if to invoke the spirits at this crucial moment that will determine a relationship between two families that is supposed to last forever. As Bitouala is about to present the "Mouanga-Loumbou" to Hakoula, this is partially what the narrator chants:

> Oh! mystérieux Amour, inexplicable Aimant qui fait balloter en épave la sensible nature, terrible Inconnu qui dompte les plus rebelles, Amour indéfinissable à l'entendement physique, pourquoi tiens tu enfermés sous ton manteau bleu-rose deux cœurs qui se sentent irrésistiblement attirés l'un vers l'autre? Pourquoi fais-tu agiter de frayeur, comme un roseau, ce fier épervier prêt à voler vers son pôle positif? (22)

> [Oh mysterious Love, unexplainable Lover which roles sensitive nature around in flotsam and jetsam; terrible Unknown which tames the most rebel, undefinable Love to physical understanding, why do you keep enclosed under your blue and rose coat, two hearts which feel irresistibly attracted to each other? Why do you make this proud sparrowhawk ready to fly towards its positive pole, shiver with fright?]

Everybody involved in the marriage customary rites knows what to do. Bitouala after offering the cloth to Hakoula invites her to drink the palm wine that has been brought for the ceremonial performance.

She drinks from the earthenware container and gives it to Bitouala to also drink from the same container. It is a sign of acceptance of Bitouala's offer of marriage. Custom also forbids the mother and the son-in-law from seeing each other at this stage, and the narrator explains this to the reader. That the narrator is constantly conscious of his European audience is evidenced at this stage of the narration, when he explains what an "inga-M'Bougou" is. It is a symbol of wealth that some African dignitaries used to wear in the past to show off their wealth. Malonga does not refer to this practice as peculiar to a specific ethnic group. The use of the term "African" underscores the narrator's intended audience of his narration—the European. Later on, the narrator tells the reader that it is perhaps necessary to explain to him or her the ceremony of Hakoula's arrival at the husband's house. He thinks the reader would not forgive him for not narrating in detail what he calls "l'épisode le plus intéressant de l'histoire d'une fête aussi mémorable dans les annales de toute la contrée de Kadi-Kadi" (27). [The most interesting episode of the story of such a memorable feast in the annals of all the Kadi-Kadi region]. But is it not only a stylistic device to justify narrating this part of the story which he could have chosen to say in only a sentence? After all, how does the reader (particularly the European reader) know that it is the most important event in a girl's life if the narrator who is an insider does not say so?

As we witnessed in Boni's novel, the offering of a dowry is an important part of the marriage ritual in most African communities. It legalizes the marriage and is a kind of endorsement by the whole community of this new relationship that has been established between the two families. The family of the woman can be witty when it comes to negotiating the bride price. As we read in Chinua Achebe's *Things Fall Apart*, even within neighboring villages the practice might vary. Some haggle over the dowry, whereas others have a more refined way of negotiating by using broomsticks to represent the amount of money they are demanding or offering. In Malonga's novel, Bidounga does not demand any dowry, but he is being witty in creating a false impression that he is not really asking for anything, because he does ask for a lot of gifts instead. He calls them "petits cadeaux" [small gifts]. What is respected in elderly people is their art of speech. Bidounga uses it to his advantage as do all elderly people in such important negotiations as marriage. As emphasized already, the ability to outwit others through speech is an art that is learned with years of experience. Bidounga is not trying to outwit his new in-laws but he knows that his ability to manipulate them through speech will win him more respect, especially in the eyes of the young ones. It is what distinguishes the old from the young and inexperienced.

As the narrator reveals the intricacies of the customs of this society to us, we see unravel before us, a love story. In the first part of the novel, Hakoula begins to have extra-marital affairs with other men, including the husband's relatives and even his slave. When the slave lover is caught red-handed making love with her, she flees and the slave is killed. It is striking how in exile alone, she accepts her guilt and wishes she could have the chance to pay for her crime against somebody she thinks she loves deeply. When there are rumors floating around that his wife is flirting with other men, Bitouala loves her so much that he is blinded by his own naiveté. But it is this love saga that will destroy the cordial relationship that existed between the two villages and communities after Hakoula flees. The narrator tells us that in spite of Hakoula's soiled reputation, she is still legend today. The reader can therefore understand why her husband would be so captivated by his love for her that he would refuse to marry any other woman, despite pressure from the family to disown a wife who has clearly been cheating on him. Legend always borders on the unusual and the unnatural. Bitouala's behavior is not surprising as the story of the love affair itself seems surreal. In fact, when he forgives her, he manifests deep love for the wife, in spite of the tragedy she has brought upon the whole society. As for the male slave lover, who has played a role in the whole tragedy, he is punished by retributive justice. The narrator does not dwell solely on the female victim's guilt but also on the male character's contribution to the turn of events in what will become a legend.

For the legend to develop, Bitouala's willingness to forgive the unfaithful wife is crucial. The love tragedy between him and Hakoula is an important motif that helps the story develop into a legend. Hakoula's sense of guilt and Bitouala's apparent naive love for an unfaithful wife are motivating factors in the reader's appreciation of these characters as hero and heroine in the legend. Having been initiated by the father before being formally accepted into the family of the husband, Hakoula was made a legendary heroine. She undercut this image of herself through her unfaithfulness to the husband. But she has recuperated this image by her gesture of true love to the one she thinks she has wronged. By their capacity to reconcile, Hakoula and Bitouala are able to re-establish the equilibrium in society that they destroyed through their marred relationship. Hakoula in particular plays a crucial role in pacifying the ancestors through her devoted love to the son whom she brings up in the wilderness. It is through her that a legendary hero is created, thus expiating her of any desecration she might have committed on the earth through her infidelity to the husband. It is not uncommon in African folk tales or legends to have this turn of events in a story.

But it is in the evocation of religious practices of the people who are portrayed in his novel, that Malonga breaks all rules of verisimilitude and realism. He takes us into the world of the unnatural, the unknown, and the unexplainable. Hakoula's beauty and natural endowment make her the envy of all men and it makes her so charming that the husband's love for her blinds him. He is not able to see and acknowledge her weaknesses as a human being and as a woman. But what makes Hakoula an even more extraordinary character is the supernatural powers that are endowed upon her as she begins her new life as a wife in another village.

Bidounga the Chief brings his daughter to officially give her away in marriage. To be able to communicate with the spirits, he does not eat anything. He only feeds on cola nuts and juice of a sacred plant. He is seated on a panther's skin which becomes the medium through which he will perform his initiation of the daughter. Once Hakoula gets into the magic circle, she is initiated and becomes from now on the priestess of the Clan Totem:

> La recouvrant alors du tapis rouge, le père remet les insignes du pouvoir spirituel à son enfant et lui glisse à l'oreille quelques mots dont le secret sera gardé envers tout le monde. La novice passe ensuite à trois reprises entre les jambes écartées du père, puis, assénant d'un coup sonore le gong de la famille, elle dit: "Mânes de N'Tsoundi, prouvez aujourd'hui que je suis de votre Maison. Obéissez à ma voix, éxecutez mes ordres." (33)

> [Then picking her up from the red carpet, the father gives back the insignias of spiritual power to the child and whispers in her ears a few words whose secret will be kept from everybody. The novice then passes three times under the opened legs of the father, then hitting the family bell hard, she says: "Spirits of N'Tsoundi, prove today that I am of your House. Obey my voice, carry out my orders."]

But what follows after the initiation is a test and a proof of the supernatural powers bestowed upon Hakoula. A herd of crocodiles lines up to form a bridge across the river. Hakoula and the family can walk across safely. Marvelous realism is the ability to go beyond the natural to make things happen out of the ordinary. The narrator reacts to what he imagines would be the reaction of his readers; disbelief: "Doutez! lecteurs, si vous le voulez, mais pour les spectateurs oculaires ayant vécu le fait, leur condition est absolu" (35). [Doubt! readers, if you like, but for the eye witnesses who saw it, their condition is absolute]. Marvelous realism is an integral part of life in this society. There is no divorce between the people's religious life and their daily activities. This initiation prepares the reader for what Hakoula is able to do and the supernatural powers she later hands down to the son born in exile—a son who becomes the hero of the legend that has interested Malonga.

There is therefore a direct correlation between the events we witness in this scene and the rest of the story in the sense that it determines to a large extent the marvelous things the reader is bound to witness in a legend. We are told in a footnote that the song that Hakoula sings to call upon the crocodiles to line up to create a bridge across the river ("Bouloungou de N'Konongo") is dedicated to the god of the waters, Boloungo. We are told that the legend is tied to a mythology. The witnesses to these events are not surprised when in the evening, Hakoula climbs to the top of Bitouala's hut and flies over the whole village while playing on her antelope horn. The people of Mandzakala also jump into the fire prepared in front of the Palace of Mi N'Tsembo without burning themselves. Through these concrete external manifestations of their supernatural powers, the N'Tsoundi family proves its superiority in the domain.

Malonga is nostalgic for a past in which African communities had direct links with the ancestors and the world beyond through these religious manifestations. The legend of M'Pfoumou Ma Mazono is about a lost paradise, a discourse which echoes the ideology of the Negritudists of the period in question. The narrator makes a direct link between this past and the present by lamenting the loss of the heritage that was handed down to Hakoula by the parents:

> Le voyageur qui se rend à M'Bamou, par la route de Kibouendé, peut encore, de nos jours, visiter les lieux de la traversée miraculeuse que nous venons de décrire. A quelque distance de l'embouchure de la M'Boté, principal affluent de la Madzia, on se sert encore aujourd'hui du gué de Hakoula. Malheureusement, au lieu de voir les fameux pachydermes, c'est du roc qui forme le fond du gué surnaturel que doit se contenter d'admirer le touriste. Nos Génies se sont-ils laissés influencer par forces extérieures au Pays. Personne ne peut l'affirmer ni l'infirmer. (37)

> [The traveler who goes to M'Bamou through the Kibouendé road, can still, in our times, visit the place of the miraculous crossing that I have just described. A little distance from the mouth of the M'Boté, main tributary of the Madzia, today people still use Hakoula's ford. Unfortunately, instead of seeing the famous crocodiles, it is rock which forms the bottom of the supernatural ford that the tourist has to contend himself with admiring. Our Spirits have allowed themsleves to be influenced by forces ouside the Country. Nobody can either confirm or invalidate it].

Legends do not answer all the questions. In fact, very often they raise questions that test our own understanding of the story that they narrate. How much has outside influence been responsible for the turn of events in the society? Malonga does not offer answers. He only raises the question and thus, invites the reader to ponder over the issue.

In the second part of the novel when we see Hakoula living in exile, the religious manifestations of the first part of the novel begin to affect significantly the outcome of events in this part of the story.

Hakoula is pregnant and a spirit appears before her to confirm her suspicion that the child is Bitouala's. The spirit is that of her grandmother—Esprit de Masonga. She is forgiven for her sin against a husband that she says she still loves, but she has to repent in a concrete way for her crime against him. This part of the story poses some problems to the reader in terms of verisimilitude. How did Hakoula deliver the child alone? Did she have any difficulties? We do not know, because the narrator does not tell us. We are supposed to assume that since Hakoula is protected by the spirits, she must have been capable of doing the unusual—that is, being able to deliver her child alone without any problems. This marvelous realism is reinforced when later we are told that Ma Mazono who is already a grown-up, hears the spirits chanting during a hunting expedition alone in the bush.

Later on, as the character Ma Mazono develops into an adult who will represent social and political evolution in his society, we witness another stage of his initiation into the world of the spirits. Mountsombo, the magician from Mouyondzi, teaches him more about his origins. The knowledge of the past, of one's history is a prerequisite to the ability to communicate with the ancestors and the spirits at a higher level. Mountsombo himself throws a challenge to whosoever would like to test his supernatural powers. In African belief systems, it is often a way through which people make a public manifestation of their superior powers, and one does not throw a public challenge without being sure of impressing his or her audience. It is often at such occasions that sorcerers test each other's powers. Mountsombo is apparently wounded by gun shots intentionally inflicted on him, but he gets up as if nothing has happened to him. Then, he is able to climb into the empty air using smoke as if it were a rope:

> Effectivement, aussi paradoxal que cela paraisse, le magicien, aggripé à la fumée noire, monte, lentement dans les airs, suspendu au-dessus du grand feu qui pourlèche ses pieds. L'ascension est à peine perceptible, mais progressive. (117)
>
> [Actually, as paradoxal as this seems, the magician, holding hard onto the black smoke, climbs slowly into the air, hanging above the big fire which licks his feet. The climbing is hardly noticeable but progresses].

As for the dancers, they compete in demonstrating their supernatural powers at the same time as they entertain the crowd. For instance, Mapouata is a good dancer, and the crowd showers him with gifts. As head of the clan he needs to prove to his audience why he merits this title. So he asks for a wild cat's skin:

Mapouata a bondi vers le flambeau le plus proche pour y brûler l'emblème sacré. Trois coups de sifflet...et on le voit maintenant tenir en laisse un splendide chat-tigre qui se pelotonne à ses pieds. Pour finir, il est venu se courber avec déférence devant Mi N'Tsembo et rejoint sa natte, ayant convaincu l'assistance de son savoir-faire. Des ovations enthousiastes ont honoré l'exploit. (135)

[Mapouata jumped towards the nearest flame to burn the sacred emblem. Three whistle blows...and they now see him keeping on a leash a spendid tiger-cat which snuggles up to his feet. To finish, he came to bow down with respect in front of Mi N'Tsembo and to sit on his mat, having convinced the spectators of his know-how. Enthusiastic applause ackowledged his exploits].

That the audience applauds Mapouata is significant, because the audience is never passive at such religious manifestations. The spirits are invoked and do respond because the individual represents the community and his or her ability to communicate with them is in a way endorsed by the community at large. It is this larger community which will judge him or her if he or she fails to live by the regulations imposed by the ancestors on individuals who are endowed with supernatural spirits. They may be able to perform as individuals, but they temporarily become the medium through which the spirits talk to the community at large; thus the importance of the public manifestation displayed by Mapouata. His success in calling upon the powers of the ancestors means that the society and the audience are at peace with the gods, and this is primordial.

Mazono, as a principal character in this legend, appropriately demonstrates his supernatural powers and proves himself before his people worthy of being crowned the chief of the new-found community:

Mais l'exploit ne s'arrête pas là. Ma Mazono, stable sur les épaules paternelles, se balance de gauche à droite, d'avant en arrière sans perdre l'équilibre, frappe trois coups sur ses mains et siffle doucement. Quatre magnifiques panthères, sorties on ne sait d'où, comme des chiens bien dressés, viennent se coucher paisiblement aux pieds de Mi N'Tsembo bouleversé. Les gros chats battent doucement le sol de leurs longues queues. Coup sur coup, Ma Mazono tire de brefs sons de sa corne d'antilope, puis d'un sifflet en os de perroquet. Au premier appel, un essaim d'abeilles bourdonnantes s'abat sur l'assistance épouvantée. Au second, une nouée de vautours noirs se répand sur la Cité et s'attaque indistinctement aux animaux, aux femmes et aux enfants éperdus. (138)

[But the exploit does not end there. Ma Mazono, stable on the father's shoulders, balances from left to right, from front to back without losing balance, claps three times and whistles softly. Four wonderful panthers, coming out of nowhere, like well-tamed dogs, come to lie peacefully at the feet of Mi N'Tsembo, who is overwhelmed. The big cats tap the ground gently with their long tails. At the same time, Ma Mazono blows a little on his antelope horn, then whistles on a parrot bone. At the first call, a swarm of buzzing bees fall on the terrified audience. At the second call, a cloud of black vultures spread over the town and indiscriminately attack the distraught animals, women, and children].

This passage is significant because it invites the reader to enter the utopian world that the narrator will create for Ma Mazono as he develops as a character. In this public manifestation of the surreal, he is a center of attraction. At the narrative level, he symbolically retains the attention of the reader during this moment and at the thematic level, he becomes the *bona fide* character around whom the legend develops. He participates actively in the unfolding of the legend of which he is the central character.

When Ma Mazono is invested with "L'Ordre de M'Pou" and enthroned as M'Pfoumou Ma Mazono, there is a surreal atmosphere that surrounds the whole incident. The narrator has prepared us for the edenic kingdom that he will create; because we have just been witnesses to his test as a new leader for his community. This extraordinary person creates a society that will be envied because there is no precedent of such an egalitarian system. An extraordinary character creates an extraordinary world which unfolds before us as the story progresses.

To provoke our nostalgia for this mythical past created by Ma Mazono, the narrator relates the past to the present as he has already done before. He tells us that the market that Ma Mazono created—Boukondzo-boua-Ma Mazono—is still a commercial center today that people love to go to. In fact, the last sentence of the novel is very significant. It evokes and justifies at the same time the nostalgia for the past. In this last sentence of the novel, Malonga is trying to authenticate through this narrative, the relevance and the importance of the legend that he has just told. The novel ends like a legend that has been orally narrated to an audience. The narrator or story-teller often gives a moral lesson at the end of his or her narrative; or he or she ends the story by relating it to concrete things with which the audience can identify. In this case, our narrator tells us that all the socio-political institutions that were created by Ma Mazono have collapsed. Only the market is a living tribute to his glory and honor:

> De toutes ses institutions sociales et économiques, il ne reste plus que le centre commercial, Boukondzo boua Ma Mazono, sur les rives de la M'Boté. (155)

[Of all its social and economic institutions, only the commercial center Boukondzo boua Ma Mazono still exists on the banks of the M'Boté].

Thus, we can lament with Malonga, the loss of such well-formed and thriving institutions of the past. For the European reader, the message is that Africans had their own socio-political institutions before the advent of colonialism.

Yet, this nostalgia for the past through legend also raises the issue of how we need to question certain of our past establishments because they encouraged inequalities in society. Ma Mazono is a hero not only because of his unusual origins and his ability to do the unnatural through the supernatural powers he has inherited, but more importantly because he establishes an egalitarian system that had not existed before. He abolishes slavery and replaces it with a socio-political structure in which there is a new and more acceptable type of relationship between members of the community.

Part of the education that Hakoula gives to his young son is to explain to him the status of a slave in the culture. Chance has brought Mazono and the two hunters, Bileko and Boumpoutou, together and through this chance meeting is determined the rest of the legend and the outcome which is the new order created by Mazono. The chance meeting obliges the mother to explain human relationship and power structure in the society to Mazono. This part of the narration depicts a young boy who has just discovered the injustice in his society and reflects upon it. The narration breaks the rule of verisimilitude or realism, when it is revealed to us that Mazono understands the circumstances under which the mother cheated on the father before she had to flee. But we know that the narrator is manipulating Mazono's psyche in order to make the young boy's ability to comprehend the nature of the unjust society in which he lives seam real, and to prompt the actions that he later takes to bring about revolutionary changes. He declares to the mother that he will maintain his name Mia Mazono as a symbol of their past, their history, but that past will be radically amended to rid it of its despotism and cruelty: "Ici, c'est le royaume de la fraternité; le mot esclave et tous ses dérivés ont disparu du vocabulaire" (106). [Here it is the kingdom of fraternity. The word slave and all its derivatives have disappeared from the vocabulary].

Ma Mazono might have brought revolutionary changes to his society, yet one crucial aspect of their customs does not seem to have changed much—and that is the status of women. Without necessarily suggesting this is a feminist novel, we need to examine critically Malonga's depiction of the relationship between men and women in this society, and especially in terms of how men perceive women in the power structure as well as how the women perceive themselves. Even far away from the rest of society and without having been subjected to the usual education that boys undergo under the influence of their fathers, Mazono has the same complex about women's inferiority like other men of the society. He says to his mother as the latter educates him on her past: "Mon langage qui semble t'effaroucher et te blesser, peut-être, est celui d'un Homme. Car, 'Force' si considérable que tu paraisses être, tu n'es, en définitive, qu'une femme" (96). [My language which seems to shock and offend you is that of a Man. For, in spite of such considerable "Strength" that you seem to be, when all is said and done, you are only a woman]. Hakoula, recognizing that the son is only an adolescent, strives to educate him on the importance of recognizing the role of women in society: "Je constate que toi aussi, comme tous ceux de ton sexe, tu te fais une mauvaise opinion de la femme. Pour les hommes, la femme est une "Force" Inférieure" (96). [I realize that you too, like all those of your sex, have a bad opinion of women. For men, women are an inferior "Strength"]. She then goes on to make a diatribe about the beauty and charm of women and what makes them special in life. Malonga at this stage in his story clearly makes Hakoula a spokesperson for women in his society. Through the long speech Hakoula makes to her son, Malonga evokes the misconceptions about women in African society and questions the reasoning that men have always used for their relegation of women to an inferior status in many social and political activities. Ali Mazrui has commented in one of his series *The Africans* that the relegation of women to work in the kitchen (in Africa) actually goes against tradition; for women were not meant to be relegated to that status. They were actively involved in all the daily affairs of society. Malonga glorifies motherhood by explaining through Hakoula how motherhood is the very essence of creation:

> Dans la procréation, la femme détient la plus grande responsabilité...Mère, elle est incontestablement l'agent intermédiaire entre la "Force-Suprême" et la création...Pourquoi, dans ces conditions, l'homme engendré et nourri par elle, qui lui doit tout, qui n'a qu'un rôle secondaire de soutien dans la famille, dans le clan, la traite-t-il en être insignifiant et inférieur. (97)

> [In procreation, woman has the greatest responsibility...Mother, she is unquestionably the intermediary between the "Supreme Power" and creation...Why, in these conditions, does man, born and fed by her, who owes her everything, who only has a secondary role of support in the family, in the clan, treat her like an insignificant and inferior being?]

This diatribe suggests that if women are assigend any inferior role in the society, it is an invention by men in their attempt to create their own privileges vis-à-vis women in society. Malonga makes a poetic defense of the symbol of woman as pillar of society in a manner that resonates Negritudist discourse. Senghor in particular has sung the praises of the African woman in some of his poems. The critics of Negritude who claim that its adepts merely sang the praises of women without doing much that was concrete enough to affect positively their status in society, sometimes forget the historical contexts of these texts. Negritude was a reaction to Euro-centric perception of Africans at the time. Gender issues did not then surface as a major concern in the colonized African writer's revalorization of African culture in the face of Western hegemony. The creation of a mythical Africa for the European reader took precedence over more concrete attempts to champion the cause of women in their society.[1]

Malonga's diatribe about the African woman is an attack on African men's relation to their female counterparts. It questions attitudes that have been institutionalized and accepted as status quo by the society. But, through Hakoula, he also makes an apologetic attempt to educate his Western reader of the time on misperceptions about African women.

For the events and the characters to fit together in the legend, Malonga recourses to the use of chance as a major factor in his narration. To create the surreal atmosphere that surrounds most of the action in a legend, a narrator resorts to the use of chance as an element that catapults the progression in the narrative. There are many instances of the role of chance as a major factor in the novel. While in exile, Hakoula becomes fatalistic. She leaves her destiny to chance: "Fataliste, elle a confié son sort entre les mains du Destin, de l'Inconnu, du Hasard" (85). [Fatalist, she has confided her fate to the hands of Destiny, of the Unknown, of Chance]. It is chance that brings Ma Mazono and his hunter friends together the first time; and chance that brings Hakoula, Ma Mazono, and the husband and father, Bitouala, together. How do we explain the fact that it is Bitouala who is chosen as the head of the emissary of the people who want to recuperate their slaves from the new community that has sprung up as a result of Ma Mazono's ingenuity? It is also chance that is on the side of Ma Mazono as he wins all his battles against the enemies. Chance becomes virtually a character in the legend. It is chance that makes the marvelous seem real and commonplace to the people. The characters believe strongly in the role of destiny in their lives.

In the role of chance is the theme of sin and forgiveness. Hakoula has sinned against the husband by cheating on him, yet his faith, trust and love for her is not shaken. The outcome of the story would have been different if Bitouala had reacted differently towards the tragedy of discovering his wife's unfaithfulness to him. It is this unfaithfulness that provokes the war between in-laws who have always respected one another. But chance will have it that the major characters in this drama that unfolds, Hakoula and Bitouala, react differently from the other characters who could shape the course of events. They are willing, against all odds, to reconcile. This stance determines the outcome of the legend.

To influence the outcome of the story he tells, the narrator resorts to several techniques which are characteristic of historical fiction. For instance, he uses footnotes to explicate the meaning of words and expressions as well as names of places that would be unfamiliar to the reader. In the following quotation referred to already in this chapter, he explains the cultural symbolism and significance of a "corde nouée" [knotted rope] as "moyen de communication télégraphique chez les lari pour s'annoncer la date d'une visite ou d'une grande manifestation. Autant il y a de nœuds à la ficelle, autant il y a de jours de la petite semaine ou de la grande à couper" (13). [Means of telegraphic communication among the Lari to announce the date of a visit or of a big event. The number of knots on the string indicate the number of days of the small or big week to cut] (13). The use of footnotes avoids an interruption in the flow of the narrative. In another example, he explains the cultural significance of a "mouanga-loumbou":

> Littéralement: dissolvant de harem. Étoffe en cotonnade, à fond bleu foncé, piqueté de points blancs et terminée en franges claires. On l'appelle aussi N'Kelé-pintade-à cause de ses points blancs symbolisant des œufs. La pintade est considérée comme la meilleure pondeuse des oiseaux. Donner ce tissu à une femme, c'est lui reconnaître des qualités de mère de famille; l'en priver, c'est la mépriser en lui déniant toute possibilité de maternité. D'où de nombreux divorces qui découlent de ce jugement. Mouanga-Loumbou est donc un dissolvant de harem, quand on ne peut ou ne veut pas le donner pour satisfaire l'amour-propre de sa femme. (19)

> [Literally: harem dissolvent. A coton cloth, with light blew coloring, studded with white spots and finished with light edges. They also call it N'kelé-guinea-fowl because of its white stitches symbolizing eggs. The guinea-fowl is considered the best layer among the birds. Giving this cloth to a woman is recognizing her qualities as family mother. Depriving her of it is despising her by denying her any possibility of motherhood. Thus, the numerous divorces which result from this judgement. Mouanga-Loumbou is therefore a harem dissolvent, when one cannot or does not want to give it to satisfy the self-esteem of his wife].

Thus, the reader can see the cultural significance of Bitouala offering this cloth to the would-be fiancée—Hakoula. He manifests great respect for her and her family. Sometimes too, the footnote is a translation into French of a song in the indigenous language. Some other footnotes explain family lineage. For instance, "bissi-N'Tsembo" is a:

> Descendant du côté maternel du Clan N'Tsembo. Bissi, les hommes ou les femmes de...a pour singulier moussi. C'est un superlatif de la particule reliant l'individu ou la famille à la descendance matriarcale. (31)

> [Descendant of the maternal side of the N'Tsembo Clan. Bissi, the men or women of...has as singular "moussi." It is a superlative of the particle connecting the individual or the family to the matriarchal descendance].

In the page that follows this footnote, he explains what a "minguengué" is:

> Tribu lari qui peuple la rive gauche de la Loufoulakari, tandis que les Bissi-M'Poutou occupent la rive droite. Les Minguengués sont réputés pour leur intelligence et sont les meilleurs artisans du Bas-Kouangou. Ils sont paisibles, mais racuniers, vaniteux et un peu nerveux. (32)

> [Lari tribe which lives on the left bank of the Loufoulakari, whereas the Bissi-M'Poutou live on the right bank. The Minguengués are reputed for their intelligence and are the best artisans of Bas-Kouangou. They are peaceful but quarrelsome, vain and a little nervous].

This last footnote reveals a subjective opinion that Malonga has about an ethnic group that the reader is not familiar with. Just as he sometimes intrudes in the narrative to express his opinion or his admiration for a character endowed with unusual qualities, he makes his subjective commentary here in a footnote without affecting the flow of the narration.

Yet, there is one footnote which places the narrative in an important historical context. In the narrative itself, he makes allusions to the way some ethnic groups participated in the European slave trade in that region of the continent. In a footnote towards the end of the novel on page 152, he tells us that Bissi-M'Poutou are called those of the west, of the other side of the ocean because of their collaborative alliance with the Bakongo considered as traitors to the race for their role in European slave trade. The theme does not become a strong motif in the novel, unlike in Hazoumé's *Doguicimi*. This is so because it is not a major part of the legend of M'Pfoumou Ma Mazono.

The footnotes create an illusion of reality especially since the narrator cites names of real places and persons that are verifiable in the real world. As in the other novels under study, the author creates what is called the "illusion du réel." Names of real ethnic groups like the Lari and the Bakongo give the legend a sense of being about the real world, even if we are constantly exposed to the marvels of the supernatural world.

The narrative itself is sometimes expressed in poetic language. The beginning of the novel itself evokes nature with a rather poetic description of the scenery, underscoring the telluric value attached to the legend that will unfold. Before we are introduced to the characters, the narrator describes the setting for the legend: "La nature, parée de ses atouts les plus féeriques, semble sortir d'un bain au cours d'une soirée très douce" (9). [Nature, prepared with its most magical assets, seems to be coming out of a bath during a very calm evening]. When later, we find Hakoula in exile, she is protected by the spirits in the wilderness. It is in the wilderness that the supernatural operates through nature. There is an equilibrium that should not be disturbed, as happens when the two clans go to war over Hakoula's infidelity and subsequent disappearance.

The narrator also intervenes very frequently to address the reader directly because he knows that there is a possibility of an inability to comprehend the nature of things as they occur and the reaction of the characters. He uses such terms as "il faut en effet dire au lecteur" (25). [In effect, I should say to the reader]; "doutez! lecteur si vous voulez..." (35). [Doubt, reader, if you want]. He anticipates the reaction of his reader and responds to it. There is an influence of oral narrative technique, as the narrator seems to be dialoguing with the audience. Nonetheless, in trying to transpose oral narrative form into novel, Malonga's direct intervention in the text sometimes interrupts the flow of the narrative. As Dorothy Blair has lamented, his habit of intervening apologetically between the text and the reader is irritating to the reader (70).

Yet, there is a lack of realism in the way the narrative sometimes progresses rather fast. The length of the novel and the legend necessitate less detail of certain parts of the story. We see Ma Mazono grow up very fast. The narrator says at one instance:

> Nous allons nous permettre d'user de nos droits et de nos facultés de narrateur pour abandonner un moment le nourrisson à sa mère—qui en est d'ailleurs fort jalouse, et ne le représenter au lecteur qu'une fois devenu un beau petit gars qui a déjà atteint l'âge de quatorze saisons sèches." (76)

> [I am going to use my rights and my powers as narrator to leave the infant for a while with its mother—who moreover is jealous of him, and to introduce him to the reader only when he becomes a handsome small man who is already fourteen seasons old].

In oral narrative, the audience would object to a summary of parts of the story if it is deemed an interesting legend. All the details of the legend are important. In the written, novel form, Malonga can manipulate his narration in a different form—by cutting off details he deems unimportant. In the novel, the reader has no choice but to trust the wisdom of the narrator in not telling us what happens in Ma Mazono's life before we meet him again as an adolescent.

The main characters of the novel evolve with the narrative. Ma Mazono develops physically and psychologically. He matures in age as in his immersion into the world of the psychic and the supernatural. Hakoula develops physically into a woman and a wife. At the same time, the father initiates her into the world of the supernatural when she is crowned a priestess on the day of her official marriage into Bitouala's family. She also matures as a woman as we see her evolve from a young lady obsessed about flirting outside the marriage to someone who understands and accepts her plight as she lives in exile. She becomes more sophisticated as we witness her speaking in poetic and philosophical language to the young Ma Mazono about the beauty and charm of being a woman. It is this psychological development that allows her to meet the challenges of her life in exile and the education of a son who is being introduced to the world outside—the place of exile in the bush—for the first time.

Bitouala also evolves from a naive young husband not prepared to accept the reality that his wife cheated on him, to a father suddenly propelled into another world; the reality of having to live with a wife who was unfaithful in the past but who has repented, and of facing the reality of an unexpected fatherhood. All these characters are manipulated by destiny, even if they evolve as the story progresses.

Malonga's narrative uses a French which is fairly easy to comprehend and the structure of the story itself is chronological. There are no flash backs. We learn that M'Polo's father, Mi N'Tsembo, wants one of her daughters for his nephew. Mi N'Tsembo explains that he wants a woman who can replace the wife he has lost. The narrator does not tell us about the life of the wife because presumably, it would not add to the progress of the narration. It is not essential to the main story in the narrative. Thus, Malonga does not resort to unnecessary flash backs or digressions.

As a narrative technique, he does not use much metaphor or other forms of imagery that obscure the meaning of the story. Also, unlike other African novelists, he does not use proverbs to enhance the local color which he creates through the use of names of real people and places. On one occasion he uses what could be a proverb to express the lust of Hakoula for N'Dzingoula, the husband's friend: "Ce que femme veut, les Mânes le tolèrent en fermant les yeux" (39). [What a woman wants, the spirits tolerate with eyes closed].

In his novel, Malonga uses some techniques of the traditional heroic stories. In many ways, Ma Mazono could be compared to a legendary hero in an African epic. He grows up in exile and completely changes the course of events in society. Talking about traditional story telling in one of his studies, Ahmadou Koné points out that: "le récit héroïque est à la fois réaliste et merveilleux"

(1985, 48). [The heroic story is both realist and marvelous]. This could be said of Ma Mazono's exploits as we see him develop as a character in exile. Exile creates the atmosphere for the marvelous. In the initiation rites we witness in this novel, Malonga is inspired by the myths of the people. Koné explains that whereas the epic story gets its source from history, initiation rites are inspired by myths. Thus the novel that Malonga creates has as its source both in real history and myth. Koné again points out that heroic, epic, or initiation stories were meant to educate the people according to certain values considered sacred. Thus the storyteller had to show competence in entertaining the people as well as in the expression of these ideas (Koné 64). The characters participating actively in this process in Malonga's novel are conscious of their role and their duty towards their audience. Malonga on his part as the one who transforms this oral tradition into the novel form, is conscious of his duty towards the audience, the reader. Malonga goes beyond the role of storyteller and marks the history of the people he writes about with his own creative talents. Koné comments thus on *La Légende de M'Pfoumou Ma Mazono*:

> Ici, l'écrivain n'est pas un simple traducteur. Il est une caisse de résonnance, un noyau rythmique qui dépasse très vite ses fonctions de relais et de transcripteur. Il pose sur l'histoire ancienne son empreinte non dissimulée de créateur. (1985, 78)

> [Here, the writer is not merely a translator. He is a resonance chamber, a rhythmic nucleus which quickly surpasses its role of relay and of transcriber. He makes his undisguised mark as creator on ancient history].

Malonga thus transforms history and myth into novel form. This makes his historical novel unique in a way. Though Hazoumé's and Boni's novelistic creations are also influenced by myth and legend, it is not at the same level as Malonga's. But they are also more successful in transforming myth, legend and folktale into novelistic form than Malonga.

Blair has criticized Malonga for writing a novel instead of a folktale, because according to her Malonga did not master the conventions of the novel form well enough to transpose traditional material into a foreign mould. She thinks that Malonga has tried to fuse too many genres—a moral tale of sin and redemption, a philosophical account of a Utopian state, a romance of sensual and ideal love, as well as traditional folk-lore with its mythic and supernatural elements (71). But if Malonga has not written a very successful novel, the reason lies in a lack of mastery of the novel form rather than in his fusing of many genres. Other African writers have been more successful in this respect than Malonga. In fact, his novel is just one example of what francophone African writers have done with the European historical novel as a genre. It is a product of an attempt to create a European type of novel by transforming African oral narrative into written form in a European language.

4

Ahmadou Kourouma: *Monnè, outrages et défis*

This chapter examines a historical novel closer to our times. Whereas Hazoumé, Boni, and Malonga wrote during the colonial era (even if Boni's novel was published in 1962), *Monnè, outrages et défis* deals with a larger scope of African history. The novel is inspired by the history of the continent covering the pre-colonial period to contemporary Africa. In his first novel, *Soleil des Indépendances*, Kourouma examined through fiction the influence of colonialism on African peoples and also touched on the abuse of power in certain traditional systems. This first novel (like the second one) focused on the Mandingo people of West Africa. Through recourse to dictions, proverbs, and a certain "indigenisation" or "malinkesation" of the French language, Kourouma allows us in his first novel to see how the main character struggles to face up to a changing world brought about by colonization of the continent.

Soleil des Indépendances, as Fírinne ní Chréacháin has suggested in an article, was not a Negritudist discourse as certain critics would like us to believe. On the contrary, the novel is an attack on those Mandingo traditions which created a class society and especially permitted the exploitation of women and encouraged the abuse of religion (Chréacháin 242). This interest for history by Kourouma is manifested again in his second novel, *Monnè, outrages et défis* which is the object of study in this chapter. Kourouma creates situations of tension and conflict at several levels in this novel. History thus becomes important because it allows us to discern the antagonisms at play in colonial hegemony as well as the abuse of political power by those who control political discourse in contemporary African society. This chapter examines closely the use of power as a motif that shapes the lives of the characters.

The Negritude movement was severely criticized for its tendency to glorify and mystify the history of Africa and of black peoples in general in the name of ideological solidarity. *Monnè, outrages et défis* goes beyond Negritudist tendencies to reveal the evils of colonialism and its untold consequences on African peoples, and without the sentimentalism that characterized some of the Negritudist discourse. The introductory chapter of this book evoked some of the definitions of historical novel that have been proposed in the past. One of these was Veynes' postulation that history is a true novel and that the conception that history makes of historic "causality" is exactly the same as that which a novelist makes of causality and puts to work in his novel. This rapprochement between history and historical novel can be read through Kourouma's *Monnè, outrages et défis*.

Kourouma creates a historical novel through his recourse to the history of the Mandingo people, with a narrative technique inspired by orality. Through several characters, power becomes a symbol in the narrative. Kourouma is very critical of the abuse of power by the Mandingo king Djigui and his entourage. Symbolically, the narrative begins with a ritual sacrifice by King Djigui to demand protection for his dynasty. It is the dictatorship, the atrocities sanctioned by this dynasty which will be the focus of the narrative of the novel. The narrator "goes back to the sources" not to glorify the history of the Madingo King, but to reveal to the reader how power was exercised in the history of the kingdom:

> Les premières saisons de son règne, il ne s'était livré à rien de vrai qu'à épouser de nombreuses vierges—il était le plus fort et le plus beau. Se faire célébrer par les adulations et les griots—il était le plus grand. Transformer ses esclaves en sbires et en sicaires—il était le plus intelligent du Mandingue. (15)
>
> [The first seasons of his reign, he had committed himself to doing nothing real except marrying a lot of virgins. He was the strongest and the most handsome. Making himself extolled by adulation and the griots; he was the greatest. Turning his slaves into henchmen and sicaires; he was the most intelligent of the Mandingos].

A Negritudist reading of the novel would see only a glorification of a traditional African political system. But a close reading will allow us to discern in the language of the narrative itself a sharp critique of the exploitation of women and of the possession of slaves.

Already in *Soleil des Indépendances*, Kourouma had alluded to a cast and class Mandingo society as Chréacháin argued in her article. In *Monnè, outrages et défis* too, we can discern an aspect of the history of the people that Kourouma invites us to examine:

> C'était une société arrêtée. Les sorciers, marabouts, les griots, les sages, tous les intellectuels croyaient que le monde était définitivement achevé et ils le disaient. C'était une société castée et esclavagiste dans laquelle chacun avait, de la naissance à la mort, son rang, sa place, son occupation, et tout le monde était content de son sort; on se jalousait peu. (20)
>
> [It was a society that did not evolve. The sorcerers, the marabouts, the griots, the people of wisdom; all the intellectuals thought that the world had finally come to an end and they said so. It was a caste and slave society in which each one had, from birth to death, his class, his place, his occupation, and everyone was happy with his fate. People were not very jealous of one another].

Kourouma wants to suggest that the society of the time had its own socio-political systems before the advent of colonialism. These systems have been destroyed or at least transformed through colonial hegemony. But we also know that Kourouma is critical of some of these traditions. They had their shortcomings. The system allowed people like Djigui to exercise power which was not always in the interest of his people. The people were united by their respect for the power of the king. But we can discern the critique in the evocation of this history of the Mandingo people:

> Certes, ce n'était pas le bonheur pour tout le monde, mais cela semblait transparent pour chacun, donc logique: chacun croyait comprendre, savait attribuer un nom à chaque chose, croyait donc posséder le monde, le maîtriser. C'était beaucoup. (20)

> [Certainly, it was not happiness for everyone, but it seemed transparent to each one, thus logical. Each one thought he understood, knew how to give a name to everything, therefore thought the world belonged to him and that he could control it. That was a lot].

Colonialism brought its atrocities, but before the arrival of the colonizers, the people lived under the dictatorship and atrocities of their own king; dictatorship sanctioned by the religion, an issue that will be discussed further on in this chapter. Kourouma is critical of the atrocities caused by the king in the name of the defense of the autonomy of his kingdom. The narrative does not leave us indifferent in the face of human sacrifices:

> Et le roi était encore dans le sang et le fumet des immolations exposés pour remercier mânes et divinités lorsqu'un autre messager se présente. (20-21)

> [And the king was again in the blood and the aroma of the immolations which were exhibited to thank gods and divinities when another messager introduces himself].

If Kourouma's novel had been published at the period Hazoumé published *Doguicimi*, some of the criticism raised in the earlier chapter on Hazoumé would have been relevant here. We are dealing with a contemporary readership that is relatively better educated about African civilization than that of the colonial era.

Samory is a king worthy of mention in the history of the colonial period. He had conquered the French in several military encounters. He represents a fierce anti-colonial force; thus becoming a hero in the history of African resistance to colonialism. Yet, Kourouma invites us to see Samory's personality in its totality to demystify this important personality in the history of the region. Samory obliged all the kingdoms to ally themselves with him: "Samory combattait et détruisait les royaumes qui rejettaient son alliance" (25). [Samory fought and destroyed the kingdoms which rejected his alliance]. Hegemonic power was not the monopoly of the colonizers.

Kourouma deplores Samory's act of offering three beautiful virgins and eighteen slaves as gifts to Djigui.

Yet, we discover that there is nonetheless a positive aspect in the portrayal of Samory as a fictional character. In a way, he symbolizes honor because he resisted colonial invasion of his territory much like the characters in Boni's *Crépuscule des temps anciens* discussed in an earlier chapter in this book. Samory confronts the whites and defies their hegemonic discourse; the uncircumcised would be conquered by the circumcised. Nonetheless, Samory has something in common with Djigui; he represents the abuse of power in traditional Africa. Djigui submits his war victims to inhuman treatments:

> Le roi vaincu, sa cour et ses généraux arrivaient à cheval jusqu'au premier rang des guerriers. Ils descendaient des montures et marchaient entre la double haie des vainqueurs balançant en l'air leurs fusils. Les guerriers hilares tout le long du trajet proféraient des insultes à l'endroit des malheureux battus. A six pas du roi victorieux, le vaincu et ses suivants se croisaient les bras dans le dos et se prosternaient. Parfois on exigeait d'eux qu'ils frottent la bouche contre le sol comme les poules le font avec le bec pour fouiller les immondices. Les griots se taisaient. Le roi vaincu parlait... (44)

> [The defeated king, his court and his generals arrived on horses at the first line of the warriors. They got down and walked between the double hedges of the victors swinging their guns in the air. The beaming warriors lined up on their way insulted the unfortunate defeated. Six feet from the victorious warrior, the defeated king and his followers crossed their hands behind the back and bowed down. Sometimes they were asked to rob their mouths against the ground as hens do with their beaks to search in the refuse. The griots were silent. The defeated king spoke...].

The humiliation of the war captives is an initiation into their new status as "subjects." Honor being important in their society, stripping them of every human dignity and honor is suppressing their political power. Reducing them to the level of a chicken is a way of stripping them of their human dignity to submit them to the sovereign power of Djigui. The griots represent the word of the king and his subjects. In this scene, they give up the word to the defeated, but it is to allow them to publicly declare that they have no power anymore. Therefore, they are not really given the power of the word. Rather, they are deprived of the power of the word. Thus, there is a symbolism in the decision of the griots not to sing, not to represent the word in their traditional role as guardians of the word. As Amadou Koné has explained, the malinké griot (called *djeli*) tells his story in the way his talent allows him to, while at the same time keeping to the traditions of his masters who taught him. He is not free to use the "parole" [word] the way he wants (1985, 25). Here, the griot recognizes his role as gaurdian of this "parole" which is the source of power of his people. He is a story-teller who mediates between the king and the people because of his special position. Like the story-teller who must be conscious of his listeners because they are active participants, the griot here is conscious of how much he allows his audience (the victors) to have control of the "parole."

This authentification of Djigui's power over the conquered is again assured when they are obliged to drink the "degué" as a mark of their submission. Djigui can exercise this power over the conquered because his absolute power is endowed upon him by tradition. Kourouma also suggests that this abuse of power allowed forced conversion of the conquered to Islam. It was not only European colonizers who sometimes used forced conversion. Some African kings like Djigui used religion to subjugate and impose forced conversion on territories they conquered.

But abuse of power as a motif in the novel is well portrayed in the history of colonization that Kourouma evokes. As argued in the chapter on Boni's *Crépuscule des temps anciens*, some African leaders collaborated with the colonial invaders. In *Monnè, outrages et défis*, the Mandingo people have no more power after their defeat by the French. This new status is symbolized by the threat of the griot Diabaté that he will leave. As griot, he represents the word in the empire. It is the griot who authenticates King Djigui's power through his word. He has nothing for which to sing praises anymore since Djigui will no longer have any "authentic word". He will not be able to represent his people anymore through the word of the ancestors, because his power (and consequently that of his people) will be subordinate to that of the colonizers who now represent the new concept of power. Diabaté's complaint is significant for our comprehension of the consequences of colonial hegemony on the continent:

> Je ne peux pas: les cordes de ma cora ne vibrent plus; j'ai oublié la généalogie des grandes familles; ma voix, elle aussi, s'est éteinte. Seuls me restent mes bras; seul me convient le labour. Je suis Diabaté de la grande lignée des grands griots[...]. J'irai cultiver jusqu'à ce que de nouveaux exploits de ceux que mes aïeux ont loués des siècles durant m'appelent des lougans. (42)

> [I cannot. The cords of my cora do not vibrate anymore. I have forgotten the geneology of the important families. My voice too has shut off. What is left is my hands. Only plowing is appropriate for me now. I am Diabaté of the long tradition of the great griots...I will go and farm until new exploits of those of whom my ancestors sang praises for centuries call me from the farms].

The griot's complaint marks the beginning of the collapse of the Mandingo socio-political system. Kourouma is critical of the hypocrisy in the so-called civilizing mission carried out by France in its colonies in Africa. The French claim to have established peace at their colonial conquest. The French flag becomes the symbol of subjugation of the colonized. Yet, Kourouma evokes this tragedy with sarcasm when he makes the white captain say:

> [...] Avec la capture de Samory, les nazaréens français instaurent leurs paix et force dans toute la Négritie, du sud au nord. Gloire et joie aux vainqueurs! Malheureux aux vaincus! [...] Regardez bien ce drapeau, aimez-le, retenez bien ses trois couleurs; jamais plus il ne vous sera permis de les ignorer. Sur les terres et les mers sur lesquelles elles flottent, il n y'a pas d'esclaves; pas un esclave dans un pays conquis par la France. (53)

> [...With the capture of Samory, the French institute their peace and power in all the lands of the Blacks, from south to north. Glory and joy to the victors! Unfortunate for the defeated!...Look at this flag well; love it, remember well its three colors. You will never be allowed again to be unaware of them. On the lands and the seas on which they fly, there are no slaves; not a single slave in a country conquered by the French].

It is through this sarcasm and irony that Kourouma depicts the colonial situation which, as Albert Memmi wrote, cannot be modified but has to be destroyed (*Portrait du colonisé*). The sarcastic language is the suggestion that colonization did not create any servitude in French territories. Kourouma creates this effect by making the captain say it himself instead of making an authorial intervention. The interpreter himself is sarcastic (becoming the voice of the author) in the way he transmits the words of the whites: "je traduis les paroles d'un Blanc, d'un Toubab. Quand un toubab s'exprime, nous, Nègres, on se tait, se décoiffe, se déchausse et écoute. Cela doit être su comme les soucrates de prière, bien connu comme les perles des fesses de la préférée" (54). [I am translating the words of a White man, a Toubab. When a toubab says something, we, Niggers, keep quiet, take off our hats, remove our socks, and listen. This must be known like the soucrate of prayer, well known like the pearls of the buttocks of a lover]. Humor is a weapon Kourouma uses to depict tragic situations.

The revolt of the people, even if only at the symbolic level, is represented by the refusal of the griot to authenticate the words of the white man with his songs when the interpreter translates the words of the latter: "[...] il n'accompagnait pas ses dires, ne les reprenait pas, ne les commentait pas comme ceux d'un noble. Le griot s'excusa; il ignorait que le langage de la force et du pouvoir blancs avait besoin de la voix des griots pour s'imposer" (54). [He did not follow up his words, did not repeat them, did not comment upon them like those of a noble. The griot apologized. He did not know that the language of white force and power needed the voice of the griots to impose itself]. Thus, through the griot, the author makes a sarcastic commentary on the imposition of colonial rule on Africans.

Colonialism perpetuated the subjugation of women. Women are offered as gifts to the Whites. They are given the most beautiful women of the country: young Fulani women with light skins and pointed noses. There is the suggestion here that the light-skinned women are more acceptable because they are closer to the white skin. That race was a factor in colonial enterprise in Africa is an element of Kourouma's discourse here. The darker skin suggests inferiority vis-à-vis the white person.

The inability of the interpreter to translate the new laws on forced labor to the people signifies the lack of true dialogue, and the lack of equality between French and colonized. The treatment of black women as economic objects recalls slave trade which sent millions of Africans to the Americas:

> Le lieutenant sélectionna, parmi les filles peules vierges, les quatre ayant la peau la plus claire et le nez le plus droit: elles furent réservées aux deux Blancs. L'interprète commanda qu'on les conduisit au marigot et les nettoyât dans tous les recoins et particulièrement sous les cache-sexe; elles étaient trop sales pour être consommées crues. (56)
>
> [The lieutenant selected among the Fulani virgins, the four who had the farest skin color and the straightest nose. They were reserved for the two white men. The interpreter ordered that they be taken to the creek to be cleaned in all the hidden parts and especially under the G-string. They were too dirty to be consumed raw].

The choice of words itself underscores the cruelty in the colonizer-colonized relationship and the powerlessness of the latter. It is Aimé Césaire who said that colonization dehumanizes the colonizer and the colonized. He calls this phenomenon "chosification" [making a thing]. The whites and the collaborators, the "tirailleurs," have no respect for the young ladies who are offered them as gifts; and as for the toubab this is what they say: "C'est une chance pour elles et pour Soba. Nous ferons de nombreux mulâtres, des demi-Blancs pour soba qui sera une grande ville et vous un grand chef" (57). [It is good luck for them and for Soba. We will make a lot of mulattoes, half-whites for soba, which will be an important town and you an important chief]. Kourouma creates sarcasm here through the mouth of the characters who are the targets of his ridicule.

The French colonizers put in place a system of education which created and re-inforced the myth of the purity of the white color, as opposed to the evil that the black color was supposed to represent. This is a phenomenon that Frantz Fanon studied in his work *Peau Noire Masques Blancs*. In a subtle way, Kourouma criticizes the myth of superiority of one race over others; a myth inculcated by the whites in Africa. The toubabs's utterances quoted above thus evokes a whole history of race relationships and perceptions which becomes a major motif in the novel.

But race is not the only issue Kourouma evokes in his critique of colonial enterprise in Africa. He also suggests that colonization brought about the commercialization of the system. This new mode of commerce is a threat to the well-established traditional sense of family, clan, and community solidarity. A capitalist system is introduced into a society which thrives on family links which have always been more important than material wealth. Moreover, the French destroyed this fabric of the society with lies. They introduced disguised slavery by claiming that "le grand dessein de la colonisation est de faire gagner de l'argent à tous les indigènes. L'ère qui commence sera de l'argent" (57). [The main design of colonization is to make all indigenous peoples earn money. The era which begins will be that of money]. The interpreter translates this apparently important message with a lot of humor: "Quand il échappera un pet avec de l'argent, tout le monde s'en accomodera; mais, sans argent, tu ne sera ni couché ni assis" (58). [When you fart with money, everybody will get used to it. But, without money, you will be neither lying nor sitting down]. The African does not express himself or herself in the same manner as the French. This in itself suggests that a cultural conflict is inevitable in the colonial enterprise.

Capitalism as a new mode of life has introduced new tastes that people did not know before. Forced labor, which was an important ingredient of French colonialism in Africa, deprived the people of an important work force, thus affecting the capacity to produce. Yet the colonizers would lie that the people who are subjected to forced labor are fed and lodged free. The reality is that they are fed through their own labor. Forced labour was capitalist exploitation at its best in the continent, and Kourouma uses his fictional characters to convey this message. Through humor and sarcasm, he invites his reader to relate this history to contemporary Africa.

That Africans were used as collaborators by the invading colonial forces was discussed in the chapter on Nazi Boni. In Kourouma's novel, the "tirailleurs" are used to better subjugate the local people. In the process, a class society is created, for the "tirailleurs" are turned into privileged people in society: "Vous serez les mieux nourris, les mieux logés, les mieux payés. Vous pourrez arracher aux autres indigènes leur nourriture, leurs bêtes et leurs femmes" (62). [You will be the best fed, the best lodged, the best paid. You can seize food, animals and women from the other indigenes]. Women are reduced to the same status as animals. This privileged class introduced by colonialism will develop into an elite class in society. The new elite in Africa will change the notion of values in society. Capitalism introduces corruption, for people like the interpreter Soumaré are promoted. Speaking of his promotion he says: "C'est une promotion que j'ai méritée pour mon rôle dans la pacification rapide, sans effusion de sang, des pays de soba" (70). [It is a promotion which I have deserved for my role in the rapid pacification, without shedding of blood, of Soba country]. Kourouma is being sarcastic here. The reader knows that Soumaré does not merit promotion and that Soba was not pacified but rather drawn into political and social conflicts. We can also discern in the direct translation from malinké, the link that Kourouma makes between the history of colonialism and dictatorial regimes in contemporary Africa.

Kourouma is particularly critical of African leaders fictionally represented by Djigui in the novel. They collaborated with the colonizers because they naively believed that would help their people develop economically. Djigui has the illusion that he has never been subjugated and that he has never lost his power. What Kourouma suggests is that he was naive and allowed himself to be manipulated by the French.

Religion plays an important role in this manipulation of the people by the colonizers. Christianity might have been used sometimes to manipulate the mind of the African, but Djigui too always invokes Allah to justify the suffering of his people. His people become more vulnerable to exploitation when he makes them construct "un palais aussi grandiose que [ses] rêves" (82). [A palace as grandiose as (his) dreams]. Effectively, Kourouma alludes here to African leaders who have palaces built for them, not to mention the building of a cathedral in a country where the majority of the people, like in most other African countries, suffer economic misery. Djigui the fictional character, thus represents corrupt African leaders of the colonial and post-colonial periods. To suggest that the people have no confidence in the colonizers, Kourouma evokes a malinke proverb": "Jamais les singes rouges ne croiront aux civilités des chiens chasseurs" (87). [Red monkeys will never believe in the civility of hunting dogs]. In other words, red monkeys cannot be naive enough to think that hunting dogs have become their partners. The mass of the people cannot be naive enough to believe that their exploiters (the colonizers) can become their good partners.

Kourouma's discourse here suggests that dictatorship creates personality cults. Djigui is believed to have spiritual powers that can heal people. Here, Kourouma makes a sarcastic allusion to autocratic African leaders who create religious cults around themselves to exploit their own people by instituting regimes of terror.

That colonization dehumanizes the colonized as well as the colonizer, as Césaire eloquently remarked, is evidenced in the sadomasochist personality of the colonist Mark:

> Le Toubab Mark exploitait un chantier à quelque distance de la capitale et avait une curieuse pratique pour sanctionner les Nègres déserteurs, voleurs et menteurs; il les faisait grimper sur des branches et les descendait à la carabine comme on descend un gibier dans une partie de chasse. (91)
>
> [The Toubab Mark was working on a building site a few miles from the capital and had a curious way of punishing deserting, stealing, and lying Blacks. He made them climb branches and shot them down with a gun like one shoots game in a hunting expedition].

In this passage, Kourouma uses neither irony nor sarcasm but depicts Mark as the cruel personality he is. Africans are reduced to the level of animals. The passage shocks the sensibility of the reader by revealing the dark side of human personality and more specifically of that of those who exercised colonial power over others. The text literally speaks for itself.

The political maneuvering which characterized African politics in the past is still in place in contemporary society. Thus history becomes important in the writer's crusade as voice of his people:

> La méthode!...La méthode!...Qu'en dire? Rien. Ceux de Soba comme tous les Africains plus tard vivront l'ère des présidents fondateurs des partis uniques, dont certains décréteront que tous les habitants du pays sont membres du parti et préléveront comme la capitation des cotisations qu'ils feront encaisser sans attribuer ni carte ni acquit. Avec les fonds jamais comptabilisés ou contrôlés, au nom du combat sacré pour l'unité nationale. (266)
>
> [The method!... The method!...What does one say about it? Nothing. The people of Soba, like all Africans later on, will see the era of presidents founders of one-party systems, some of whom will decree that all the inhabitants of the country are members of the party and will impose levies such as poll taxes which they will collect without giving any card or receipt. With funds that are never well accounted for or controlled, in the name of the sacred fight for national unity].

Here Kourouma makes a direct attack on political discourse in Africa. The critique here is very direct and blunt. Some of the systems put in place by colonialism thrive today in the continent. Certain traditional structures combined with the vestiges of colonialism have created a complex socio-political atmosphere in contemporary society of which the writer is a witness. Multi-party systems introduced by colonialism have, in some cases, been turned into one-party states, thus creating political terrorism (253). For example, in the novel, Chief Béma ostracizes Mody Diallo a teacher, and Kouassi a doctor (as well as their families) from the village because they refuse to align themselves with the new party. With the introduction of party politics, the mass of the population has often been alienated from political and economic power through the maneuverings of the party that forms the government. There is an allusion to this state of affairs in the narrative, suggested through the constant misunderstandings created by the bad interpretation of French into malinke. Here is an example:

> Les malveillants, Kélétigui et ses codetenus, les ennemis de Béma, avaient traduit le mot progressiste par *progressi* et les Malinké n'avaient retenu que les consonances terminales *sissi*, qui signifient "fumée". Toujours par malignité, les mêmes avaient prétendu que les initiales PREP se disaient *prou* qui est le son de l'échappement d'un éhonté pet à un mauvais mangeur de haricots. Personne à Soba ne voulait passer pour un *sissi* ou un *prou*. (265)

> [The malicious ones, Kélétigui and his fellow detenees, the enemies of Béma, had translated the word "progressiste" as *progressi* and the Malinké had retained only the last consonants *sissi* which mean "smoke." Still by malice, the same people had claimed that the initials PREP were pronounced *prou* which is the sound produced by a shameful farting of a bad beans-eater. Nobody at Soba wanted to be a *sissi* or a *prou*].

This humor lays bare the ridiculous nature of imposing a foreign system on the people. The new political system has also created frictions and divisions in families. For example, Béma tries to manipulate his father Djigui against his own brother. The narrator also tells us at the end of the novel when Djigui dies, that he had betrayed his people by welcoming the colonists when Samory's defeat was imminent. Thus, Kourouma's fiction suggests that the knowledge of history is important if Africans want to come to terms with a situation in which some of its leaders continue to betray their people on the political, economic, and cultural fronts. The ones who exercise power have monopoly over the word in modern society. They manipulate history and the process itself of telling history: "C'est toujours nous les Nègres qui avons ni agence de presse ni TSF, ni journaux, ni porte-parole pour le dire, toujours nous qui tirons les premiers sur les autres" (282). [It is always we the Black people who have no press agency, TSF, newspapers or spokesperson to say it. We are always the ones who fire on the others first]. The narrator deplores the cowardly act on the part of the "tirailleurs" who shoot at the people of Soba. The "nous" here is the mass of the people, and the "tirailleurs" represent the government and its army and police forces which often control the news in Africa. The end of the novel justifies the interest in history and Kourouma's commitment as a writer. The committed writer in Africa becomes the voice of the people who have no control over the news media:

> La Négritie et la vie continuèrent après ce monde, ces hommes. Nous attendaient le long de notre dur chemin: Les indépendances politiques, le parti unique, l'homme charismatique, le père de la nation, les *pronunciamientos* dérisoires, la révolution; puis les autres mythes; la lutte pour l'unité nationale, pour le développement, le socialisme, la paix, l'autosuffisance alimentaire et les indépendances économiques; et aussi le combat contre la sécheresse et la famine, la guerre à la corruption, au tribalisme au népotisme salmigondis de slogans qui à force d'être galvaudés nous ont rendus sceptiques, pelés, demi-sourds, demi-aveugles, aphores, bref plus nègres que nous ne l'étions avant et avec eux. (287)
>
> [The world of the Black and life continued after this world, these men. Our long hard route awaited us. Political independences, one-party, charismatic man, father of the nation, pathetic *pronunciamientos*, revolution. Then the other myths. The fight for national unity, for development, socialism, peace, food, self-sufficiency, and economic independence. And also the fight against drought and famine, war against corruption, tribalism, nepotism; a hotchpotch of slogans which by being made trite, have made us sceptical, bald, half-deaf, half-blind, like aphorisms, in a word more black than we were before and with them].

This passage sounds like a political diatribe. Kourouma is very didactic here. The narrator, "nous," identifies himself with the mass of the people in the continent.

Yet, in this portrayal of the exercise of power, the novel stands out among the historical novels under consideration in this study as an attack on the subjugation of women carried out in diverse ways. There is a sense of appeal to the reader's sensibility in the way women are treated by the male counterparts. Women have no word and the novel is replete with examples of how they are treated like food or animals. They are property of the men; objects of pleasure for the men. This status explains why they are offered to the invading colonists as gifts.

In his narrative, Kourouma deplores the humiliation and degradation of women. In the name of religion, Djigui treats his wives like children. They have no voice. In fact, he does not even know the number of wives he has. When he goes on a religious pilgrimage, he is obliged to reduce the number of wives he has. So, he renounces all the wives "sauf Moussokoro la préférée officielle et les deux, plus jeunes du harem" [except Mossokoro the official favourite woman and the two youngest ones of the harem] (226). The laws of the koran are manipulated to satisfy the sexual pleasures and the power of the king. Women are reduced to objects without any power:

> Souvent aveugles et percluses, elles attendaient patiemment à Toukoro au fond des cases, près des feux au milieu des haillons et des rats. Leur répudiation consiste en ceci; on leur fit contracter des mariages blancs avec un petit-arrière-fils de moins de cinq ans." (226).

[Often blind and crippled, they waited patiently at Toukoro at the bottom of the huts, near the fires in the middle of the rags and rats. Their renouncement consists of the following. They were made to contract false marriages with a great-grandson less than five years old].

Like articles for sale, the king gives them away in "marriage" "sans exiger...un seul cauri de dot" [without asking for a single cowry as dowry] and the new "husband" has the power to send away his "wife." (227). Moreover, the woman is considered worthy of this type of marriage because she is "croyante et honnête" [a believer and honest]. It is not for her husband to prove himself worthy of marrying her. She has no voice. It is the man (in this case the king) who speaks in her name as if she were not capable of speaking for herself. Thus, in all circumstances, she has no control over her own life, her destiny.

The female voice is suppressed and old women are only important in so far as they serve as objects to legitimize the power of the king. To accomplish his religious duties, the king needs the same ladies that he has rejected, preferring the younger ones. Kourouma underscores this in sarcastic language:

Donc, seul, Allah, quand Djigui effectuait le second pélérinage, connaissait le nombre exact de ses épouses. Même si le nombre fatidique de quatre a pu être valide: le Tout-Puissant, nous ne cessons de le proclamer, est miséricorde. (228)

[Therefore, only Allah, when Djigui made the second pilgrimage, knew the exact number of his wives. Even if the fateful number four could be valid, the All-Powerful, we do not stop saying it, is all-forgiving].

The exploitation and "chosification" of women is legitimized and legalized by a traditional system represented by the king's power. The king believes that it is the duty of a woman to prove herself worthy of a man:

Une femme ne s'aime jamais avant [...]. Une femme s'aime après un long usage, après qu'elle s'est montrée suffisante à notre service, après que ses calmes et humanismes ont valu, plus que ceux des autres femmes, après qu'elle s'est révélée plus chaude que les autres (250).

[One never loves a woman before...One loves a woman after using her for a long time, after she has proven to be good for our use, after her calm and humanisms have been shown to be worth more than that of other women; after she has shown herself to be hotter than the others].

Men have absolute power over women. Moussokoro can be given away as wife to Djigui against her will. The old lady who shelters Moussokoro when she tries to escape, expresses how women are resigned to their fate in society: "Dans ce monde, les lots de la femme ont trois noms qui ont la même signification: résignation, silence, soumission." [In this world, woman's fates have three names which have the same meaning: resignation, silence, submission] (135). The freedom of a woman can only be sanctioned by a male. For example, a girl must have an "age group husband" to be allowed to go out to dance in the evening moonlight. But Moussokoro revolts against a custom which requires that a woman be a virgin when she marries. She has slept with Abdoulaye, the boyfriend, thus creating what is tantamount to a scandal. Kourouma does not develop a female counter-discourse beyond the symbolic revolt put up by Moussokoro.

Tradition also allows the deplorable act of killing the wives of a deceased king and of putting some in the harem to spend their life praying for the deceased king. Kourouma reveals these atrocities without any authorial intervention in the narrative.

As a committed writer, Kourouma employs several narrative techniques which embellish his fiction and underscore the inhuman atrocities that his fictional characters are subjected to by others. He uses mainly humor, sarcasm, and irony to depict tragic situations in his novel. This technique is reinforced by his frequent recourse to malinke proverbs; thus giving an important role to his knowledge of traditions in his creation of historical fiction.

Humor is used in *Monnè, outrages et défis* to make a caricature of characters, to ridicule them by unmasking their hypocrisy (as in the case of the colonists), or their ignorance. For example, to underscore the lack of real communication between colonists and the people, Kourouma ridicules the interpreters and the griots:

> Le griot poursuivit. Le prénom Jean devint Zan (prénom bambara) dans le discours du griot qui, après cette rapide "malinkisation" (Zan Traoré) qu'il appela islamisation, demanda au brigadier les raisons d'un débarquement aussi insolite que la rencontre des cynocéphales pêchant des carpes dans le courant. (174)

> [The griot continued. The first name Jean became Zan (a Bambara first name) in the griot's talk, who after this quick "malinkisation" (Zan Traoré) which he called islamisation, asked the brigadier for the reasons for a landing as unusaul as the encounter of the dog-faced baboons fishing carps in the current].

Kourouma ridicules the lack of understanding created by the imposition of French political systems on the colonized:

> Le Blanc parla, se perdait dans de longs développements politico-historiques. Il parla, trop et vite, avec des néologismes; fascisme, pétainisme, gaullisme, marxisme, capitalisme, le monde libre [...]. L'interprète a dit *gnibaité* pour liberté; dans les commentaires du griot, cette

gnibaité est devenu *gabata* qui littéralement signifie "vient prendre maman". La liberté; la *nabata* avait, pour ceux de Bolloda cette dernière signification. Le Centenaire déconcerté se demandait pourquoi de Gaulle voulait absolument équiper tous les Noirs d'Afrique, nous garantir à nous tous des porteurs de vieilles mamans. (217-218)

[The White man spoke, lost in long speeches about politico-historical issues. He spoke for a long time and quickly with neologisms: fascism, petainism, gaullism, marxism, capitalism, the free world...The interpreter said *gnibaité* for freedom. In the commentary made by the griot, this *gnibaité* became *gabata* which literally means "come and take mama." Freedom, *nabata* had the latter meaning for the people of Soba. The disconcerted Hundred Year Old Man wondered why de Gaulle wanted at all cost to equip all the Blacks of Africa, guarantee all of us as carriers of old mothers].

Or again, when Djigui undertakes to learn French, the reader is treated to scenes of quid pro quo: "Il fallait répéter mot à mot et à haut voix, 'Mamadou amène sa sœur', phrase qui très mal prononcée et déformée par le griot devint '*mamadou à mina ka sirii*'. Ce qui signifie en malinké Mamadou saisis-le et attache-le" (231). [One had to repeat word for word and loudly "Mamadou brings her sister," a sentence which badly said and deformed by the griot became "*mamadou à mina ka sirii*" which means in Malinké "Mamadou catch him and tie him"].

The misunderstandings are provoked by bad translation from the French language. For example, the word "progressiste" is translated as *progressi* and the Mandingos retain only the last consonants *sissi* which means "smoke."

Sometimes, the humor is directed by one character towards other characters. The concept of joking brothers among the Mandingos is exploited by Kourouma. Fadiga can say:

Un authentique Kuruma se reconnaît à ceci qu'il croit aux paroles et se dévoue toujours à des causes qui ne valent pas le pet d'une vieille grand'mère. (187)

[An authentic Kuruma is recognized by the fact that he believes words and always devotes himself to causes which are not worth the fart of an old grandmother].

Kourouma's recourse to humor is enhanced by his knowledge of Mandingo proverbs. For example, when he talks about the advent of colonialism, he says: "Celui qui craint la destruction de ses épis par les singes demeure dans son lougan" (54). [The person who fears that monkeys will destroy his crops stays in his farm]. The griot replies to the interpreter by saying: "Quand tu as entrevu, dans un fourrage, la croupe d'un éléphant, tu dois deviner que ce que tu as aperçu n'est qu'une insignifiante partie de la bête" (57). [When you see in the fodder, the croup of an elephant, you must guess that what you have seen is only a small part of the animal]. In other words, colonization will bring much more profound changes than they have seen so far. To suggest that Africans cannot trust the French colonizers: "Jamais les singes rouges ne croiront aux civilités des chiens chasseurs" (87). [Red monkeys will never believe in the civility of hunting dogs]. Just as monkeys distrust hunting dogs, so do the colonized have to be distrustful of the colonizers. To explain to the whites why he cannot mobilize more people for the war, Djigui reasons: "La limite de la bête est sa queue; il n'y a pas de forgeron qui à force de frapper transforme le cuivre en or et aucun éreintement ne peut faire taire l'eau de la pierre" (110). [The limit of the animal is its tail. There is no blacksmith who can change copper into gold by beating it, and no slating can stop the noise of the water in the stone]. The interpreter replies: "La force comme la lune est haute et comme la lune elle ne peut suivre les soucis des minuscules fourmis perdues sur la terre" (110). [Strength like the moon is high and like the moon it cannot follow the worries of the small ants lost on the land]. He advises that the Mandingo people should stay in the good books of the French colonizers, because "quand une femme ne donne plus satisfaction, on en épouse une autre" (110). [When a woman does not provide satisfaction anymore, you marry another one]. The colonized people are like a woman that the husband can divorce because he feels he no longer gets satisfaction from her. Referring to the conflict between Djigui and his son Béma, we read that "On n'appelle pas au secours quand le couteau qu'on porte à sa ceinture vous transperce la cuisse: en silence, on couvre sa plaie avec sa main..." (129). [You do not call for help when the knife you are carrying in your belt cuts through your thigh. You silently cover your wound with the hand]. In other words, Béma being Djigui's own son is like the knife that cuts its carrier.

It is through proverbs that Kourouma employs symbols which create local color. Historical fiction evokes places, characters and dates that we can identify in real life. The proverbs are often metaphors taken from the behavior of animals and human beings, as well as from nature and this creates local color. We will analyze a few of them. To suggest that the French are losing the war, what Kourouma evokes is the Mandingo concept of cowardice: "En authentique Keita, je ne répondais jamais aux hommes qui, surclassés sur l'aire de la lutte rentraient se défouler sur leurs pauvres épouses" (112). [As an authentic Keita, I never responded to men, who, outclassed in fight went back home to let off steam on their poor wives]. Instead of recognizing their cowardice and their weakness, the French want to exculpate themselves : "comme le matou fainéant qui, pour excuser sa couardise se plaint des souris qui mordent les chats dans les lèvres. Quand chacun doit se retourner contre moins forts la bise souffle contre la calebasse vide: les Français étaient des cornus qui ne donnaient des coups qu'aux bêtes décornées" (113). [Like the lazy tomcat which, to excuse his cowardice, complains about the mice which bite the cats in the lips. When each one must turn against a weaker person, the North wind blows against the empty calabash. The French were horned animals which only hit dehorned animals]. Here we have images of human and animal behavior but also the role that nature plays in human behavior. To say that Djigui does not know the new Commandant, the narrator compares the situation to the brightness of a light that the person born blind has never seen (113). To explain the reason for his visit to king Djigui, Soumaré the interpreter explains "Ce qui m'amène ressemble à la cause qui oblige le crocodile à sortir de l'eau pour aller lécher la rosée des herbes" (115). [What brings me is like the cause which obliges the crocodile to come out of the water to lick the dew from the grass]. This behavior of the crocodile is unusual and rare. The preceding paragraph had explained to us that "Soumaré allait rarement au Bolloda" (115). [Soumaré rarely went to the Bolloda]. Thus, his visit to the king at the moment is an unusual act motivated by a serious incident; the misunderstanding between the king and the new Commandant.

To describe the threatening attitude of Commandant Bernier towards Africans, the narrator compares what this attitude forebodes to the "nuages qui charrient l'orage et le tonnerre" (120). [Clouds which sweep along thunder and lightening]. Also, when the eunuch tries to discourage Moussokoro from attempting to escape, he compares him to the sheep that tries to escape and ends up tightening the grip of the rope around the neck (140). Béma will have other chances to get rid of Yawuba the new marabout who is an obstacle to his political ambitions. The narrator compares this to "une souris narquante qui a son trou dans le mur de la case de votre mère. On aura d'autres chances à la retrouver". [A flouting mouse which has its hole in the wall of your mother's hut. You will have other occasions to find it]. All these metaphors embellish the language of the narrative, while creating local color, even if it poses a problem of comprehension for the non-initiated reader who has no notion of Mandingo proverbs. The title of the novel itself has an important word (*"monnè"*) that cannot be well translated into French. Metaphorical language is very poetic. Kourouma is like a griot who castigates his society in metaphorical language. But *monnè* also symbolizes the inability of colonizer and colonized to communicate, because it is not a dialogue of equals.

Thus, Kourouma resorts to his knowledge of the customs of his people to create real-seeming characters who relate in a way that creates caricatures of fictional historical figures. He is an engaged writer in the Sartrean sense. According to Sartre (cited in the introductory chapter) the committed writer knows the importance of the word. He knows he cannot be impartial when he commits himself to unveiling the human condition. In his historical novel, Kourouma takes sides against the oppressor.

Yet the beauty of Kourouma's novel does not only lie in his use of humor, satire, and proverbs but also in the technique of narrative voices as well. Sometimes, the reader needs to read closely to be able to identify the source of discourse. Kourouma frequently uses the free indirect speech narrative form. In his novel *Madame Bovary*, the nineteenth-century French writer Gustave Flaubert used free indirect speech. But Flaubert gave importance to narrative itself, without any ideological motifs. Kourouma, on the contrary, is not interested in narrative for its sake. There is an obvious ideological motif as we have seen in our analysis of the novel. The reader is sometimes confused as to whether it is Djigui, the interpreter, or the griot who is narrating.

In the story, there is an omniscient narrator. This narrator is often (with reason) identified with the author of the novel, Kourouma. He is the one who comments on events and creates a link between the other narrative voices, thus creating a "dialogue" with the reader. Kourouma has created multiple voices manipulated by the main narrator. Identifying the speaker or the intended audience of the speech is not always obvious. Yet we know that Kourouma is the one who manipulates the multiple voices. In realist writing, sentences are arranged in such a way that the reader can identify the narrator(s) of the story. However, *Monné, outrages et défis* sometimes defies this relationship between the reader and his or her text.

At the beginning of the novel, for example, the narrator identifies himself as belonging to the king's society" "Lui qui était notre roi" (15). [He who was our king]. This is important because the sentence reassures the reader that being an insider, the narrator knows the history of the area well. He talks of a king and of a people with whom he can identify and recounts the history of a people to which he belongs. This use of the personal pronoun "nous" runs through the novel. Sometimes, by using "nous" the diegetic narrator invokes legend to make his story more authentic: "La légende prétend que cinq fois le long du chantier, Diabaté, le messager de Samory, arrêta *notre* roi; cinq fois, Djigui le bouscula" (33). [Legend claims that five times along the building site, Diabaté, Samory's messenger, stopped *our* king; five times Djigui shuffled him aside].

But why would Djigui often become narrator in the story? He identifies himself as the narrator by the use of the pronouns "moi" and "je": "Ecoute-moi Djigui, roi de Soba, je me suis réveillé, levé. J'ai décidé de parler, de marcher, de manger, de respecter mes femmes" (47). [Listen to me Djigui, king of Soba, I have woken up, gotten up. I have decided to speak, to walk, to respect my wives]. Djigui is narrator here; because these words are not in quotes. In fact, he introduces his own direct speech which follows in quotes: "J'ai demandé au chef de mes sièdes". [I asked the head of my *siedes*]:

> Tous les habitants sont-ils chassés des cases?
> Oui, Djigui Keita roi de Soba. (48)
>
> [Are all the inhabitants chased out of the huts?
> Yes, Djigui Keita king of Soba].

The novel is replete with such examples of Djigui the main character playing the role of narrator. On page 75 for example, Djigui the narrator tells us about his conversation with the Commandant concerning the train: "Pour faire arriver le train, on pouvait compter sur moi, Djigui" (75). [To make the train arrive, they could count on me Djigui]. In the paragraph that follows, he recounts the reaction of the Commandant: "Non, non, le Blanc ne me le recommandait pas. Une gare n'était pas une petite mosquée qui se construit attenante à une chambre" (75). [No, no, the white man was not recommending it to me. A train station was not a small mosque which is built adjoining a bedroom]. Then, in the paragraph which follows, the narrator, Djigui, introduces his own speech which is the reaction to the Commandant:

> Je rétorquai aux nouveaux ergotages du Blanc, en précisant que tout ce qu'il citait ne m'incommoderait réellement. "Un vacarme pour l'honneur ne pouvait fatiguer un homme d'honneur. Je veux ma gare et mon train à ma porte." (75)
>
> [I retorted at the new quibblings of the White man by telling him precisely that in reality, all the things he was quoting did not bother me. A row for honor could not tire a man of honor. I want my train station and my train at my doorstep"].

Thus, without warning the reader, the main narrator manipulates Djigui who is one moment a narrator and the next the speaker. But sometimes, one cannot easily identify the narrative voices. For example on page 103, we have in the same paragraph:

> J'allais enfin connaître le pays des Blancs [...]. Djigui eut le mal de mer et voulut demander à retourner à Soba [...] Deux fois nous jêtames l'ancre pour admirer des villes... (103)
>
> [Finally. I was going to know the country of the White people...Djigui had sea sickness and wanted to return to Soba....Twice we cast anchor to admire some towns].

The paragraph that follows this one continues the use of the personal pronoun "je" and "nous." We can identify the "je" as Djigui.

Thus, it would be Djigui who includes the other characters in the "nous" of his own narration. But then, what do we make of "Djigui eut le mal de mer" in the same paragraph? This is the difficulty posed by the use of free indirect speech in narration.

Why is it important to identify the speakers and the narrators (multiple voices) in the story? We are dealing with historical fiction which claims some authenticity in the historical facts that inspire it. Since the exercise of power is a main motif in the novel, the identification of the narrative voices is essential. The choice of historical events by a novelist, as Paul Veynes has suggested, is motivated by an ideological inclination. We need to know who manipulates discourse in the narrative and why Kourouma identifies with certain characters. The claim to "truth" and "authenticity" become important in historical fiction. The choice of events by Kourouma in the fictional world he creates in the novel is motivated by an ideology.

The use of free indirect speech by Kourouma demonstrates his ability to manipulate the language of the colonizer as a weapon. The beauty of his art is reinforced by his deep knowledge of traditions of the region. Like the "anciens," he alludes to in his novel, Kourouma has the gift of the word.

The narrative structure itself is chronological. It begins with the fall of Samory followed by that of Djigui and ends with the advent of colonialism and the creation of political systems in contemporary Africa. However, there are some important flashbacks which have a significant effect on the narration. The division into six parts follows the historical chronology, except the flashbacks which tell us about Béma's birth. It does not interrupt the progress of narration. Kourouma does not indulge in long digressions which have no rapport with the story. The epigraphs of the sections invoke in proverbial and metaphorical form the central theme of the sections.

Like the other African historical novelists considered here, Kourouma's novelistic creation is influenced to a great deal by traditional story-telling. Sometimes, he tells his story like the "griot" (praise singer). But the writer has some freedom that the griot could not enjoy. As Ahmadou Koné says in his study of the influence of oral narration on the African novel, "les moyens et les conditions d'expression donnent à l'écrivain une liberté que le griot n'avait pas" [the means and the conditions of expression allow the writer a freedom that the griot did not have] (1985, 83). He goes on to explain that the traditional African narrator followed a certain pre-existing pattern. Creativity was limited to the "langage" [language] and style of the artist. These pre-existing patterns must have been created by some artists in the first place. So there was some kind of "pure" creation of art. But the fact is that because the collectivity was more important than the individual in this society, the originator of

Ahmadou Kourouma: *Monnè, outrages et défis*   121

the story remained anoymous. This was especially the case because the notion of "author" did not have the same importance or the same significance as it does today (Koné 25). Kourouma who has mastered the techniques of the griot, has transformed traditional art (through proverbs, metaphors and so forth) into an art that is recognized as an individual's production; the historical novel. Nonetheless, before he wrote *Monnè, outrages et défis*, he himself had lamented (commenting on his first novel) how difficult it was for him to express cogently in French, the reactions of his fictional characters (Kone 152). But his talent is in being able to manipulate the French language to express the thoughts of his characters who express themselves in malinké.

Kourouma has demonstrated in *Monnè, outrages et défis* how the historical novel can give us a critical look at our past and contemporary society. In this novel, he goes beyond what he had done in *Soleil des Indépendances*. He gives us a new sense of what historical fiction can do in francophone Africa. He is critical of his society, yet unlike Ouologuem (in *Le Devoir de Violence*), he does not create a myth of Africa in European image. Commenting on how Kourouma uses history in *Monnè, outrages et défis*, Irele wrote:

> An introspective quality thus informs Kourouma's novel, a quality that turns largely on the association of the historical vision it embodies with the forms of an indigenous orality, felt as a necessary dimension of the mode of expression of this vision. The novel illustrates the way in which there is often a double articulation of narrative in the historical and cultural context of contemporary Africa—of the literate form of the novel as both the medium of an engagement with history and as creative transformation of orality within writing in its formal realization. (1993, 167)

Thus Kourouma's latest novel is a testimony of what the African writer has done with history and orality in fictional form. The focus on power structure in the novel in this chapter has underscored the interplay between history and narrative and the struggle by the characters to control discourse in various forms in the process.

Using the language of the colonizer or former colonizer, the African writers considered in these first four chapters "translate knowing into telling," as White says in his study of narrative. They address the African as well as the outsider. White argues that though we may not be able to comprehend specific thought patterns of another culture, we have relatively less difficulty understanding a story coming from another culture. Thus he sees narrative as a meta-code, a human universal on the basis of which transcultural messages about the nature of a shared reality can be transmitted (1987, 1). Through narrative, the African writer shares with humanity what would otherwise be considered an experience that is culture-specific.

Narrative helps to make that culture-specific experience an ideological message to readers in general.

One common trait in these novels is the influence of oral tradition. In her study of the question of orality in the African novel, Eileen Julien has taken the position that it is no longer viable to see traces of oral traditions in the novel as a sign of African authenticity. She argues that, "when we look at [the interaction of orality and writing] in literary genres, it therefore should not be in an effort to prove or disprove cultural authenticity but rather to appreciate literature as a social and aesthetic art" (24). Much as the argument about not defining an African writer as "authentic" or not by using the recourse to orality as a criteria is valid, we cannot overlook the fact that Negritudist writers themselves considered their use of orality as a counter-discourse to the myths that Europeans created about African society. Consequently, for them, the use of such modes of orality as proverbs, oral narrative form, riddles, dictons and so forth, was a form of authenticity, both in terms of defining themselves as writers and as a way of revalorizing their own culture in the face of colonial hegemonic discourse. In more recent writing in European languages from francophone Africa, novelists like Ahmadou Kourouma have used orality to create a new form of counter-discourse to challenge the hegemonic discourse of the colonizer and neo-colonizer, as well as that of the ruling elite class estranged from the mass of the population.[1]

5

Léonard Sainville: *Dominique Nègre Esclave*

This chapter will examine *Dominique Nègre Esclave* by the Martiniquan writer Léonard Sainville. The proposed thesis is that for Sainville, the revalorization of the image of the maroon is crucial in the Antillean's search for an authentic cultural identity. By studying in his historical fiction, the process of "chosification" (to borrow a term from Césaire) that characterized the treatment of the slave in the Antilles, Sainville reveals a strong sense of ideological commitment. His fiction was motivated by a desire to subvert the Euro-centric discourse of the "Other" by intimating that the maroon was a hero who was denied his rightful place in the history of the Antilles. In *Dominique Nègre Esclave*, he presents marooning as a counter-discourse to the dominant discourse of the slave master. This chapter will demonstrate how the slave master created "otherness" in slaves and how the slaves reacted to this predicament in a way that enables Sainville to see them as the heroes of their own emancipation.

Like Glissant after him, Sainville demonstrates through fiction that Antilleans must first try to understand themselves. In the process of creating an authentic discourse of their own, they must initially strive to understand the discourse of the ancestors against the backdrop of European colonial hegemony. In *Dominique Nègre Esclave*, Sainville identifies the oppositional discourses of the slavery era and then demonstrates how they worked against each other.

An early supporter of the Négritude movement, Sainville also believed in the necessity of adopting a Marxist approach to the liberation of oppressed peoples—a belief that was partly responsible for the confrontation with the French government. In *Dominique Nègre Esclave*, Sainville creates an anti-colonial discourse that makes him a committed writer in the Sartrean sense of the word. According to Sartre, a committed writer cannot ignore what is happening in society. Writing is, for him, a form of engagement with society, and it should be used as propaganda, as a means of declaring one's solidarity with one's times. Sartre argues that writers need to ask themselves what aspect of the world they want to reveal, and what changes they want to bring about as the result of this revelation. In his view, "revealing" the world represents an attempt to change it. For this reason, he contends that the committed writer should abandon the impossible dream of painting an objective or impartial picture of society and of the human condition in which it participates (781). Sainville's writing is dictated by his commitment to changing the human condition: to rehabilitating the place of black people in history. In revalorizing the image of the black in Dominique, he, like other Negritude writers, is declaring his solidarity with his times.

Like his African counterpart, the Antillean historical novelist has experienced the effects of European colonial rule. By the time Sainville wrote *Dominique Nègre Esclave* in 1948, slavery had been abolished in the French Antilles a hundred years earlier and Martinique had become a part of France—a "Département d'Outre Mer"—two years previously.[1] Within this context, Sainville's discourse in *Dominique Nègre Esclave* is that of an angry "subject" of a French domination that had promulgated many false stereotypes about his race. The novel is Sainville's response to a situation in which his own people had been relegated to the periphery by a dominant Euro-centric discourse. Influenced by his background as a professional historian and political activist, his choice of a specific period in the history of Antillean slavery resulted from his own scholarly research in the area. In a doctoral thesis that he presented several years after his novel appeared, he explained the importance of the fictional version of his research work, emphasizing that, by marooning and by persistently defying the system that had turned them into beasts of burden, Antillean slaves had themselves brought about the dismantling of the institution of slavery (1970, 1294). Therefore, his choice of specific events was clearly motivated by a sense of pride in his people and in his culture. He desired to re-write that part of Antillean history which had always been distorted in Euro-centric discourse. The medium he chose was the subversive discourse of the revolted slave.

Toumson has commented that Afro-Antillean writing developed from the writing about Africa that French fiction writers of the eighteenth and the twentieth centuries had developed. The theme of slave revolt was nothing new. Creole antiabolitionist novelists of the twentieth century had dealt with this theme in their writing (Toumson 337). Léonard Sainville, and Glissant after him, were therefore directly influenced by a theme that had been developed before they began writing fiction. Toumson also argues that the character of the "maroon" was not an invention of Afro-Antillean protest writers. The maroon as a character was remolded to assign to him or her the moral nobility and the heroic dignity of which he or she had been stripped. According to Toumson, it was German romanticism which had made the literary figure of the outlawed a fashionable one:

> Le roman du marronage [...] avait repris, en l'adaptant, cette figure archétypale. Dans le roman antillo-guyanais de l'après-guerre, le marron se présente comme une réalisation de la même figure générique, à la différence notable près que l'on quitte la dimension de l'histoire anecdotique[...] pour celle du mythe idéologique et de la rédemption. (338)

> [The novel on marooning...had mimicked this archetypal figure in an adopted form. In the Antillano-Guyanese novel of the post-war period, the

maroon is depicted as a realization of the same generic figure, except for the significant difference that it abandons the domain of anecdotic history (...) in favor of that of ideological myth and redemption].

Maroons as we see them in Antillean literature, therefore, personify the archetypal "nègre romantique" and become the central figure of the "négateur."

Sainville's revalorization of the image of the slave in *Dominique Nègre Esclave* was actually inspired by the development of Antillean discursive processes that are quite similar to those described by Michel Foucault in *Surveiller et punir*. The systematic attempt to dehumanize and deculturalize the slave was one manifestation of what Foucault analyzes as the exercise of power. In *Surveiller et punir*, he traces the history of the prison and shows how, through the years, French society viewed physical punishment as a corrective method. The dehumanizing treatment of the slave cannot be divorced from this concept of punishment in French society during the period depicted in Sainville's fiction. From the concept of bodily chastisement, French society moved toward the idea that the chastisement of the soul was a more effective method of punishment. This shift in attitude occurred during the nineteenth century. In Sainville's *Dominique Nègre Esclave*, the slave was subjected to the chastisement of body and soul. According to Foucault, the French regarded punishment as a means of intensifying society's awareness of the severity of a crime. The crime itself had to be brought to light through confessions, speeches, and other activities that served to publicize it. Punishment was thus supposed to be inflicted in public so that the culprit would be appropriately humiliated (Foucault 59).

Foucault's analysis of French society and its concept of punishment could also be applied to the situation of the Antillean slave and especially to the revolted maroon who was often publicly humiliated. Sometimes his body was even mutilated in the presence of the other slaves. In spite of the "Code Noir" that was passed by the French government to monitor the way slaves were handled by slave masters, the severest punishment that could be inflicted on a slave master for breaking the law was a mere scolding. This situation, as Sainville testifies in *Dominique Nègre Esclave*, helped reinforce a clear division between the races by defining the black "Other" as a slave. The dehumanization and public humiliation of slaves were intended to make them "confess." These measures were also addressed to other slaves who might contemplate the act of marooning. However, this "chosification" of the black is the starting point for the emergence of an important counter-discourse on the part of the maroons in Sainville's historical novel. In speaking about the birth of the concept of punishment in French society, Foucault explains:

> Le supplice fait partie de la procédure qui établit la réalité de ce qu'on punit. Mais il y a plus: l'atrocité d'un crime, c'est aussi la violence du défi lancé au souverain. C'est ce qui va déclencher de sa part une réplique qui a pour fonction de renchérir sur cette atrocité, de la maîtriser, de l'emporter sur elle par un excès qui l'annule. L'atrocité qui hante le supplice joue donc un double rôle: principe de la communication du crime. (59-60)

> [Punishment is part of the process which establishes the reality of what one is punishing. But there is more: the atrocity of a crime is also the violence of the challenge thrown to the sovereign. It is what will provoke in him a retaliation which is meant to underscore this atrocity, to master it, to get the upper hand over it by extremes which nullify it. The atrocity which haunts the torture therefore plays a double role: principle of the communication of the crime].

The crucial idea in this passage is the perception of crime as a challenge to the power of the sovereign. The atrocity of the punishment brings out the truth; it also certifies the power of the sovereign. It is part of a ritual which ends in the triumph of power.

The same ritual is re-enacted in *Dominique Nègre Esclave* where the maroon is punished in a way that supposedly undermines the rationale for his or her revolt against the system and underscores the power of the white béké. If crime is a challenge to the power that the sovereign exercises over the people, the main actor in this social drama is, as Foucault points out, the people themselves; their real and immediate presence is required for the "ceremony" to have the required effect.

The system that existed in the Antilles during the centuries of slavery was indeed a testimony to the power that the European master exercised over the "inferior" Other. Perceived primarily as an economic object, the Antillean slave was subjected to a "justice system" that obliged him to recognize his powerlessness before the law. In contrast, the white béké was untouchable before the law and could disregard it at will. He represented the status quo which the whole system had been devised to maintain as it was. However, the maroon subverted this system through the persistent revolt that Sainville portrays in his fiction as a crucial factor in Antillean history.

Dominique Nègre Esclave calls into question the entire discourse that justifies this status quo. For Sainville, the maroon was the "négateur" of a system analogous to the one that Foucault examines in his study. Césaire was also responding to this situation when he wrote:

> Et ce pays cria pendant des siècles que nous sommes des bêtes brutes; que les pulsations de l'humanité s'arrêtent aux portes de la négrerie; que nous sommes un fumier ambulant hideusement prometteur de cannes tendres et de coton soyeux et l'on nous vendait sur les places et l'aune de drap anglais et

la viande salée d'Irlande coûtaient moins cher que nous, et ce pays était calme, tranquille, disant que l'esprit de Dieu était dans ses actes. (*Cahier*, 38-39)

[And this country cried out for centuries that we are brutish beasts; that the heartbeats of humanity stop at the doorsteps of the Black race; that we are itinerant bastards hideously promoting the production of tender sugar cane and silky cotton and we were sold in public squares, and the alder of English cloth and the salted meat of Ireland cost less than us, and this country was calm, peaceful, saying that the spirit of God was in its actions].

In this passage, Césaire is demonstrating the dehumanization imposed upon black people by slavery. Many European intellectuals had justified this practice. According to them, the slave was a mere economic object. Césaire's anger at this scandalous situation resembles Sainville's own desire to re-valorize the image of the maroon in his historical fiction. As Césaire had done before him, Sainville depicts graphically the predicament of the slave, but he also presents the maroon as a hero who refuses to accept his situation docilely.

In the novel, Dominique and Azaïs (the head of the maroons) symbolize one aspect of Antillean history that has been neglected or distorted in Euro-centric history. They persistently refuse to be objects in the eyes of the slave masters. Thus, the slave masters' exercise of power fails to eliminate the counter-discourse of the maroons. Dominique, Azaïs, and their companions subvert the "subject" image that the white men were seeking to impose on them. In the process, they also subvert the image the whites have created for themselves. In effect, the maroons are challenging the dominator-dominated relationship on which this white self-image depends. In other words, the confrontation of the maroons with the white béké creates a new type of relationship and proves that the white masters' definition of the relationship is not the only possible one. Black people had not been created to be dominated by Europeans, as the latter contended. In fact, Sainville's portrayal of the confrontational relationship between the maroon and the slave master undermines assumptions that had always been taken for granted in the dominant European discourse.

In his preface, Sainville claims that his novel was inspired by the true history of Azaïs and Hibo, two maroons accused of having killed another maroon, Moco. In the novel, he uses their authentic historical names, and Azaïs actually has the personality of his historical model. As Sainville reports, there is an archival account of what transpired in Guadeloupe between Azaïs and his captives in 1837:

Le 21 et le 22 ont été jugés Azaïs et Hibo accusés de meurtre avec préméditation sur la personne du nommé Moco. Azaïs, marron dans les bois de la Souffrière, s'était mis à la tête d'esclaves fugitifs et avait construit un camp. Au nombre de ses compagnons se trouvaient Anne, sa sœur, Moco, au sieur de Blainville, Hibo, au sieur Cardonnet. (9-10)

[On the 21st and the 22nd, Azaïs and Hibo were judged, having been accused of murder of the named Moco with premeditation. Azaïs, a maroon in the woods of the Souffrière, had made himself head of fugitive slaves and had built a camp. Among his companions were Anne, his sister, Moco, who belonged to Mr. de Blainville, Hibo, who belonged to Mr. Cardonnet].

This preface needs to be read as part of the discourse of the entire novel. It prepares the readers for the character they will discover in Azaïs, because the fictional Azaïs in the novel corresponds closely to the historical Azaïs of the preface.

Like his historical homonym, Azaïs creates a power structure around himself in a way that defies the subject image that is commonly associated with slaves by their masters. For the slave master to exist in the image he has forged for himself, he needs to maintain the image of the inferior "Other" that he has imposed on the slave, but Azaïs' discourse subverts the image that white békés like Donzolet have of themselves.

The novel itself opens with an example of the white béké's discourse of power—the flogging of Jean-Pierre on the "quatre-piquets." Donzelot creates an image of superiority around himself in order to keep the slaves in a perpetuallly subservient state: "Il voulait avoir l'allure terrible, car on procédait à un chatiment et tout 'l'atelier hommes' avait été convié à la cérémonie" (13). [He wanted to have a terrible look, for they were going to do a flogging and the "men's workshop" had been urged to attend the ceremony]. This quotation reveals the existence of the same power structure that Foucault analyzes in his work. Donzelot's "allure terrible" emphasizes the power he exercises over the subject "Other." Making sure that all the slaves witness the punishment meted out to the "culprits" is a way of "legitimizing" the whole process, of making it an established institution in the eyes of the slaves. It is a concrete way of defining the slaves' Otherness in a system where the white béké's power determines how society functions.

Jean-Pierre was being punished because he dared to behave in a way that was not in the interest of the slave masters:

Ne s'était-il pas laissé surprendre avec les trois autres sacripants à mâcher de la canne, la veille au soir, peu après le retour des champs! Ne savaient-ils pas tous ces Nègres, que leurs vols répétés causaient le plus grand dommage aux propriétaires? Ne leur donnait-on pas la nourriture en suffisance? (14)

[Had he not allowed himself to be caught with the three other rogues eating sugar-cane the previous day in the evening, shortly after coming back from the sugar-cane fields! Did all these Niggers not know that their theft caused the greatest damage for the owners? Were they not given enough food?]

In this passage, Sainville adopts an ironic tone to underscore the white béké's opinion about a slave who is eating sugar cane to avoid starvation. The author's description of the slave master's reaction seems detached, but its sarcastic tone draws attention to the predicament against which the maroon was revolting.

The maroons in *Dominique Nègre Esclave* do not docilely accept the image of themselves as mere economic objects. Freedom is crucial to them, and living in the mountains under the leadership of Azaïs is an open defiance of the whole economic and political system based on slavery. If slavery in the New World stripped Africans of their human identity and dignity, the stance of the maroon represents their fight to regain a fully human status:

> A l'échelle des marrons vivaient et prospéraient les intérêts, les sentiments, les vices, les vertus, qui formaient le complexe psychologique et social de la grande société de laquelle ils s'étaient mis en marge; mais il y manquait l'esclavage et l'avilissement. (58)
>
> [In the rangs of the maroons one could see flourishing interests, sentiments, vices, virtues, which made up the psychological and social complex of the big society from which it had seperated itself. But what was lacking was slavery and degradation].

Azaïs personifies authority, an authority which poses a threat to the status quo. Under his leadership, the maroons exercise self-discipline. In fact, the system they create for themselves living in the mountains is an uncompromising rejection of the image of the "Other" that had been imposed by Euro-centric discourse. The rules and regulations established by the maroons for themselves disprove the myth of the slave as a being who was incapable of doing anything for himself.

Colonialism thrived on the myth that Africans, Blacks, were backward people who needed European civilization. The activities of the maroons contradicted the assumption on which this myth was based. According to the myth, Africans and other colonized peoples were incapable of making progress by themselves. They needed somebody else to tell them what was good for them. Needless to say, that somebody was by definition the white man. By organizing a maroon society in the mountains, Azaïs effectively subverts the power exercised by the white béké and by all those in Europe who benefit from slavery. His character effectively symbolizes the pride of Antilleans, descendants of slaves, in their ability to seize the historical initiative. However, the maroon who best represents this pride in the ancestors is the main character Dominique himself.

By comprehending the nature of Dominique's "adventures" with different slave masters, the reader achieves insight into the life of a slave in the French Caribbean. Dominique is a picaresque-like hero—persistently challenging the status quo, revolting and marooning at every opportunity, and becoming more hardened and more witty after his experiences with each new master. For Sainville, this attitude makes Dominique a symbol of the anti-colonial discourse that rejects all that the institution of slavery represented.

Dominique serves the ideological purpose of Sainville's anti-colonial discourse in the sense that he embodies the history that is being rewritten in the Antillean writer's search for a viable cultural identity. He symbolizes a rejection of the exercise of power by French society as it has been defined by Foucault. Through Dominique, Sainville demonstrates that the slave was not a passive "subject" in a purely assimilationist system. A maroon of the first order, Dominique resents the system from the beginning and constantly poses a threat to it. Even during his childhood, he is a potential hero. Even then, he desires to liberate himself from his subject state and yearns to create an anti-colonial discourse that would accurately represent the history of his people. In the eyes of the whites, however, Dominique incarnates the devil image they associate with all maroons.

Precisely this image provoked Sainville's anti-colonial discourse in the first place, for he reverses its significance. Ironically, the negative image associated with the maroon makes him a hero in the eyes of the black Antillean, and this image makes him an appropriate symbol of the writer's anti-colonial discourse. In the eyes of the whites, blacks are incapable of the love that one human being can feel for another. This stereotyped idea is illustrated during the trial of Azaïs and the other maroons when the whites express surprise that a slave could love a woman the way Moco loved Azaïs' sister:

-Tiens, les Nègres peuvent aimer à ce point, comme des Blancs? s'étonna le "cinq ficelles". Bizarre, n'est-ce pas? fit le Gouverneur avec un gros rire. (95)

["What? The Niggers can love to this extent like Whites"? 'five strings' said astonishingly. "Bizarre, isn't it"? commented the Governor with a big smile].

This conversation encapsulates the European's implied perception of the slave as being incapable of normal human sentiments.

In his relationship with the white masters, however, Dominique demystifies such stereotypes. For example, he endures physical torture, a daily occurrence in the life of a slave, with courage. He defies the power of the white béké, refuses to cry as he is tied to the "quatre piquets" and then flogged:

> Le colon connaissait bien Dominique. Il le tenait pour une des brebis galeuses de l'atelier, une de ces "têtes de nègres" obstinées, vindicatives, "sournoises", un véritable "enfant de garce" que les mauvais traitements, l'emploi même des moyens de terreur semblait ne pas pouvoir réduire. (16)
>
> [The colonist knew Dominique well. He considered him one of the spoilt sheep in the group, one of these obstinate, vindictive "sly" "nigger heads", a real "slut child" whom the bad treatments, even the uses of terror seemed not to be able to subdue].

When Dominique spits in disgust as he is tied to the "quatre piquets," he challenges the image that the white society has created for itself, underscoring his own dignity as a member of the black race.

Slavery was an inhuman institution that sought to deprive blacks of their human dignity. Sainville creates a positive counter-image of the slave and of black people in general through his portrayal of Dominique:

> Ni les blessures du fouet et celles de l'amour-propre, ni les affres de la faim ou celles du désespoir n'avaient porté atteinte à la personne physique ou morale du grand gars Dominique. Il appartenait à la lignée millénaire et toujours renouvelée des parias qui refusent la misère de leur condition, et il portait en lui, toute vibrante, la dignité de l'homme noir. (17)
>
> [Neither the wounds of the whip and those of self-esteem, nor the pangs of hunger or the wounds of dispair had done damage to the physical or moral being of the huge man Dominique. He belonged to the millennium and constantly revived tradition of social outcasts who refuse the misery of their condition, and he had in him, powerfully, the dignity of the black man].

Through Dominique, Sainville expounds his Negritude ideas. Significantly, Dominique is not a mulatto, but a pure black. Even though Dominique's mother had slept with many men, his father was certainly a black man: "Dominique, câpre 'cent pour cent', n'était certainement le fils d'un béké ni d'un mulâtre" (20). [Dominique a "hundred per cent" caper was certainly neither the son of a béké nor of a mulatto]. Sainville emphasizes the family lineage of his hero because, according to him, it makes the latter more appropriate as a symbol of his anti-colonial discourse.

But Sainville's portrayal of Dominique differs from the way his compatriot Roland Brival portrays his hero Macouba in *La Montagne d'Ebène*, which was inspired by the same historical events. Although a pure-blooded African like Dominique, Macouba was not born into slavery. Sainville seems to suggests that, for his hero to be a more authentic representative of Antilleans' quest for identity, he needs to be born into the system like Dominique.

Dominique's initiation into adulthood is accompanied by his early encounter with sexuality. Made to join the "petite bande" [small group][2] at the age of ten, he undergoes a metamorphosis as his eyes are opened to the realities of slavery. For him to become the hero of a later maroon revolt, he must first experience a physical and psychological initiation:

> Comme tout jeune esclave, il prenait de plus en plus conscience de l'immense fossé qui séparait les hommes à peau noire ou brune de ceux qui l'avaient blanche. Il réalisait journellement, dans l'impossibilité d'exprimer sa personnalité, dans le refoulement constant de ses moindres désirs, ce que c'est qu'appartenir à un autre. [...] Il cherchait à être un esclave moyen parmi trois cents autres esclaves et à refréner toute individualité, en même temps que violente, mais réprimée, se développait la haine des hommes blancs et ceux qui, servilement, se soumettent à eux. (23-24)

> [As a very young slave, he was more and more conscious of the great divide which separated black skinned or brown skinned men from the white ones. He realized everyday in the impossibility of expressing his personality, in the constant repression of his smallest desires, what it meant to belong to another person [...]. He strove to be an average slave among three hundred other slaves and to hold any individuality in check. Violent but at the same time repressed hatred of white people and of those who servilely submit themselves to them, was developing in him].

As a result of having experienced the dehumanizing conditions of slavery, Dominique realizes while still a child that he is no more than a commodity in the eyes of the white man. The impulse that is triggered by this insight enables him to gain back his human dignity and thereby to become a symbol of black dignity and pride. He does not hesitate to hit a supervisor who had been cruel to him, despite the fact that he will be imprisoned for his "offense" and subjected to utterly inhuman treatment.

Even in prison, Dominique fights to defend his own humanity. By doing so, he categorically rejects Euro-centric myths about the black man's inherent dependency and docility—myths that were used in European discourse to justify the inhuman treatment of slaves:

> Il [Dominique] était un esclave. Mais il voulait vivre, il voulait être fier, il ne voulait pas être broyé par la machine. Il voulait être lui. (28)

> [He (Dominique) was a slave. But he wanted to live; he wanted to be proud. He did not want to be crushed by the machine. He wanted to be himself].

Dominique's "prise de conscience" in this passage underscores his pride in himself, in his race. His determination to survive the rigors of slavery is the driving force that ultimately enables him to undercut the power of the white béké.

In their rejection of the image of the "Other" imposed on them by the white béké, Antillean slaves revolted in a variety of ways. Apart from marooning, they often resorted to poisoning as a way of creating a counter-discourse. Poisoning the masters' animals diminished the economic power that was also reflected in the "chosification" of the slave:

> A la mechanceté, ils répondaient par une méchanceté plus grande. Le sadisme du maître trouvait, en face de lui, une fureur de vengeance et de destruction qui semblait inapaisable. (276)
>
> [He returned wickedness with a greater wickedness. The master's sadism was confronted by him with a fury of vengeance and of destruction which seemed to be unpacifiable].

By creating a counter-discourse in response to the sub-human treatment to which he and the other slaves are subjected, Dominique actually subverts the economic power base of the slave masters and thereby diminishes their power over him and his people.

Sainville also focuses on the reaction of the slaves vis-à-vis other dimensions of the cruel system that has been imposed on them. For example, Dominique's courage when he is being sadistically tortured with a hot iron arouses the reader's sensibility to the breaking point, but it also disproves the Europeans' stereotyped notion about black people:

> Un homme s'approcha du feu et se saisit d'un fer à l'extrémité complètement rougie. Dominique serra les dents et ferma les yeux pour ne point voir. Il concentra fortement sa pensée sur Léontine et sur son enfant. Il sentit la cuisson à son épaule gauche et un grand élancement. Il se raidit. Une deuxième cuisson, un deuxième formidable éclair qui traversait tout son être. (286)
>
> [A man approached the fire and seized an iron with a red-hot end. Dominique clinched his teeth and closed his eyes in order not to see at all. He concentrated his thoughts very hard on Léontine and on his child. He felt the roasting of his left elbow and a very sharp pain. He stiffened. A second burning, a second strong lightning which ran through his whole body].

This graphic description underscores the cruelty of Dominique's punishment, but it also emphasizes his ability to survive physically, to resist in a heroic manner. In this description, Sainville does not simply highlight the relationship between blacks and whites in the Antilles; more importantly, he creates an ideological basis for questioning the entire colonial enterprise and the supposedly humanitarian Western philosophies that were adduced to support it. If the French had created codes of behavior for slaves in order to keep them perpetually in a subordinate state, Dominique disregards those codes and obliges readers to recognize their inherent brutality.

In his book *Nous et les Autres*, Tzvetan Todorov analyzes the French perception of the "Other" in a way that we can also apply in our study of the relationship between the white béké and the slave in Sainville's *Dominique Nègre Esclave*. It is a relationship based on the Euro-centric discourse of the Other. In his study, Todorov demonstrates how ethno-centrism permeated the works of writers such as Pascal and La Bruyère. Reflecting French society's perceptions of other people, such works help us understand why many Frenchmen regarded it as "normal" to dehumanize the slave in the most sadistic manner. In this sense, Todorov's study illuminates the rationale behind the dehumanizing of Dominique and the significance of his ability to revolt against it.

As Todorov points out, works such as Renan's *L'Origine du Langage* assume the superiority of the white race:

> Visiblement, c'est encore la providence qui décide du rôle dévolu aux différentes populations du globe; la race blanche est seule pourvue de la dignité du sujet humain, les autres races devant s'en tenir à des fonctions instrumentales: elles n'existent pas en elles-mêmes mais seulement dans l'optique du projet impérial auquel est prédestinée la race blanche. (1989, 134)

> [Visibly, it is again providence which decides on the role alotted to the different populations of the globe. The white race is the only one imbued with the dignity of the human species, the other races being limited to instrumental functions only].

According to Todorov, Renan argues that expansionist wars were perfectly legitimate as long as they were not waged between races that belong to the superior class, but rather by peasants and people of working-class origins. Colonial wars, in Renan's view, were the ideal (134-135). For Hippolyte Taine and Gobineau too, Europeans were innately civilized; in their view "civilization" is an inherited characteristc and cannot be acquired (147). This concept permeated white Antillean society, which regarded the black person as inherently uncivilized.

Todorov goes further to point out the absurdity and hypocrisy of the official position adopted by French government officials toward the plight of slaves. For example, Alexis de Tocqueville tried to reconcile his ethical opposition to slavery with his position as a French Deputy. While arguing for the right of slaves to be free because nobody had the right to possess another human being, Tocqueville acknowledged that the wealth of the slave traders was a legitimate property (Todorov 1989, 221). In order for France not to be ruined by the abolition of slavery, he concluded, the former slave territories had to be maintained under French colonialism. Even for well-intentioned Europeans like de Tocqueville, relationships with other peoples were perceived largely in terms of the political and economic benefits they entailed for Europeans. Such discourse permeated European literary and political writing well into the colonial period. For this reason, *Dominique Nègre Esclave* needs to be read against the backdrop of colonial hegemony, for only in this context can we comprehend the counter-discourse that characterizes the Antillean historical novel and, more specifically, the role of the hero in Sainville's novel. Dominique is a victim of the system that Todorov describes. He also challenges that system.

Dominique's relationship with the white béké also introduces another crucial element of slavery—the treatment of the female slave who was in many ways the ultimate victim of European perceptions of the "Other." The slave was an economic object, but the female slave was even more completely stripped of her dignity, for she was obliged to satisfy the sexual needs of her fellow slaves as well as those of her lecherous masters. Beverly Ormerod has shown how the conception of a child fathered by a white man represented a female slave's only hope of obtaining better living conditions and upward social mobility for her descendants (Ormerod 58).

Ormerod also shows how the female slave was deprived of her right to determine the sexual uses to which her own body was put. Required to become a breeding machine for future labor, the female slave was obliged to sleep with whichever male was chosen for her by the slave master. In his *Discours Antillais*, Edouard Glissant touches upon the bestialization of the female slave as an object of production:

> Le maître entend que l'esclave lui appartienne, jusque dans la fonction de reproduction. Le plaisir ni la jouissance de l'esclave ne sauraient être pris en compte, tout de même que pour un étalon. Sa marge de manœuvre sexuelle est contrainte à la marge bénéficiaire du maître [...]. La jouissance n'est pas un acquis, n'est pas un projet, c'est un dérobé. Ce n'est pas un prolongement de soi; c'est ce qui est déduit de l'Autre, l'Autre toujours présent, voyeur invisible et réprimant. (294)

> [The master means that the slave belongs to him even to the extent of the function of reproduction. Neither the pleasure nor the delight of the slave would be taken into consideration, just as for a stallion. His scope of sexual activity is limited to the scope of the master's pleasure (...). Pleasure is not an acquired thing. It is not a project; it is a secret. It is not an extension of oneself. It is what is deduced from the Other who is always present; an invisible and suppressed voyeur].

As Glissant explains, the male slave considered sex with the female slave (even if it were rape in the sugar-cane fields) as a theft of the master's power and as a means of gaining revenge on the master. If the master was truly a "voyeur," the male slave's "flirting" with the female slaves became a subtle way of defying the latter's power (293-302).[3]

The female slave cursed her own pregnancy and often resorted to abortion, which was not uncommon because it was regarded as preferable to bearing a child who would be enslaved from birth. Even in the slave ships that transported them to the New World, the female slave was dehumanized by constant rape by the "slave owners." Glissant underscores the psychological and sociological importance of this phenomenon in Antillean history, and as can be seen in Sainville's *Dominique Nègre Esclave* and in his own *Le Quatrième Siècle*, the "chosification" of the female slave represented a crucial dimension of this process. Glissant makes this point poignantly in the following text:

> Dans l'univers absolument fou du bateau négrier, là où les hommes déportés sont annihilés physiquement, la femme africaine subit la plus totale des aggressions, qui est le viol quotidien et répété d'un équipage de marins rendus déments par l'exercise de leur métier; après quoi, au débarquer sur la terre nouvelle, la femme a sur l'homme un inappréciable avantage: elle connaît déjà le maître. (1981, 297)

> [In the totally crazy world of the slave ship, where the deported men are physically annihilated, the African woman undergoes the most absolute aggression which is the daily and repeated rape by a team of sailors made demented by the exercise of their duty; after which on debarking on the new land, the woman has an inappreciable advantage. She already knows the master].

For this reason, the "chosification" of the female slave is more profound than that of her male counterpart. The female slave not only has to contend with a denigration of her race, but also with a demeaning image of her sex.

Her humiliation as a female reinforced the white world's view of her as a symbol of the subjugated inferior black race. As René Depestre explains:

> La femme esclave en tant que valeur d'échange et *d'usage*, était encore plus réifiée et aliénée, car elle devait satisfaire à la fois les besoins sociaux du maître et ses besoins sexuels: à l'heure du repos le "sexe-guerier-blanc" immolait joyeusement ses préjugés raciaux dans le sexe somptueusement incolore de la femme noire. (97)

[As an object of exchange and *use*, the slave woman was still more reified and alienated, for she had to satisfy at the same time the social and sexual needs of the master: at bedtime, the "sex-warrior-white" joyously immolated his racial prejudices into the sumptuously colorless sex of the black woman].

In other words, the woman symbolizes an objectified Otherness. Sainville's use of this insight can be seen in the fact that Dominique must live with the pain of knowing that his "wife" Léontine has slept with white males. For him, sleeping with a white girl would be an appropriate revenge on the race that has dehumanized his own. The omniscient narrator of the novel even allows the reader to enter into the psyche of Dominique as the latter contemplates his plan to avenge the lecherous activities of the white béké with black female slaves. Unfortunately, Sainville does not endow the female slave with the same subversive power that he accords to Dominique, who actually challenges the assumptions on which the bestialization of the female slave are based. He, not Léontine, confronts the power of the white béké on behalf of the women who are the ultimate victims of the white man's lechery.

For Dominique, the fact that the white béké can sleep with black female slaves whenever he desires to do so represents one form of degradation of the black race. It reminds him that he is not a free man, but only an object to be exploited for the profit of the white béké. This insight makes him more determined than ever to subvert the false image imposed on his race. He creates his own counter-discourse by establishing an amorous relationship with Marguerite Marinois, his master's daughter. Their relationship is not a simple love adventure. It is a symbolic relationship because it represents the type of relationship that would not be acceptable in a society based on the unequal status of white masters and black slaves.

Dominique breaks the barriers established between races in this society, and his act has a profound significance within the context where it takes place:

Trois siècles de colonisation unissaient cette fille de l'Europe et ce descendant d'indigènes africains. Trois siècles d'esclavages, un monstrueux amas de préjugés, l'orgueil d'une race avilie et torturée continuaient à séparer ces deux êtres. En ces premières minutes qui les rapprochèrent, frémissants et angoissés, tous les complexes nés de cette histoire habitaient peut-être leurs cerveaux. (271)

[Three centuries united this girl of Europe and this descendant of indigenous Africans. Three centuries of slavery, a monstrous heap of prejudices, the pride of a debased and tortured race continued to separate these two beings. In these few minutes which brought them together, trembling and in anguish, their minds were troubled by all the complexes created from this history].

When Dominique makes love with Marguérite for the first time, he is engaging in a symbolic act because he is calling into question centuries of supposed European superiority. In his relationship with her, he puts himself and his race on the same level with the race of the dominator—the white béké—an equivalence that the Euro-centric discourse of the slave master had denied. By revealing the hypocrisy of this discourse, Sainville invites his reader to reflect on the whole enterprise of colonialism and its attendant consequences.

If the institution of slavery created a barrier between races, Dominique and Marguerite realize that love can transcend these barriers. In this sense, Sainville seems to be suggesting that harmony between the two races is possible. The account of a love affair between Dominique and Marguérite demonstrates that, far from being a devil, the black slave can be attractive to white women. Besides, the relationship between Dominique and Marguerite is not a banal love story. Sainville uses it to create a positive image of the slave and to subvert the false image of the Black race in Euro-centric discourse.

Among the masters under whom the picaresque-like Dominique serves, only Marinois has a human attitude towards his slaves, but he goes bankrupt and is ejected from the system.[4] Marinois' sense of morality makes him different from other members of the béké society to which he belongs. He is too human to survive in a system that thrives on the dehumanization of the "Other." The picaresque experiences of Dominique afford him the opportunity to comment on the nature of other slave masters and to recognize how different they are from Marinois. Like the picaresque hero, Dominique becomes increasingly hardened as he experiences life under the iron hand of different masters, but his experiences take on a symbolic significance because they encapsulate the experiences of all slaves.

As in the case of picaresque heroes in European literature, chance plays an important role in Dominique's life. For example, after Dominique and his lover Léontine have been separated for a long time, chance brings them together at one of the occasional meetings when slaves gather at nightfall for music and dancing. Another example is the capsizing of the ship in which Dominique and other slaves are escaping to Antigua, an incident that leads to the adventures Dominique experiences on that island. A chance occurrence thus affords readers the opportunity to discover the extent of Dominique's determination in his quest for freedom. The creation of a picaresque-like hero in Dominique is an ideological statement in that it enables Sainville's hero to be exposed to a broad range of authentic discourse at the "periphery" of the French colonial system. After all, the picaresque hero belongs by definition to the lower class, and

Dominique's wanderings permit Sainville to depict the historically complex context in which the maroon revolts took place.

In his subversion of Euro-centric discourse, Sainville not only creates a black hero, he also attacks the hypocrisy of Christianity which was used to deculturalize colonized peoples and to inculcate in them a sense of blind obedience toward the master. Sainville's Marxist ideology surfaces in his portrayal of the hypocritical missionaries who played such an important role in perpetuating the inhuman system of slavery. In *Dominique Nègre Esclave*, Christian proselytism was an instrument for creolizing slaves, and creolization was the beginning of the dehumanizing process for them. In this context, creolization involves the loss of cultural identity that occurred when blacks were obliged to adopt Western values in lieu of the ones they had brought with them from Africa. The whole enterprise of Christianization in the Caribbean was based on the argument that Africans did not have a religion and could only attain salvation by acknowledging the Christian God.

In the novel, Léontine believes what she has been taught from the Bible, and her naiveté has a strong effect on her psyche because it convinces her that she and others like her are inferior to white people. According to Christian-influenced Euro-centric discourse, blacks are descendants of Ham who was cursed by his father Noah. Dominique himself rejects this idea; he himself is an atheist. In fact, he expresses his doubts about the Christian God in no uncertain terms to Léontine:

> Ton bon Dieu, ce n'est pas le dieu des Nègres: c'est un dieu pour les békes, un bon dieu pour les maîtres. S'il existe, c'est un salaud. Mais il n'existe pas [...]. Dis-moi, ton bon Dieu, pourquoi il nous a laissés, nous les Nègres esclaves, pourquoi il nous a laissés dans le souci comme ça... (279-280)
>
> [Your God is not the god of Black people. It is a god for the békés. A god for the masters. If he exists, he is a bastard. But he does not exist... Tell me why your god left us, we the Black slaves, why he left us in such worries].

In this passage, Dominique questions the validity of what Christianity teaches because he finds it hypocritical in light of the plight of black people. Sainville demonstrates here that, unlike Léontine, Dominique has a "prise de conscience" with regard to the ideology behind the sort of Christianity that was taught to slaves. This "prise de conscience" enables him to become the symbol of the counter-discourse that Sainville wants to create around the maroon revolts.

Sainville does not ignore the fact that some Christian missionaries defended the cause of the slaves and wanted to see the system abolished. The difference between Catholics and Protestants is suggested by the fact that the Protestant missionaries seem to have been more human in their approach to the evangelization of slaves.

For example, when Dominique takes refuge in British Antigua while seeking to gain his freedom, he encounters Reverend Samuel, who champions the cause of the slaves and fights for the abolition of slavery at the risk of being persecuted by his own people (147). But the positive image of Reverend Samuel does not diminish the hypocrisy of the Christian churches which most whites attended in the belief that such institutions preserved their own supposed superiority. This phenomenon reinforced the idea of difference, and even today it continues to reinforce the Western system of values that prevent Antilleans from attaining their true freedom. Witness the reaction of the Catholic Church in Haïti to the practice of voodoo by its faithful.[5] Writing about the slave era in the Caribbean, Barbara Bush says that "the conversion and indoctrination of slaves was intimately linked with controlling slaves, for Christianity stressed submissiveness on earth in return for rewards in the hereafter" (157). Reaction to how this permeates contemporary Antillean society is projected in works such as those of Césaire. René Depestre in his work on Negritude comments about Césaire's reaction to the vestiges of colonialism, one of which is Christianity:

> Où le jeune Césaire tournait le regard il se heurtait douloureusement aux sordides valeurs de la colonisation: fausse respectabilité, christianisme d'espèce venimeuse, insolence militante des Békés, avec leur racisme arrogant et satisfait de ses bassesses. (58)

> [Wherever the young Césaire looked, he painfully stumbled against the sordid values of colonization: false respectability, a vicious type of Christianity, militant insolence of the Békés, with their arrogant racism satisfied with its vileness].

Antillean writers have generally denounced the role played by the Christian church in perpetuating slavery. Similarly, novels about pre-independence Africa have tended to adopt the same stance with regard to the Catholic church. In this context, it is relevant to recall how Pope Pius V decreed that all colonized peoples were pagans and should be submitted to slavery in order for their souls to be saved. Sainville categorically rejects this idea in *Dominique Nègre Esclave*.

The baptism imposed on slaves newly arrived from Africa played an important role in this acculturation process. As Maryse Condé has pointed out, the term "nègre bossale" referred to newly arrived slaves after they had been baptized. This usage of the term reveals how Europeans perceived blacks as naturally evil beings who needed the Christian God in order to be saved:

> Le nègre est sans contredit une espèce inférieure, mais le baptême par la force de la bonté divine le fait enfant de Dieu [...]. Le noir est naturellement enclin au mal, pourri de vices. Seule la connaissance de la parole de Dieu, la

discipline pénitentielle peuvent venir à bout de leurs détestables tendances. (Condé, 24)

[The black person is without question an inferior species, but forced baptism of the divine mercifulness makes him child of God...Black people are by nature inclined to do bad things, rotten with vices. Only the knowledge of the word of God and penitential discipline can make them change from their dreadful tendencies].

Maryse Condé's insight into the béké mentality is the same as that which underlines Sainville's portrayal of Christian missionaries in *Dominique Nègre Esclave*. Dominique and the other slaves are regarded as naturally evil and therefore in need of the Christian faith in order to save their souls from damnation. But this perception is only a pretext to protect the economic and political power base of the dominant white society.

As Maryse Condé further attests, everything, including the taste for food, was imposed on the slave by the master. He was made to live in a perpetual state of dependency—a situation which persisted after the abolition of slavery:

Les esprits des xviiè et xviiiè siècles n'envisageaint pas que le sauvage d'Afrique, transplanté aux Caraïbes, puisse produire une forme de culture originale et ne lui laissaient d'autre choix que d'oublier son moi précédant pour naître au sein du Nouveau Monde. (6)

[17th and 18th century mentalities did not envisage that the savage from Africa, resettled in the Caribbean, could produce a type of original culture and imagined that he had no other choice but that of forgetting his former being so that he could be born in the New World].

The whole thrust of Sainville's ideology in *Dominique Nègre Esclave* is to portray how these concepts were perpetuated through the treatment of slaves and how the slaves themselves reacted by creating their own counter-discourse.

Sainville's criticism of the church is clearly part of his anti-colonial discourse. If contemporary Euro-centric discourse about the people of the Antilles was profoundly influenced by the institution of slavery, Antillean writers need, he felt, to articulate an authentic cultural identity that does not deny this history but redefines it from their own point of view.

One aspect of Antillean history that Sainville touches upon in his novel is the class interest of the mulattoes. The mentality of contemporary Antillean society has been forged from centuries of antagonism between different classes—an antagonism that persisted after the abolition of slavery and the elevation of Martinique and Guadeloupe to departmental status in the French Republic. In

Dominique Nègre Esclave the class interests of the mulattoes and the white békés do not coincide, but the attitudes of the mulattoes also alienate them from the black slaves. At the same time they must defend themselves against the denigration imposed on them by the dominant discourse of the white béké. They are not accepted by the white béké class, and yet they refuse to identify with the predicament of the slaves. Many mulattoes even speak out against the abolition of slavery. As Sainville demonstrates in *Dominique Nègre Esclave*, slave society was a highly stratified society.

Although slaves, unlike mulattoes, were usually deprived of education, Dominique learns how to read and write at an early age, thereby disproving the myth that his race is inherently inferior in intellectual terms. Nevertheless, Sainville places his Negritude discourse in the mouth of a mulatto, Pamphile, who does recognize the syncretistic nature of Antillean culture. Pamphile is proud of the black heritage that originated in Haïti, the first independent black state in the modern world. According to Pamphile, whites owe their wealth to the inhuman exploitation of black slaves:

> Il ne faudrait pas oublier que leur fortune, leur position, ils ne les doivent qu'au travail des Noirs. Nos ancêtres étaient des esclaves. Ils sont morts sous le fouet. Nous ne devons rien à ces békés: C'est eux qui nous doivent tout. (219)

> [One should not forget that they owe their fortune and their position only to the work of the Blacks. Our ancestors were slaves. They died from the beatings. We owe nothing to these békés. They are the ones who owe us everything].

Sainville sees Pamphile's "prise de conscience" as a crucial factor in the liberation of black people from European bondage. Through Pamphile, he is making an ideological statement about the history of the Antilles. The wealth of the white population has, he insists, been acquired at the expense of the black slave.

In contemporary Antillean society, social class is partly determined by skin complexion. To a large extent, skin color determines one's status in Antillean society. As Frantz Fanon has convincingly demonstrated, Antilleans have grown through the centuries to hate themselves. In their attempt to make themselves acceptable to the "center," they have failed to create an authentic discourse of their own. In *Dominique Nègre Esclave* Pamphile symbolizes this predicament. The task that Sainville set for himself in his historical fiction was to rehabilitate black people and to give them back their rightful place in history. He does this by demonstrating how Pamphile, symbol of the syncretistic Antillean culture, shows pride in his origins. In this sense, he differs greatly from other mulattoes, who, in the eyes of the slaves, are part of the oppressor class.

Sainville's Marxism predisposes him to place considerable emphasis on class interests, which he regards as intimately related to race interests. He recognizes that the dominant position of Eurocentric discourse has been determined to a large extent by economic interests. As he demonstrates in the novel, slaves are conscious of the economic interest they represent for the "center", and in their struggle for freedom, they often threaten these economic interests. They do so by marooning and by descending, from time to time, on the masters' plantations, which they often destroy.

Through the exercise of power, Europeans created a world in which their discourse was perceived as universal. By correcting the inaccuracies of European accounts of Antillean history and by revalorizing the image of the maroon, Sainville subverts the discourse of the center and challenges the view of human nature by means of which it justifies itself. Because Dominique's adventures imply a three-hundred-year "chosification" of black slaves during a time when a Euro-centric discourse was evolving to justify European exploitation of the Other, Sainville's narrative tends to follow a traditional chronological pattern that exposes readers to the reality of historical evolution in the Caribbean. A major innovation in Sainville's novel is his depiction of the way in which people living on the periphery systematically undermined the dominant discourse. Using a single omniscient narrator throughout *Dominique Nègre Esclave*, Sainville tells about historical events that took place in the 18th and 19th centuries. He even specifically dates certain parts of his narrative, thereby clearly locating the whole narrative in a concrete historical period. For example, he refers to the slave revolt of St. Pierre in 1831 (76), and the last chapter of the novel is titled "1848"—a significant date for the French Caribbean because it was the year slavery was abolished in the Antilles. Significantly too, the "story" ends at a point when the slaves revolt and Dominique runs away to join the others in freedom. The use of specific and verifiable dates in historical fiction is significant because it helps create a sense of verisimilitude. Within this context, his revolt against the dehumanizing situation of the slave and his action at the end of the novel served to rehabilitate the image of the maroon and to place it within a "real" historical context.

Dominique Nègre Esclave opens with a chapter about the "quatre-piquets"—a brutal practice intended to condition slaves into docilely accepting the image of them created by the slave masters—and it closes with a chapter about the emancipation of the slaves in 1848. This structure clearly reinforces Sainville's ideological message. The conclusion of the novel is a "happy ending" that contrasts with the tragic opening of the novel, for it suggests that the slaves earned their own freedom, as Dominique himself did when he escaped from prison to join the other revolted slaves:

> Il [Dominique] la [l'émeute] suivit partout. Avec elle, il remonte vers les Mornes du Prêcheur. Avec elle, il revint le soir dans la ville. Les révoltés l'avaient débarrassé des durs anneaux de fer. Le soir, il donna l'assaut à la maison où complotait la contre-révolution. Il suivit l'incendie, il parcourut les rues où régnait la terreur. Libre, farouche il applaudit la révolution victorieuse et la liberté proclamée. (295)
>
> [He (Dominique) followed it (the uprising) everywhere. He followed it up the Mornes du Prêcheur. He followed it back to the town in the evening. The revolted slaves had freed him from the hard iron rings. In the evening, he attacked the house where the counter-revolution was breeding. He followed the fire, he ran through the streets where terror reigned. Free, fierce, he applauded the victorious revolution and the proclaimed freedom].

This dramatic ending suggests an optimistic perception of cultural "métissage" in the Antilles—a society in which the historical legacy of maroons needs to be recognized. Significantly, it is Dominique's fellow former slaves who release him from the shackles that still bound his hands when he escaped from prison. Dominique has acquired an almost supernatural power to defy the béké and to walk into freedom with the other former slaves. The closing of the novel is therefore an ideological statement which suggests that Dominique and the maroons in general succeeded in creating a concrete counter-discourse to the discourse of the white béké.

All the novels discussed in this study were inspired by historical events. It is of course a truism to contend that history is characteristic of the "historical novel," but as Paul Veynes has argued, historical fiction articulates the specificity of historical events and makes them intelligible on a human level. Sainville accomplished this goal by creating fiction around the maroon revolts in the nineteenth century.

Like Hazoumé and Boni, he too was inspired by true historical events, and like them, he refers to historical facts in the novel. As he himself explains:

> Si le personnage central est une fiction, il n'en est pas moins représentatif d'une condition, et sa psychologie que je me suis efforcé de rendre authentique n'est que le reflet de celle de l'homme noir antillais en lutte contre le régime qui l'opprimait, il y a un siècle, et comme elle m'est apparue à travers les textes. (11)
>
> [If the main character is fictional, it does not make him less representative of a condition, and his psychology which I tried to make authentic is only the reflection of that of the black Antillean man fighting against the regime which oppressed him a century ago and as it appeared to me through the texts].

Although Dominique and the other characters in the novel are partially fictional, they symbolize the reality of Antillean history—a reality that can be verified in actual historical documents. Dominique's experiences were inspired by three centuries of slavery in the Antilles, and the fictional portrayal of them marries fact and fiction to create an authentic discourse of the Antillean people.

Dominique is the main character in the novel. However, the particular historical incident that Sainville cites in his preface as the inspiration for his fictional creation does not involve Dominique, but rather the trial of Azaïs and the other maroons, of whom Dominique was one. Toumson has acknowleged that by the time Sainville wrote this novel, Azaïs had become a legendary hero in Antillean writing. He was involved in the slave uprising around 1657 in which the slaves slaughtered their white masters (Toumson 340).[6] But, although Azaïs is an important character in the novel, most of the action revolves around Dominique. Thus, in his fictional version, Sainville shifts the reader's attention to a character who is not the real hero in the particular historical incident that inspired his fictional creation in the first place.

Azaïs, Hibo, Moko, and Anne are actual historical characters, but Hippolyte (the maroon to whom Azaïs wants to give his sister forcibly against her will) is actually Dongar according to actual historical documents. Maintaining the original names of historical characters does influence the reading of historical novels like *Dominique Nègre Esclave* because it forces the reader to reflect upon the way in which fiction can draw attention to historical meanings that might otherwise be overlooked or misunderstood.

Like Hazoumé and Boni, Sainville uses footnotes to explain words and terms that are likely to be unfamiliar to the non-Antillean reader. These footnotes heighten the impression of verisimilitude because they locate the narrative events within the specific geography and history of the Antilles. By explaining the referents in the novel, Sainville creates "l'effet du réel" [the impression of reality]. His footnotes explain social factors that enable readers to understand contemporary Antillean perceptions of life. For example, in one footnote, he explains that the game called "calibandjo" is a "jeu pratiqué par les enfants antillais, et qui consiste à se lancer du haut d'une colline herbeuse en se tenant en équilibre sur la partie ligneuse d'une feuille de cocotier" (21). [Game played by Antillean children involving throwing oneself from the top of a grassy hill while holding oneself in balance on the line part of a coconut leaf]. "Mulâtres," he explains on another occasion, are "hommes de couleur ayant un épiderme se rapprochant plus de celui des Blancs que de celui des Noirs" (20). [Men of color who have a skin color closer to that of whites than to that of blacks]. A "bel-air" is an "espèce de quadrille costumé dansé au rythme d'un chant satirique" (80). [A kind of danse performed in costume in a square done to the rhythm of a satirical song]. Such distinctions and socio-historical factors enable the reader to enter into the world of the Antillean people and their discourse.

Not only does Sainville cite true historical dates and places, he also authenticates the historical incidents he incorporates into his fiction through the footnotes. In one footnote, for example, the plight of Azaïs and his "accomplices" is authenticated by referring to specific legal documents:

> En réalité, seul figure dans les annales judiciaires de 1837, transcrit dans la correspondance générale de la même année, le procès d'Azaïs et d'Hibo (Cour d'Assises de Pointe-à-Pitre, 1re session). (108)

> [Actually, we can find in the judicial records of 1837 only written in the general correspondence of the same year, the trial of Azaïs and Hibo (Court of Assizes of Pointe-à-Pitre, first session)].

By citing such historical happenings, Sainville is bringing history to bear upon the present predicament of the Antillean. The trial of Azaïs and Hibo is significant in Sainville's revalorization of the maroon because they represent a rejection of the image of the "other"—an image that had been imposed on the slave and continues to be imposed on his descendants.

In another footnote, Sainville heightens the sense of historical authenticity by assuring his readers that Antigua actually did serve as a refuge for slaves seeking to free themselves from bondage on the French islands:

> C'est le régime de contrainte et de surveillance auquel furent soumis les Noirs des Antilles britanniques entre la proclamation de l'abolition de l'esclavage et sa suppression définitive (1er août 1834-1er août 1838). (127)

> [It is the regime of constraint and supervision to which Blacks of the British Antilles were subjected between the proclamation of the abolition of slavery and its final elimination (1st August 1834 to 1st August 1838)].

There is a fundamental difference between a work of art and a historical document. As Sainville's novel demonstrates, historical fiction transcends the boundary between reality and the imagination. But even though a work of art is not the simple mirroring of a given situation or the faithful transposition of the world, it can lead to the real. History gives a meaning to anti-colonial discourse in Africa and the Caribbean. It also gives meaning to the writer's creation of a new discourse. Thus, history authenticates the writer's discourse, subverts the dominant Euro-centric discourse, and creates an authentic discourse in which Africans and Antilleans are no longer merely objects but rather the core of their own discourse. With this new sense of history, writers of historical novels also succeed in subverting the very notion of center and periphery.

The "effet du réel" creates a sense of verisimilitude in *Dominique Nègre Esclave*. This sense of verisimilitude has an ideological function because it underscores the anti-colonial thrust of Sainville's discourse. In effect, it prompts readers to learn more about the historical events that inspired the fictional variations on history in the first place. Sainville's choice of specific historical events was motivated by a sense of pride in his people and in his culture. He desired to re-write that part of Antillean history which has always been distorted in Eurocentric discourse. Yet the success of the novel as an ideological statement does not disguise his neglect of artistic quality. In fact, Toumson, among other critics, has criticized Sainville for this, asserting that, "attachante [*Dominique Nègre Esclave*] est entachée d'imperfections formelles qui peuvent surprendre chez un connaisseur aussi averti de l'art" (340-341). [Captivating as it is (*Dominique Nègre Esclave*) is marred by imperfections in form which can be surprising coming from such a well-informed expert in art]. René Menil has also criticized Sainville for not paying much attention to art itself in his fiction:

> L'erreur du romancier c'est, faisant un roman, de laisser le roman s'échapper du genre romanesque (qui a ses lois et ses exigences) sous prétexte d'obéir aux impératifs de la politique, sous prétexte de courir au plus pressé. (187)

> [The mistake of the novelist is that in writing a novel, he creates a novel (which has its rules and particularities) outside the novelistic genre under the pretext of following the dictates of political demands, under the pretext of meeting the most urgent need].

Clearly, Sainville's novel is not the sort of artistic creation we find in other Antillean historical novels such as those of Glissant.

The focus in this chapter has been on the importance of the subversive discourse of the revolted maroons. For Sainville, the image of the maroon represented a rejection of the false image that had been imposed on black Antilleans as a consequence of slavery. The subhuman state in which the slave was maintained to protect the interests of the "center" made the confrontation of discourses inevitable. In his historical fiction, Sainville demonstrates that there was not just the dominant discourse of the slave master. There was also the counter-discourse among slaves themselves. Euro-centric discourse tried to deny the existence of this counter-discourse, but Sainville employed his historical novel of marooning to reaffirm its existence and to show how it functioned.

6

Edouard Glissant: *Le Quatrième Siècle*

Like Sainville, Glissant revalorized the image of the maroon when he developed his own discourse of Antilleanity in his historical novel, *Le Quatrième Siècle*. It too reflects the author's quest for a viable cultural identity through historical fiction. The novel is about slave revolts and about the importance of the maroon to any authentic Antillean discourse. To repossess the past, to understand it, Antilleans need, Glissant asserts, to understand their history; they need to re-write their own history against the backdrop of Euro-centric hegemonic discourse.

Some critics have tried to undermine the importance of the "black element" in Glissant's discourse because, according to them, Glisssant's position on Negritude shows that he believes in a "métisssage culturel" that does not lend more importance to any single element of Antillean culture. However, this argument undermines the minority discourse in Antillean culture because it seeks to justify the dominance of Euro-centric discourse on the grounds that Glissant does not really believe in the search for a genuine black identity.

Historical factors have made the search for an authentic cultural identity quintessential for the Caribbean writer, and like Sainville, Glissant places primary emphasis on the revalorization of the image of the maroon. As he explains in *Le Discours Antillais*:

> [...] le Nègre Marron est le seul vrai héros populaire des Antilles, dont les effroyables supplices qui marquaient sa capture donnent la mesure du courage et de la détermination. Il y a là un exemple incontestable d'opposition systématique, de refus total. (104)

> [...The maroon is the only real popular hero of the Antilles of whom the horrifying punishments which marked his capture show the degree of courage and determination he had. There is in it an unquestionable example of systematic opposition, of total insubordination].

Like Sainville, Glissant emphasizes the maroon's capacity to survive inhuman conditions and his ability to create a counter-discourse to the image imposed on him through slavery. In this way, he too is proposing a counter-discourse to demystify the Euro-centric discourse of the Other.

In the novel, Papa Longoué's family lineage symbolizes the maroons who refused to accept docilely their condition as slaves. The Beluse are a rival family whose members live on the plantations. They represent the docile slaves who had nothing of which they could be proud at the moment of emancipation. Papa Longoué and the Beluse therefore represent diametrically opposed world views that emerged during the history of slavery in the Antilles. The dichotomy between the maroons and the slaves of the plantation is not itself the major point. The real difference between the two families is the element of rejection in the maroon's revolt. For Glissant, the maroon represents a concrete formulation of the black person's rejection of the discourse of the "Other." He argues that the role of the maroon in Antillean history must be emphasized because it has persistently been misinterpreted in Euro-centric history.

Papa Longoué represents a spiritual link with the ancestors and with the Africa from which they first came. Moreover, his African spiritual powers enable him to maroon soon after he arrives on the islands. Thanks to the barrel which gives him supernatural powers, he escapes without being pursued by the slave masters and their dogs. Moreover, he is able to cover his own traces in a mysterious way of which he alone knows the secret. Later, he invokes the power of the ancestors to liberate himself from the white béké. Glissant is particularly interested in the powers that link Papa Longoué with Africa, because they represent the basis for the articulation of a viable identity that is not dependent on Euro-centric discourse and its stereotyping of Antilleans.

Subsequently, we learn how Papa Longoué kidnaps Louise, who becomes his wife:

> Il avait marqué des signes connus de lui seul sur des sentiers par où on pourrait le poursuivre: des branchages croisés pour égarer celui qui s'engagerait dans un autre; et à un troisième croisement le nœud invisible qui attire le danger. (86-87)
>
> [On the paths where he could be pursued, he had made some signs only he understood; crossed branches to make the person who took the other one lose his way; and at a third crossing the invisible nut which attracts danger].

By employing the knowledge he had acquired before he left Africa, Papa Longoué manifests an ability that later saves him from the domination of the white béké. This ability is symbolically linked with the power of the ancestors; similarly, Glissant believes the source of Antilleans' spiritual well-being lies in an understanding of their past.

In his eyes, Papa Longoué demonstrates how Antilleans need to maintain the link with the ancestors because it is their identity. This link to the past is through a belief system entrenched in the history of the maroons. In *Le Quatrième Siècle*, even ten years after the marooning of Papa Longoué, the barrel's power has such an effect on the white béké La Roche that he himself returns it. He believes so strongly in its power that he even refuses to chase Melchior Longoué for fear that he himself will be humiliated. André Ntonfo observes that

Glissant's image of Longoué is not that of a defensive individual who is preoccupied with preserving his freedom. He points out that Longoué and the other maroons are dynamic characters whose marooning is a positive action undertaken on their own initiative. Contrary to the stereotyped images of Euro-centric discourse, the maroon as portrayed by Glissant is not a sub-human animal who is constantly being pursued by a slave master and his dogs; in reality he is a human being who attacks, who harasses his pursuers, who sacrifices his own private interests to overthrow the established order that oppresses him and others like him (Ntonfo 199). In this way, Glissant creates a counter-discourse that goes beyond a simple description of the dehumanization imposed on slaves by the white béké.

Longoué's eventual victory over the slave master is presaged the day he arrives in the new land:

> Il n'avait pas offert au commandant Duchêne le spectacle de la bête affolée qui regarde et se débat devant l'entrée de l'enclos préparé pour elle. (55)

> [He had not given to Commandant Duchêne the spectacle of the terrified animal which looks and wonders within itself in front of the enclosure prepared for it].

By his demeanor, Longoué defies the myth of the "bon sauvage," and later he proves to be a brave fighter, disproving the myth of the slave master's superior power and his supposed invulnerability vis-à-vis the slave. The slave masters' belief in Longoué's spiritual powers suggests that their own discourse is hardly impervious when challenged by the "Other," whom they regard as inferior. Significantly, La Roche dies on the last boat that smuggles slaves into the islands against the laws of the republic. The slave ship "Rose Marie" was a symbol of white dominance over the slaves, and La Roche's death on it symbolizes the victory of the revolted slaves over the institutional structure by means of which the slave masters had sought to exercise power over them. In fact, it was on these slave ships that the rape of the female slave was institutionalized: to be perpetuated after the slaves were brought "safely" to the islands. Bernadette Cailler (1988) and Cilas Kemedjio (1994) have commented on the widespread practice of rape on female slaves throughout the era of slavery. Kemedjio has called it the "rape and reproduction of slave bodies" (59). The death of La Roche, a slave master, on a slave ship therefore becomes a symbolic subversion of the institution that he represented.

In *Le Quatrième Siècle*, the young Mathieu is the symbol of a characteristically Antillean yearning. He wants to understand himself, and this desire can only be satisfied by delving deeply into the history of his people. The product of hegemonic colonial encounters in the Antilles, Mathieu not only seeks to shed the identity that has been imposed on him, but to create an authentic discourse based on the actual experiences of the people. He needs to go through a metamorphosis in order to comprehend the nature of the Euro-centric discourse that imprisons him in its false myths and stereotypes. Papa Longoué is the custodian of oral tradition, he imparts knowledge to the young Mathieu and allows him to fill the gaps in the Euro-centric history he has learned at school. Webb has pertinently remarked that "Glissant contrasts the quimboiseur's intuitive vision with Mathieu's penchant for documents and chronologies" (48). The interaction of two generations through the two characters reveals the problems of history and identity for Caribbean people.

Through the diegetic narrator Papa Longoué, readers discover the unfolding of the history that has fashioned contemporary Antillean life. He recounts the history of slavery as it had been handed down to him orally by his forefathers. What Mathieu learns from Papa Longoué's account of the slave era is that maroons were heroes. This image of them thus offers an alternative to the French perception of the slave and provides the basis for articulating a counter-discourse to the dominant one that Mathieu had assimilated at school.

The importance of Mathieu's "dialogue" with the "anciens" (represented by Papa Longoué) is that he discovers the truth about colonial encounters in the Antilles. This truth is that colonialism and slavery were not in any way justifiable and that the colonialists perpetuated a false image of the colonized in an attempt to maintain the status quo.

In the dehumanizing process, the slave was transformed into an economic object. In *Le Quatrième Siècle*, however, Glissant refutes the validity of this reductive image by creating the same sort of anti-colonial discourse that Sainville had deployed in his novel. Papa Longoué revolts and maroons as soon as he debarks from the ship which brought him from Africa. Glissant's point is that the discourse of the slave master was not the only discourse in Antillean history; there was also, as he shows, the counter-discourse of the slave, the dominated.

Because the vestiges of the slave era persist in the minds of contemporary Antilleans, Glissant insists that they must undergo a process of re-awakening. Daniel Guérin says:

> Ici [...] nous nous trouvons en présence d'un des nombreux reliquats du passé esclavagiste. Parce qu'aux siècles précédents le maître blanc a dû dévaloriser idéologiquement l'épiderme de l'esclave pour justifier son asservissement, le blanc d'aujourd'hui, aux Antilles, ne se contente pas d'exploiter économiquement l'ouvrier de couleur, il continue à lui manifester, sous les formes les plus diverses, sa prétendue supériorité raciale. (79)

Edouard Glissant: *Le Quatrième Siècle*

[Here we are confronted with one of the many vestiges of the slave era of the past. Because in the previous centuries the white master had to devalorize ideologically the skin of the slave to justify his subservience, the white person of today, in the Antilles, is not just happy to economically exploit the worker of color, he continues to show him, in the most diverse ways, his claimed racial superiority].

The Antillean of today needs a "prise de conscience" to deal with the unjustified superiority complex that the white society has developed through the centuries. In *Le Quatrième Siècle*, Mathieu represents this self-awareness—the self-awareness that the young Antillean needs in order to reject the demeaning image that has been imposed on him by the French educational system. By bearing testimony to this history, Papa Longoué is accepting the shameful past that Aimé Césaire in his famous poem *Cahier d'un retour au pays natal* exhorted Antilleans to take pride in asserting, for as Césaire pointed out, their assertion of pride in this past is a first step in the revolutionary project of rejecting the Euro-centric perception of themselves. As suggested in the chapter on Sainville, this assertion of pride is necessary because enlightened Antilleans know that various methods have been used throughout the centuries to maintain the slave in a sub-human state. They also know that they must challenge the assumptions behind such practices if they ever hope to liberate themselves.

For the slave master, maintaining an inferiority complex among the black slaves was one way of preserving the European's perception of himself and of projecting it onto the world. In other words, Europeans viewed themselves as being at the center of the world, and they assumed that their own values were universally valid. This assumption emerges clearly in Glissant's depiction of the slave master, for to exist according to the image he has forged of himself, the slave master needs to posit the existence of an inferior "Other." This inferior Other is the slave with his supposedly primitive or barbaric origins.

This sort of Euro-centric discourse is articulated mainly by the white békés Senglis and La Roche. The latter handles the slaves when they are unloaded from the slave ships and sold like animals in the market. In Antillean society today the white béké still seeks to maintain his position at the center of the universe by denying the validity of any discourse other than his own. By revalorizing the image of the maroon, Glissant reinforces the counter-discourse that calls into question the Euro-centric discourse that reduced black Antilleans to a less-than-human status.

Obviously, neither the slave master nor the race (or class) he represents has any interest in acknowledging the maroon's revolt as a rejection of the false image that had been imposed on him by his European masters. In their eyes, the slave was a bandit with a taste for "savage" things, and they extended the assumptions behind this image to their depictions of maroon revolts.

In order to justify the sado-masochist system of slavery, Europeans sought to inculcate in the black Antillean a sense of hatred for his own color, his own origins, which, in the minds of the whites, made him an inferior human being. The negative image of maroons was maintained by inculcating in children the idea that they were the incarnation of the devil:

> C'était la coutume de menacer les enfants de les faire enlever par un marron. Car le marron était pour les populations la personnification du diable: celui qui refuse. (129)

> [It was customary to threaten children that they would be taken away by maroons. For the maroon was for the people, the personification of the devil: the one who refuses].

Glissant alludes to this situation in his novel because he thinks Antilleans need to understand how contemporary society is still being controlled by false perceptions of the historical phenomenon of slavery.

The impression one gets from the above passage is that, in European discourse, the maroon is a "diable" because he refuses the image that has been forged for him from the moment he is captured in his ancestral African homeland. But the phrase "celui qui refuse" suggests that, for Glissant, the maroon was a hero precisely because he had been painted as a devil—that is, because he demonstrated the ability to subvert the image of the society which had reduced him to a sub-human state. He is a "personnification du diable" [personification of the devil] because he subverts the image of himself as the member of a subject race. However, in the eyes of Antillean writers such as Sainville and Glissant, he becomes a hero for this very reason. Thus, Glissant's discourse is built on a challenge to the Eurocentric discourse in which he, as the descendant of slaves, has been stripped of his human dignity, deprived of his rightful place in the human race.

Mathieu is the symbolic link between the younger generation and the past, which is represented by Papa Longoué. From the perspective of oral tradition, Mathieu's knowledge is inadequate. The books in the school library cannot supply the information Mathieu needs in order to forge a meaningful link between the past and the present. Yet for Glissant, it is not merely a matter of comprehending the past. According to him, Mathieu needs to build the future as well. He is like a child going through an initiation that will enable him to be admitted into adulthood. Mathieu had been seeking to understand how his ancestors came to be a subject race, and Papa Longoué provides him with an account of the history that he needs to know if he hopes to establish a meaningful link with the past.

Mathieu is in some ways like Glissant or the Antillean writer in general. Glissant himself acknowledged that he, like Mathieu, had been inspired by a "quimboiseur." Mathieu too experiences a re-awakening as he listens to Papa Longoué narrate the story of his ancestors. He too fills in the gaps left by the Euro-centric history he had learned at school. Before he can reject the false image that has been imposed on him by Europeans, Mathieu needs to understand his own predicament. Papa Longoué enables him to learn about the history of his people from the vantage point of an insider. In a sense, Mathieu plays the role of audience, of reader. His reaction to Longoué's narrative typifies the way in which many Antilleans found their history difficult to comprehend. The knowledge they had acquired in French schools was inadequate because it contained their own history only as it was perceived from a European point of view.

At one point in the novel, the young Anne plays the role of the French while the young Liberté plays the role of the English. Their children's game becomes a symbolic role-playing scene that recalls the antagonisms between the colonial powers in the Caribbean. More significantly, it recalls how the slave was the ultimate victim in these conflicts. According to the dominant image, he was only an insignificant Other—an economic object—whose destiny was shaped by those who had the monopoly of discourse. Glissant underscores the misery of the slaves, describing how children start working in the sugar plantations as early as four years of age:

> Leur bande de fantômes hagards de faim, blêmes sous la peau noire d'avoir mangé la terre, les fruits verts ou pourris, tous les débris de l'existence animale et végétale, enfants-vieillards, qui savaient déjà qu'ils leur faudrait se soumettre au double pouvoir, l'un officiel et l'autre obscur, qui les maintiendrait toute leur vie sous le joug. (70)
>
> [Their group of phantoms distraught with hunger, deathly pale under the black color from eating the earth, green or rotten fruits, all the debris of animals and vegetables, old-looking children, who already knew that they would have to submit themselves to the two power system, one official and the other hidden, which would keep them all their life under the yoke].

Like Sainville, Glissant graphically paints the sub-human state to which the slave was reduced. By starving the slaves, the white béké hoped to impose his power more effectively upon them. But Glissant, like Sainville, suggests that the slave was a hero who survived such inhuman conditions. By persistently revolting and marooning at the risk of losing a leg or a hand, or of being flogged to death, they showed how wrong the myth of the dependent slave actually was.

The dehumanizing process started the moment that slaves were captured in Africa. During the long journey across the Atlantic, however, they already began to revolt against this process. In *Le Quatrième Siècle*, Papa Longoué describes a typical scene on a slave ship:

> Mais tout avait été laissé sous la pluie: les fouets à plombs, les lanières roidies, la potence aux pendus (en vérité plus impressionnante qu'un gros mât), et le bâton crochu qu'on enfonçait dans la gorge de ceux qui tentaient d'avaler leur langue, et le grand baquet d'eau de mer où les marins plongeaient la tête quand ils remontaient suffoqués des profondeurs de la cale, et le fer à rougir, fourchette implacable pour ceux qui refusaient le pain moisi ou les biscuits arrosés de saumure, et le filet par lequel on descendait les esclaves, chaque mois, dans le grand bain de la mer: filet pour les protéger des requins ou de la tentation de mourir. (21)

> [But all had been left in the rain: the lead whips, the tightened lashes, the gallows for hanging (in reality more impressive than a big pole), and the claw-like stick which they stuck in the throat of the ones who tried to swallow their tongue, and the big tub of sea water where the sailors stuck the head when they came back up suffocated by the depths of the holds, and the red-hot iron, an implacable fork for those who refused the mouldied bread or the biscuits spread with brine, and the net that was used to lower the slaves, every month, into the big bath of the sea; a net to protect them from the sharks or the attempt to die].

What emerges clearly in this passage is the dehumanization of the slaves. Glissant demonstrates how they were perceived as economic objects. If the slave traders wanted to protect the slaves from being eaten by sharks, they were merely protecting their economic interest. Committing suicide by refusing to eat or by swallowing one's tongue was a form of revolt against "chosification." In fact, the slaves' revolt was not a passive one; on the contrary, it was the concrete articulation of a discourse to counter the Euro-centric discourse of the Other. It was articulated under the most inhuman conditions and often by individuals who had been members of royal families in their African homelands. Antilleans can be proud of this revolutionary impulse in their own past. In fact, Glissant implies that they must become proud of it if they ever hope to recognize the truth about their own situation.

René Depestre has argued that the Antillean writer is faced with the problem of decolonization, of breaking with the obsessive conflicts inherited from the slavery era. According to him, the Antillean writer's quest for identity must confront the ambiguous situation of the "subject" Other in European discourse. The capitalist West, says Depestre, did everything possible to assure that the subjugated labor force lost not only its freedom but also the collective memory and the imagination that might have allowed them to pass the truth and experiences of their social and cultural vitality from one generation to the next (98). Glissant's novel is a testimony to Depestre's assertion, for it is his attempt to reconcile the Antillean present with this past.

As André Ntonfo observes, Glissant's narrative also underscores the slave master's persistent ridicule of the slave. Even on the day of emancipation, when officials call out the names of the slaves, they consciously undermine everything that might give relevance to emancipation as they seek to preserve everything associated with the world of the béké. For example, even the names of the slaves Zéphir, Alizé, Sapin, Maisance, Capotte are treated with contempt and the ceremony itself is calculated to demean the newly emancipated former slaves:

> Famille Tousseul, un, répétait le second commis. Il tendait le certificat d'existence, sinon d'identité. (176)
>
> Tousseul family, one, the second clerk repeated. He gave out the certificate of existence if not of identity].

In this scene, the slave master and the officials still determine the discourse, for they still hold the power. They are the ones who give an identity to the former slaves. The connotation of the word "give" is that the slaves themselves did not win a new identity for themselves, and of course this impression is precisely the one that the Europeans desire to perpetuate. The idea that the new identity of the former slaves should be authenticated by the ones from whom they have just won their freedom is ironic.

In describing the predicament of the ancestors, Glissant employs a liberating language, a language that is not static but dynamic. In fact, he sees hope for a better future in their proud acceptance of their "certificat d'existence." This pride in the role the maroons played in their own emancipation is a counter-discourse to that of Europeans who themselves claim credit for having abolished slavery. According to Glissant, the pride exhibited by the maroons at the time of emancipation provides the basis for a rewriting of Euro-centric histories of slavery.

During the emancipation ceremony, the evocation of the Longoué family name has a revealing impact on the census officials.[1] The Longoués clearly represent a challenge to the status quo because they symbolize the maroon's rejection of the identity that had been imposed on all black slaves:

> Ils [les commis] furent vite au bout de leur science. Ce fut à ce moment-là qu'ils entendaient une voix qui les fit sursauter disant: Famille Longoué. Ils se redressèrent vivement—Comment, comment, glapit le premier

commis?—Famille Longoué, dit Melchior. Un homme Melchior Longoué; un garçon; Apostrophe Longoué; une fille: Liberté Longoué; une femme: Adémie Longoué. (177-178)

[They (the clerks) quickly finished their job. It was then they heard a voice, which made them startle, which said: "Longoué family." They sat up brusquely. "How, how"? the first clerk yelped. "Longoué family," Melchior said. "One man Melchior Longoué, a boy Apostrophe Longoué, a girl Liberté Longoué, a woman Adémie Longoué."]

Like the first Longoué who marooned soon after debarking from the ship that had brought him and other slaves from Africa, the Longoué family continues to challenge the dominant discourse of the white béké. The present generation of Longoués represents, in a sense, the collective memory of Antilleans. For Glissant, the discourse embodied in the attitudes of the Longoué family lives on. It has survived centuries of persistent European attempts to create an imaginary otherness in all black people.

The Euro-centric discourse that justified the practice of slavery deprived transported Africans of a knowledge of their past, their history, their legends, and their systems of belief. By rehabilitating this past, Antillean writers such as Glissant destroyed the myth of the subject Other and became the voice of collective memory for the descendants of slaves who had sought to re-assert their concepts of selfhood in the contemporary world.

To destroy the myths created around the Antillean "being" and to assert the Antillean's right to control the discourse about his own identity, Glissant places considerable emphasis on oral tradition, particularly in terms of its relation to the role played by Papa Longoué. This emphasis reflects Glissant's rejection of Euro-centric discourse and his definition of an authentically Antillean discourse with which to replace it.

As Peter Hulme suggests, the basic motivation behind colonial discourse was the need to produce something for Europe, to articulate procedures, modes of analysis, kinds of writing, and clusters of imagery that reinforced the European view of the Other (56). There is no reason why the biased written accounts of history by slave owners should be more reliable than the oral history handed down by the slaves themselves, and Glissant's portrayal of Papa Longoué obliges readers to recognize the validity of this observation.

Because oral tradition is an important part of Antillean history, the fusion of it with literate European traditions in the writing of authors such as Sainville and Glissant has helped to produce an authentic Antillean discourse. For Glissant, Antillean history would not be complete without an acknowledgment of the essential role played by the "quimboiseur" in recapturing the unrecorded elements of

Antillean History. As Papa Longoué says to Mathieu: "Tu ne peux pas, je te dis, tu ne peux rien si tu ne remontes pas la source". [You cannot, I tell you, you cannot do anything if you do not go back to the source]. Mathieu cannot comprehend the complexity of the history of his people without going back to the roots. The first Longoué symbolizes the past which Mathieu needs in order to come to terms with his own quest for a viable identity.

Establishing the link between oral and written literature, Glissant explains in *Le Discours Antillais* that the contemporary Antillean text can be situated between the spoken and the written as well as at the confluence of several languages, of which creole is one (265). According to him, the synthesis of these various elements requires the creation of new genres in conjunction with the reconsideration of ethical and political principles. The attempt to create these new genres produced the complexity of his own writing.

Frederic Case reproaches Glissant for having written fiction in a language that is impenetrable to the "uninitiated" reader. According to him, the intricate structure and verbal complexity of *Le Quatrième Siècle* obscure the novel's message (Case 1985). How can the writer's ideology be effectively communicated, he asks, if the text is so difficult to comprehend? How "good" a novel is *Le Quatrième Siècle* if it can only be understood by a small elite class of readers? The answers to such questions are not simple, but one needs first to recognize that Glissant's use of symbolism reflects Antillean reality. The complexity of this reality is parodied in Glissant's employment of symbols drawn from Guadeloupean and Martiniquan landscapes. For example, the discourse of the revolted maroon—his rejection of the image imposed on him by the slave master—is reflected in his ability to survive the harsh life he is obliged to live in the mountains. His willingness to accept such conditions is a concrete demonstration of how much freedom means to him.

As opposed to the slaves of the plantations, the maroons took the initiative to free themselves. For this reason, the maroons in *Le Quatrième Siècle* descend from the mountains at the moment of emancipation with a certain amount of pride. Unlike the plantation slaves, who are still known by the names given them by the masters, the maroons have given themselves their own names:

> Les anciens esclaves des Plantations étaient là, y compris les femmes. Mais aussi, majestueux dans leurs haillons, traînant comme une parure de dignité leur boue et leur dénuement, et les seuls d'ailleurs à être armés de coutelas, les marrons [...]. Leur particularité (en plus du coutelas) était qu'une fois arrivés près de la table, ils annonçaient d'eux-mêmes leur nom et celui de leurs proches, au contraire de la masse qui eût été généralement bien en peine de proclamer des noms ou d'exciper d'une vie familiale. (176-177)

[The former slaves of the plantations were there, including their wives. But also, majestic in their tattered clothes, dragging like a costume of dignity their mud and their destitution, and moreover the only ones to be armed with cutlasses, the maroons... What was particular about them (apart from the cutlass) was that once they got near the table, they announced their names and that of the ones near them, unlike the masses who would generally have found it difficult to proclaim their names or to plead a family life].

As we see in this passage, the cutlass of the maroons becomes a symbol of their freedom from oppression. Ironically, it is also one of the tools with which the slaves worked on the plantations and a symbol of oppression in the sense that it was the instrument used by the slave masters to mutilate the bodies of re-captured maroons. When brandished by the maroons, however, the cutlass was clearly a symbol of the quest for freedom. Apart from the guns that they sometimes captured from their former masters, the maroons fought with cutlasses when they raided the plantations or defended themselves against surprise attacks organized by the plantation owners. Their cutlasses also helped them to survive in the jungles of the mountains. Thus, the instrument that symbolizes oppression for the slave comes to symbolize freedom for the maroon.

The cutlass also symbolizes their hope to repossess the land, and possessing the land signifies the assumption of control over their own destiny. As slaves, they had been deprived of their human dignity, their identity, but just as the maroons had asserted their control over the mountains in their perpetual quest for freedom, their descendants need to repossess the lands they had worked for the benefit of the white béké if freedom from slavery is to be meaningful to them. This aspect of Antillean discourse had generally been ignored or distorted by Euro-centric historians, and Glissant's emphasis on it serves to correct their biased accounts of the past.

In addition to the mountains and the cutlass, the rivers and the sea perform a symbolic function in *Le Quatrième Siècle*. Because the rivers were sometimes used by the slaves to escape, they, like the mountains, symbolize freedom and the slave's yearning to affirm his own authentic identity. Glissant's *La Lézarde* was published before *Le Quatrième Siècle*, and the central metaphor in it is the river which lends its name to the title of the novel. This river symbolizes the source to which Antilleans must return, according to Glissant, if they ever hope to achieve a viable sense of identity. In *Le Quatrième Siècle*, the rivers are part of the landscape the Antillean is striving to repossess and, together with the sea, they remind the Antillean of the place from which the ancestors came.

The sea can be a positive image for Glissant because it suggests the origins of present-day black Antilleans whose ancestors came across the sea from their motherland in Africa. The sea reminds them of who they are and where they came from. At the same time, the sea is a negative symbol in the sense that their ancestors were driven across it and precipitated into slavery. It reminds them that their ancestors arrived on the islands not as free people but as slaves who had been deprived of their human dignity and identity.

The wind has positive and negative connotations for them, for the wind helped the slave ships sail to the West Indies with their captives from Africa and often annihilated them in unpredictable storms. But the wind also symbolizes the freedom that the slaves achieved in 1848. In *Le Quatrième Siècle*, the wind is associated with Mathieu's hope for the future of his people. It suggests the changes that Mathieu sees blowing through the land, and it brings him the knowledge he acquires from Papa Longoué. During Mathieu's meetings with Papa Longoué, he repeatedly tries to control the rate at which Papa Longoué recounts his story, as if he wants to control the wind that is blowing.

Symbolically, this wind is a wind of hope that will help him create his own authentic discourse—a discourse that rejects the Euro-centric myths and prejudices that had been perpetuated by the inhuman system of slavery. As Wilbert Roget argues, Glissant's discourse is a calling into question of the stereotyped identity concepts of Euro-centric discourse (1989). For Glissant, the present generation of Antilleans must undergo a transformation in order to break away from the complacency that has all too often characterized their society. In this sense Glissant can be considered a progressive Negritudist who uses symbolic representation to create a new image of the Antillean.

How does the narrative form of *Le Quatrième Siècle* reflect the writer's ideology? As has been demonstrated in previous chapters, the ideology of authors who write historical novels always lies behind their choice of historical happenings within which they locate the fictional events of their narratives. Their choice of stylistic techniques is also a function of their ideological position, a fact that is particularly evident in *Le Quatrième Siècle*.

Responding to criticism of his works as impenetrable to the ordinary reader, Glissant lamented:

> Tout le monde dit que ce que j'écris est complexe, mais je me demande comment on peut écrire des choses simples sur une situation complexe comme celle des Antilles. Il n'y a pas de situation claire aux Antilles sinon on aurait, comme par ailleurs, réussi à résoudre les problèmes. (1991, 29)
>
> [Everybody says that what I write is complex, but I wonder how one can write simple things on a complex situation like that of the Antilles. There is no clear situation in the Antilles, otherwise one would have, as in other places, succeeded in solving the problems].

Thus the complexity of Glissant's writing is not gratuitous. One striking feature of his writing is the poetic nature of his prose. At times, his language is impenetrable to the "uninitiated", and the narrative structure of *Le Quatrième Siècle* is extremely complex. The problem posed by Glissant's technique in the novel is the one identified by Case, for if the novelist's language is so impenetrable that it limits his readership to a small elite group, how can his work be regarded as relevant to the larger mass of Antilleans? Yet Glissant's response to that criticism is a pertinent one.

In *Le Quatrième Siècle*, there are several narrative voices and the difficulty created by the complexity of the language makes its meaning indecipherable to the "uninitiated" reader. There is the omniscient narrator. There is Papa Longoué, who narrates the history of his people to the young Mathieu. And there are the direct interventions of Mathieu, who often complains about the complex nature of Papa Longoué's narrative. When Papa Longoué is narrating his story, Mathieu is the audience/reader. The omniscient narrator (who can be equated with the author) manipulates the other voices in the different levels of the narrative. Before writing his novel, Glissant already knows what he is going to narrate and how he is going to manipulate the narrative to suit the ideological stance he desires to communicate. Similarly, Papa Longoué knows what he is going to narrate to Mathieu, and he too manipulates his own narrative to emphasize the historical details that he deems crucial to Mathieu's understanding of the past. On another level, the omniscient narrator manipulates Papa Longoué's narrative just as the latter manipulates the narrative he is recounting to Mathieu. Thus, if Mathieu (the audience) complains of Longoué's overly complex narrative, he is merely echoing the anticipated response of actual readers of the text.

The different levels of narrative (or narrative voices) are married together by Glissant's use of "style indirect libre" [free indirect speech]. In realist writing, sentences are organized in such a way that the narrator(s) in the story can be easily identified. However, in *Le Quatrième Siècle*, readers must scrutinize the text closely to identify the source of the discourse. For example, when Papa Longoué is explaining to Mathieu how the slaves landed on the islands, there are lines that could be either Papa Longoué's direct speech or the direct intervention of the extradiegetic narrator:

> Car aujourd'hui dans leur petit coin de terre, ils se traînent, et ils ne voient pas! Où est-ce vent? Par où? Lequel? (19-20)

> [For, today in their little corner of land, they dragged themselves and they do not see it! Where is the wind? Through where? Which one?]

Because the absence of direct speech signs makes it difficult to attribute these lines to Papa Longoué, one could assume that they represent the direct intervention of the extradiegetic narrator. However, the same lines could be attributed to Papa Longoué because they might be a continuation of the dialogue between him and Mathieu.

Similarly, the following paragraph contains questions and answers that could be attributed to Papa Longoué. However, there is no punctuation to indicate that it is a direct speech. Thus a problem arises about whether it should be attributed to the diegetic narrator or to the extradiegetic narrator, who would, in this case, be entering the psyche of Longoué, the diegetic narrator. There is a punctuation mark after the first sentence, and it reinforces the idea that the whole paragraph could be attributed to Papa Longoué:

> Il en était venu des cents et des cents. Tu comprends? Pourquoi auraient-ils vu passer dans les brumes de leur souvenir, avec ses planches moisies qui pendaient sur la conque comme des bras sans mains, ce bateau-là? Celui-là précisément. Entré dans la rade, un matin de juillet, sous une pluie démente? (20)
>
> [Hundreds and hundreds of them came. Do you understand? Why would they have seen that boat passing in the mists of their souvenir, with its mouldied planks which hung on the conch like arms without hands, that boat? That one, precisely. Entered in the harbor, a July morning, under an insane rain].

The following paragraph, some of which is in parenthesis, could also be attributed either to Longoué, the diegetic narrator, or to the extradiegetic narrator.

The narrative at this point is about the slave ship at sea and about its arrival at the islands. It is chronologically consistent, but why is part of it placed in parenthesis? Does this punctuation indicate a direct intervention by the extradiegetic narrator, whereas the rest of the paragraph is in the voice of the diegetic narrator Papa Longoué? The paragraph in question reads as follows:

> (La *Rose Marie*. Elle était attendue avec impatience; on manquait de bras dans le pays. Il avait fallu toute la science du maître de bord pour que parviennent *à bon port* les deux tiers des esclaves embarqués. La maladie, la vermine, le suicide, les révoltes et les exécutions avaient ponctué la traversée de cadavres. Mais les deux tiers, ça faisait une excellente moyenne. Et le capitaine avait échappé aux navires anglais. Un marin remarquable). (20)
>
> [The *Rose Marie*. They waited for her impatiently. There was shortage of labor in the country. The master on board had had to use all his science to bring safely to shore two-thirds of the slaves shipped. Disease, vermin, suicide, revolts, and executions had marked the crossing of the corpses. But

two-thirds was an excellent average. And the captain had escaped the English ships. A remarkable sailor].

This paragraph contains a significant commentary on the condition of the slave "Other" and the status of the slave as an economic object. Whether this discourse is attributed to the diegetic narrator or to the extradiegetic narrator, we know that both fictive characters have been invented by the author. Nonetheless, identifying the originator of this discourse would enable readers to gauge its importance for the overall ideological message of the novel.

What is at stake in this question of attribution becomes evident in a direct speech by Mathieu, who serves as Papa Longoué's audience. The sentence appears in quotation marks: "Plus vite, papa, plus vite, ça c'est connu, j'ai lu les livres!" (21) [Faster, papa, faster, what you are saying is known, I read the books]. Because of Mathieu's direct interruption of the narrative, the narrative in question can be attributed to Papa Longoué. However, there is no punctuation mark to indicate that Longoué is speaking in these paragraphs. It would be logical to assume that Longoué is delivering this long discourse, especially since it might be Mathieu who interrupts by warning: "Tu vas te perdre...!" (22). [You will go astray]. However, this comment could also be a reflection, an internal monologue of the extradiegetic narrator. This confusion of narrative voices is significant because the reader is frustrated in an effort to comprehend the ideological importance of the history that is being recounted.

The complexity created by the use of "style indirect libre" is reinforced by Glissant's use of italics. Claude Duchet argues that italics in a realist discourse serve to emphasize the point being made and to emphasize the fact that the characters are products of a given society. The behavior of the characters has obviously been fashioned by the norms of the society in which they live. Duchet demonstrates how italics in a realist novel can actually devalorize the discourse in question. For example, italics underscore the irony of the fact that particular importance is attached to some characters in the narrative (143-163).

However, italics serve a different function in Glissant's *Le Quatrième Siècle*. They do not have a devalorizing purpose. On the contrary, they add emphasis and complexity to the poetic register of Glissant's narrative. Glissant uses such devices to manipulate the readers' perplexity in the face of this poetic language in order to provoke them into thinking about the history of his people, about the nature of the dominant discourse, and about the counter-discourse he has created in his novel. The last sentence of *Le Quatrème Siècle* is a typical example of this strategy:

Il entendait le bruit des chaînes qu'on manœuvrait, les *oué* en cadence, les cannes qui craquaient sous l'hélice, dans le soleil, oui, dans la grande saison chaude—c'est la fièvre c'est un monde le monde et la parole enfonce la voix gravit la voix brûle dans le feu fixe et il tourne dans la tête emportant balayant mûrissant—et qui n'a ni fin ho, ni commencement. (287)

[He heard the noise of the chains that were being manouvered, the rhythmic *oué*, the canes which cracked under the propeller, in the sun, yes, in the big hot season—it is fever it is a world the world and the word buries the voice climbs up the voice burns in fixed fire and it turns in the head carrying along sweeping ripening—and which has neither end, oh nor beginning].

This passage reads like poetry. It defies the rules of punctuation that are usually adopted in literary prose. The difficulty of interpreting this text is accentuated by the author's use of metaphoric language, which recurs throughout the novel.

How can the "uninitiated" reader decipher such passages? Yet these passages touch upon the nature of Antillean history, thus making them significant for understanding Glissant's concept of Antilleanity. Glissant has mastered the language of the dominator—the white béké—and can use it to create his own counter-discourse. The metaphors he uses help to recreate the history of his people. At the end of the novel, he makes a summary of dates and historical events that the reader would otherwise find difficult to identify chronologically. The various items in this kind of list can also function like footnotes to create the impression of verisimilitude in the text.

Glissant's text also demonstrates his control over the language used by the dominant class to impose its power in the Caribbean. By transforming this language into a poetic idiom, Glissant is proving that Antilleans can manipulate the same language that the French originally used to impose a false image of Otherness on them. Daniel Racine suggests this possibility when he argues that Glissant's intention was to deconstruct the French language in order to develop an engaged language capable of shocking his readers into awareness (620). In this sense, Glissant's power over the language of the former colonizer transforms it into an effective weapon against domination.

In his historical fiction, Glissant manipulates history to create an authentic Antillean discourse. Like Sainville, he uses true historical names, places, and events, but whereas Sainville uses a preface to emphasize the historical authenticity of his fictional creation, Glissant does not situate his narrative in relation to specific historical events.

The story of the rival Longoué and Beluse families was inspired by a whole spectrum of historical persons and events. Because Glissant does not focus on a particular historical incident or period, his historical fiction differs from that of Sainville, Hazoumé, or Boni. Nonetheless, he and Sainville have the same ideological concern—the revalorization of the image of the maroon in Antillean history. As Jack Corzani has observed, the classical scenes of Antillean history are portrayed in *Le Quatrième Siècle*: slave trade and slavery, the relationship between the colonized and the colonizer, slave revolt and emancipation (1980, 221-222). The lesson Antilleans need to learn from the past is that the European created an inferior "Other" in them by fostering a complex that they themselves have interiorized over the centuries. Antilleans need to understand this past in order to come to terms with the present and to build the future—to create a new Antillean with a new and authentic discourse of his or her own. Josaphat Kubayanda has remarked that:

> One objective of postcolonial literature from the Caribbean is to write a Caribbean ending to a very misconstrued colonial and slave beginning, which essentially was a painful rite of passage into modernity. Another goal is to counter the Eurocentric modes of representation of the Caribbean, especially its underprivileged subjects. These two desired goals (reconstructing a sense of identity and confronting the hegemony of Western culture) establish a link between Caribbean writing and postmodernist discourse in general. (1992, 181)

The preceding chapters on Sainville and Glissant have underscored their testimony to this painful "rite of passage" and how they have reconstructed a new sense of authentic Caribbean identity by confronting Western modes of discourse. Revalorizing the image of the maroon is one crucial way in which they have done this.

Although Glissant and Sainville differ greatly in their opinions about Negritude and its relevance to the development of a progressive approach to the solution of the black world's problems, they actually express similar concerns in their historical novels, for both desire to subvert the dominant Euro-centric discourse that had previously been taken for granted. *Le Quatrième Siècle* deals not only with the past, but with the present and with the future as well. Glissant was inspired by history, but he believes that a pride in the past can be coupled with concrete attempts to understand the present and to advance progressive approaches to the problems that arose during the course of history. Within this context, his revalorization of the image of the maroon serves an important ideological function in the sense that it negates the dominant discourse that has been used in the past to perpetuate the image of the colonized Other.

Conclusion

Critics have tended to define the historical novel only in terms of the classical historical novel of nineteenth-century Europe. Such definitions do not provide an adequate basis for understanding the historical fictions of African or Caribbean writers. For example, Jack Corzani believes that Glissant's *Le Quatrième Siècle* is not a historical novel because he thinks it does not follow the pattern of what has, in Europe, been considered to be a historical novel (1980). My reading of *Le Quatrième Siècle*, however, shows that, although it does not strictly follow the norms of the European historical novel, it does focus upon a historical phenomenon—slavery—in a way that links it with the African-Caribbean historical novels of writers such as Hazoumé, Boni, and Sainville. For a novel to be classified as a historical novel, it does not have to recount only specific events from the past; it can synthesize a global perspective upon the nature of such events, and that is precisely what Glissant does in his novel.

Although African and Caribbean historical novels share many traits with the "classical" European historical novel, they also differ from it in significant ways. These differences derive from the peculiar predicament of the African-Caribbean writer as a colonized or formerly colonized individual. The African-Caribbean historical novel performs an ideological function that its European counterpart does not necessarily serve. For these writers, writing becomes an act of engagement by means of which they can critique colonialism and the power it represents. The fact that they experienced the imposition of colonialism upon them makes it imperative for them to re-write history in order to question the control of discourse that had been maintained through the control of political and economic power by the colonial (or former colonial) forces. In other words, African and Caribbean historical novelists are representative of "the empire writing back" (to borrow a term from Aschcroft et al.) in response to the way that hegemonic discourses function in the world order, whereas European writers never experienced the situation of colonized or former colonized people. They do not have to write in the language of a colonizer or former colonizer and they are not necessarily confronted with the felt necessity of asserting pride in the cultural identity of an oppressed people. These ideological factors help determine the type of history that attracts the attention of writers who are obliged to confront the discourse of the "Other" that evolved in response to the colonialists' need to justify their enterprise.

Some critics have defined the historical novel as a novel in which true events from the past inspire the fictional creation—events to which the writer was not a witness. However, the cases of Hazoumé, Boni and Kourouma demonstrate that the historical novelist can be inspired as well by events they have themselves witnessed. History does not exclude the recent past. Because the same observation can be made about some recent European historical novelists, the historical novel should be redefined to include fiction inspired by contemporary events.

The African-Caribbean historical novel is characterized by a set of shared literary and ideological functions, and they largely determine the author's choice of historical materials and narrative techniques. Like the European historical novel as defined by Alfred Sheppard, the African-Caribbean historical novel has been inspired by a past that is recreated in the writer's imagination. The writers considered in this study all employ the facts of history as their essential raw material, but like European historical novelists, they use these events selectively. The choice of what to include and what to exclude is dictated primarily by the ideology that inspired their historical writing in the first place. For example, Hazoumé was inspired to a certain extent by a resentment against the role played by the Dahomeyans in nineteenth-century West Africa. At the same time, he was concerned with making the culture of these people comprehensible to the outside world, while testifying to his own respect for French culture and for what he considered to be the "civilizing role" of the French colonial enterprise in Africa. Boni's historical fiction was an expression of resistance to colonial rule and resentment against the French destruction of the Bwa kingdom and its culture. Malonga uses legend to depict the collective memory of an African people and Kourouma castigates colonialism as well as African leaders. Glissant and Sainville were concerned with a revalorization of the image of the maroon in Antillean history because the maroon represented, for them, the articulation in concrete form of a counter-discourse in opposition to the hegemonic power of European discourse at the time of slavery.

According to Jonathan Nield, a novel is rendered historical by the introduction of dates, personages, and events that can be readily identified as historical. This characteristic of European historical fiction can also be found in African and Caribbean historical novels, for identifiable dates and events are often used to enhance the verisimilitude of novels such as those that have been considered in the present study. However, the ideological factors that determined the selective use of such materials in these novels were governed by ideological factors far different from those that were operative in the work of nineteenth-century European historical novelists such as Walter Scott and Alfred Vigny. These European writers of course sought to influence readers' perceptions of history, but the task of African-Caribbean historical novelists was more complex. Desiring to re-assert pride in their cultural heritage, the latter were using the language of the (ex-)colonial master in order to reorient their readers' perception of a history that had, in the past, always been written by representatives of the colonial order.

The use of historically verifiable minor characters is common in the European historical novel. Scott used them in his novels, and so did many African-Caribbean historical novelists. For example, Hazoumé introduced important historical figures like Guézo in *Doguicimi*, but he also introduced minor characters such as the king's wives, the Vidaho, and Toffa. Boni also introduced minor characters like Térhé and Hadounfi to enhance the verisimilitude of his fictional creation. Kourouma uses more fictional characters among whom the griot for example would be a minor character in most history texts. In the case of Sainville's *Dominique Nègre Esclave*, the names of most of the slaves were actually minor characters in history; and Glissant employed identifiable minor characters such as Senglis and Mathieu. All these historical writers placed at the center of their narratives, characters who had been ignored by history as written by the colonialists. For example, the maroon had never been portrayed as a hero in official European accounts of Caribbean history. Yet Sainville and Glissant, without denying the role played by European emancipationists, persistently emphasize the role of the maroons in bringing about their own emancipation in 1848. By doing so, these writers invite their readers to re-assess the validity of the European claim that slaves themselves had nothing significant to do with the abolition of slavery, which had supposedly been brought to an end by the humanitarian activities of white people like Victor Schoelcher. In this way, African-Caribbean historical novelists rehabilitated characters who had been treated as unimportant by European historical writers.

Novelists have an advantage over historians in the sense that they can fill the gaps in documented history by inventing minor characters. African-Caribbean historical novelists took full advantage of this opportunity in their forging of what might well be described as an authentic anti-colonialist discourse. However, as Paul Veynes has argued, the choice of materials in any historical discourse introduces an arbitrary factor. The validity of this contention can easily be illustrated by examining the nature of the problems created by the ambiguity of Hazoumé's pro-colonialist discourse in *Doguicimi*. This author's arbitrary choice of historical events and his use of a pro-colonialist discourse have often been regarded by African critics as a reflection of his lack of commitment to African liberation—a commitment that these critics consider to be a crucial ingredient in any authentic African writing. Thus, his choice to focus upon human sacrifices among the Dahomeyans reflects quite a different attitude toward his subject from Sainville's choice of the maroon revolts as a model of heroic resistance to colonial injustice.

As Georg Lukács has pointed out, the historical novel is invariably linked with the great and urgent problems of the present. If historical fiction in Africa and the Caribbean was inspired by discursive practices that had evolved during four centuries of slavery and colonization, it was also influenced by the Negritude movement, which was essentially a response to the Euro-centric discourse of the "Other." Within this context, African and Caribbean historical novelists developed a particular form of counter-discourse in their attempts to address urgent contemporary problems.

Negritude discourse was itself a re-writing of history and a rejection of ethno-centric European interpretations of the past. Post-structuralist and modernist approaches have further called these interpretations into question by revealing the indefensibility of their implicit claims to universal validity. The African-Caribbean historical novel participates in this movement of ideas. If such works differ from their nineteenth-century European predecessors because their authors were writing from the perspective of colonized or formerly colonized peoples, this perspective was further differentiated from European models of the genre by the fact that the African-Caribbean historical novel was at least partly inspired by oral traditions. For this reason, it must be understood in terms of the political and social functions that it was intended to fulfill. Like other historical novels, the historical fictions that have been considered here, function as fictional works, but they also serve some of the same functions as anthropological treatises, and in some cases their ideological function often overshadows their literary qualities.

Felix Couchoro's *L'Esclave* provides a good test case for my understanding of the African-Caribbean historical novel. One of the first novels to have been published in francophone Africa, it shares with Hazoumé's *Doguicimi* some of the principal ideological concerns of a historical novel written during the colonial era. Although *l'Esclave* does not focus on verifiable historical events, its treatment of a specific historical era was, like that of *Doguicimi*, inspired by a profound familiarity with oral narratives about that era. Nevertheless, *L'Esclave* does not exactly fit into the category of the African-Caribbean historical novel as defined in this study.

Couchoro's novel relates the story of Mawoulawoé, a slave boy bought by the "father" Komlangan, who dies and, following the customs of his people, bequeaths his property to his legitimate son. However, Mawoulawoé uses Machiavelian tactics to kill anyone who stands in the way of his attempt to usurp the property of his adopted "father," although he eventually commits suicide when Komlangan's eldest son Daniel returns from his studies in Europe and reclaims his father's property. The story deals with the problems that arise in the traditional inheritance system, and it evokes universal themes such as jealousy, fidelity, and the conflict between good and evil. Sabit Salami praises *L'Esclave* as a successful synthesis of orality and written form, arguing that Couchoro's treatment of the jealousy theme elevates the novel to the level of a universally valid depiction of human nature:

> Qu'il [Couchoro] ait pu fermer les yeux sur les méfaits du colonialisme est la preuve que la littérature africaine peut transcender les préoccupations du moment. L'engagement politique n'est, après tout, que transitoire, surtout par rapport à un sujet aussi fondamental à la nature humaine que la jalousie. (225-226)
>
> [That he (Couchoro) was able to close his eyes on the evils of colonialism is the proof that African literature can transcend the preoccupations of the times. Political commitment is, after all, only transitory, especially compared to a theme as fundamental to human nature as jealousy].

In reality, however, the predicament of the writer and his people as colonized subjects is far more important than the theme of jealousy. Unlike Hazoumé and Boni, Couchoro simply ignored the problem of colonization, and this lack of concern for the dominant historical phenomenon of the era about which he was writing makes it difficult to read *L'Esclave* as convincing historical fiction.

Like Hazoumé and Boni, Couchoro uses traditional oral storytelling techniques to reinforce Negritude assumptions about African cultural authenticity, but his works also reveal how an African writer can be seduced by his exposure to a Western education. Although he claims to be propounding a progressive type of Negritude that eschews outmoded traditions, his quest for a viable cultural identity actually revolves around the African's relationship to a traditional value system. How can one import foreign values, he asks, without losing one's own cultural authenticity? He attempts to answer this question but only succeeds in demonstrating the extent to which he himself has been acculturated. For example, he clearly places more faith in the tenets of Christianity than he does in the values of traditional African belief systems, implying that the white man's religion can redeem his characters in a way that their traditional religious practices cannot. Such lines of argument do not represent a synthesis of cultures; they merely reiterate the colonialists' image of Africans.

As Adrien Huannou has argued, Couchoro is essentially a moralist, each of whose characters has a particular function to fulfill (1987, 82). In fact, *L'Esclave* might well be called a "roman à moeurs." Yet, to the extent that it exploits historical events to enhance the verisimilitude of his novelistic portrayals, it is also a historical novel. Couchoro delineates the social consequences of certain customary practices and defines the impact of Christian missionary activity on them. In *L'Esclave*, the characters tend to be type characters with specific moral qualities. For example, Mawoulawoé symbolizes ambition, and through him, the author moralizes about the need to respect social norms and customs. In *Doguicimi* and *Crépuscule des temps anciens,* the belief system is shown as fashioning people's way of life, particularly in the sense that individuals are punished for trangressing against the norms of the ancestors. Couchoro seems to be suggesting the same relationship when he portrays Mawoulawoé as a Machiavelian character who is punished for having committed adultery with the wife of his "brother."

In the novel, good eventually triumphs over evil, as it does in the historical novels of Hazoumé and Boni, for Mawoulawoé is thrown out of the house by Daniel. However, in the sense that Daniel was educated in Europe, this ending identifies Western values with goodness and traditional African ones with evil. The triumph of Western values is justified, he implies, because they represent a higher level of "civilization." Such ideologically tinged messages obviously reinforce self-serving European pronouncements about their own so-called "mission civilisatrice" in Africa.

Nonetheless, Couchoro's novel must be seen in its historical context. He himself could not have been overly critical of French colonialism at the time when he was writing. His use of traditional story-telling techniques and moralizing digressions indicate that he had not completely lost touch with his own people. Furthermore, he develops universal themes such as love, hatred, and ambition in a peculiarly African way by adopting the history, legends, and myths of his own people to a narrative that was written in the French language. In this sense *L'Esclave* is an African historical novel, but unlike other African-Caribbean historical novels, it does not undercut the colonial discourse of the West.

Senghor has been criticized for having fostered the impression that Western culture is superior to the African heritage that serves as the backdrop for his anti-colonial discourse, but his definition of the situation is illuminating in the sense that it helps explain the ambiguous position of "évolué" writers such as Couchoro. According to Senghor, the world is like a musical group in which the African is the "batteur de tam tam" [drum beater] and the European the "chef d'orchestre" [band leader] (1977). A "civilisation de l'universel" [civilization of the universal] based on such assumptions implies that Africans are morally obliged to abide by the overall direction of Europeans. However, colonization is not based on an equitable exchange of cultures, for the colonizers refuse to recognize the culture of the colonized as the equivalent of their own. In *L'Esclave,* the Western-educated Daniel saves his family from the evil machinations of Mawoulawoé, and the Christian god saves the community from the chaos caused by the former slave. Under these circumstances, there is no synthesis of cultures, but merely the triumph of one over the other.

Conclusion

On the contrary, Jean Ikellé-Matiba's *Cette Afrique-là!* is a powerful indictment of German and subsequently French, colonial atrocities in Cameroon. The novel is historical fiction inspired by a personal and a collective experience of dehumanization under German and French colonization in that region of the continent. Like Boni in *Crépuscule des temps anciens* or more recently Kourouma in *Monnè, outrages et défis*, Ikellé-Matiba's eye-witness account appeals to the sensibilities of the reader by questioning the hypocrisy of all the theories that were used to justify the scramble for and partition of Africa by Europeans. Mômha is the main character who is also the narrator. His experiences with the German and French colonizers recall Boni's people's encounter with the French invaders in *Crépuscule des temps anciens*. The colonized is an objectified being only perceived of value to the colonizer as long as he or she is a tool for exploiting his or her own land. Mômha becomes acceptable to the German colonizers and missionaries when he is well assimilated into Germanic culture. He is Christianized and speaks and writes German well. In the eyes of the colonizer, as Mômha himself puts it, he has now become a "civilized" person and the colonizer can identify with him. He has become a tool for the "civilizing mission" of the colonizer—working for him as a civil servant.

Yet, strikingly enough, after Mômha's dehumanizing experiences with both the German and French colonists, he is willing to forgive them. At the end of his narration, he evokes a Senghorian notion of brotherhood/sisterhood, of "civilization of the universal". His story is a history lesson to the young people in his audience, but it is also a moral lesson:

> Oublions tout ce que nous avons souffert. L'histoire humaine est ainsi faite. Des lendemains radieux nous attendent, j'espère. (240)
>
> [Let us forget all that we have suffered. This is how human history is made. Brighter days await us, I hope].

Like a story teller who moralizes at the end of his or her folk tale, Mômha uses his story about European colonization to admonish his audience not to harbor bitterness against their former colonizers. He is a product of his traditional African education which teaches this perception of life, but he is also a product of the Christian faith that he has imbibed from the European missionaries. Mômha is a product of these two cultures, even if the encounter between the two cultures has been that of dominator and dominated, of master and subject.

As in the other historical novels discussed in this book, *Cette Afrique-là!* evokes true historical events that we can verify in real life. Ikellé-Matiba evokes authentic names of places, people and events. Mômha, the main character has actually lived in that region. In fact, through Mômha the narrator, Ikellé-Matiba resorts to some of the techniques we have identified in Boni's and Sainville's novels in particular. For example, he alludes to Ruben Um Nyobe, an important nationalist in Cameroonian history. In a footnote, he explains that: "Il était alors Secrétaire Général des Syndicats C.G.T. de la Sanaga Maritime (229). [At that time, he was Secretary-General of the C.G.T. Maritime Unions of Sanaga]. The narrator also alludes to Arab and European slave trade in the continent (52).

Through his main character, who is also the narrator, Ikellé-Matiba creates the image of a Senghorian edenic pre-colonial Africa and in a long digression from the story, he makes a diatribe on what he calls the difference between "civilisation harmonisée" [harmonized civilization] and "civilisation stabilisée" [stabilized civilization]. His purpose is to educate his audience (and ultimately his European readers) on the importance of knowledge of African contribution to civilization—for example in the field of medicine. The narrator's sarcastic tone in alluding to European claims that they were civilizing Africans and helping them develop is an effective stylistic device that Kourouma also uses in his novels.

Through the narrative structure, Ikellé-Matiba creates a *mise-en-abyme* at several levels. There is a diagetic narrator who controls the narrative of the main character, Mômha, who is actually the one who does the narration of the whole story. Mômha's narration is therefore a narration within a narration. Furthermore, there are several *mise-en-abyme* within Mômha's own narration because he constantly quotes directly what other people have narrated in the form of letters to him. In these letters that he quotes directly to his audience, the original writers of the letters sometimes in turn quote directly from others, thus creating another level of *mise-en-abyme*. For example, Lingôm's brother's letter to Mômha (the narrator), is a narration within a narration. In the letter, we learn of how Lingôm dies at the hand of the cruel colonizers (169-170). There is a further *mise-en-abyme* when in this letter, Lingôm's own letter to the family is quoted directly. Lingôm's brother in the original letter to Mômha also quotes an eyewitness account of Lingôm's execution (169). Yet, in the eyewitness' account of this execution, he too quotes directly Lingôm's own words before he was executed when he took off his hat and said: "Je suis fier de mourir pour que vive le Kaiser" (169). [I am proud to die so that the Kaiser may live]. Ikellé-Matiba does not resort to free indirect speech like Glissant, and that is why the reader can easily identify the multiple narrative voices who create short narratives within narratives.

The adaptation of the folk tale mode of narration creates a real audience for Ikelle-Matiba's main character who does the real narration of what is the "story" in the novel. The reader is the audience for the extradiegetic narrator who only uses Mômha's story to his audience as a pretext to tell his own "story" to the reader. Thus, Ikellé-Matiba uses the setting for an oral story narration—people gathered in an African village at night to tell folk tales—to create historical fiction which undercuts the hegemonic discourse created by Europeans through their colonial activities in Africa.

This notion of counter discourse is what we witness too in Roland Brival's *La Montagne d'Ebène*, which has much in common with Sainville's *Dominique Nègre Esclave*, for it was inspired by the same historical events. An account of the nineteenth-century maroon revolts, it focuses on a main character with picaresque-like characteristics. In his search for an authentic Antillean identity, Brival, like Sainville and Glissant, finds it crucial to revalorize the image of the maroon. Writing after the publication of Sainville's *Dominique Nègre Esclave* and Glissant's *Le Quatrième Siècle*, he revives the Negritude discourse in the context of which historical fiction often serves as a means of discrediting Euro-centric discourse and the power it represents.

A maroon of the first order like Dominique, Macouba, the hero of Brival's novel, rejects the image of the other imposed on him through the institution of slavery. His revolt is not a passive one. On the contrary, it is the engaged articulation of his own concrete discourse. Through Macouba, Brival revalorizes the image of the revolted maroon, thereby subverting the image of the maroon disseminated by the discourse of the slave master. Like Dominique, Macouba persistently maroons in search of a permanent freedom, and he refuses to be cowed by the inhuman treatment inflicted upon him.

In his search for a viable cultural identity, Brival believes in a return to Africa. For this reason, he makes his hero a pure-blooded African in contrast to Sainville's creole hero and the creole descendants of the original Longoué in Glissant's *Le Quatrième Siècle*. Antillean writers might have different approaches to the elaboration of a counter-discourse in the Caribbean context, but they all have the same ultimate ideological goal.

In Sainville's novel, the critical viewpoint is that of the author himself. In Brival's novel, the critical perspective is provided by the subjective consciousness of the novel's black hero. As part of his depersonalization, dehumanization, and creolization, Macouba is obliged to accept his name, which, although it sounds African, actually symbolizes the beginning of the creation of "Otherness" in him. Significantly, Brival underscores the importance of Macouba'a reaction to this process of creolization, for he himself realizes that his renaming is the beginning of his "chosification," the beginning of his transformation into an economic object. His whole life becomes shaped by this loss of identity, and his "prise de conscience" is significant because it symbolizes the need for Antilleans to go back to their roots in order to discover who they truly are. In this sense, *La*

Montagne d'Ebène represents Brival's attempt to come to terms with the past by asserting his pride in Macouba, who rejected the image that had been imposed on him.

Whereas Sainville's Dominique was born into slavery, Brival's Macouba is an adult who remains conscious of his ancestors in Africa, conscious of his own attachment to the land and to his people. Africa was part of his psyche. In contrast, Dominique must learn at second hand about the ancestors in Africa, and as a slave, his access to this knowledge is limited to what he hears recounted by the older people and by the newly arrived slaves from the continent. For Macouba, the Caribbean land and its people are strange, and he must adapt to them. If Dominique is taught from childhood to believe in the inferiority of his race, Macouba had acquired a strong sense of pride in his heritage before he was captured and enslaved. The different backgrounds of these two characters influence the nature of the subversive discourse they articulate in response to their respective situations.

In a significant interior monologue, Macouba reflects on Africa, the motherland, and on the destiny of black people in general:

> Quel imprévisible motif eussent pu invoquer les dieux pour avoir infligé pareil châtiment aux peuples de l'Afrique? se demandait-il. Et, à supposer qu'une faute eût été commise, pourquoi ne les punissait-il pas sur les lieux mêmes de leur forfait, comme il en était d'usage? (48)
>
> [What unforseeable motif could the gods have invoked for having inflicted such punishment on the peoples of Africa? he wondered. And, supposing that a fault had been committed, why did he not punish them in the place they committed their infamy, as was usually the case?]

He is asking what theory could possibly be adduced to justify the suffering of black people under slavery. No religious justification is plausible, and Brival is clearly using Macouba's monologue as a means of confronting the destiny of his entire race. Through Macouba, he calls into question the absurd Western religious assumptions according to which the plight of black people was the result of a curse, as is supposedly suggested by the Bible.

When Macouba introduces himself to the maroons, he uses his original African name, Djakoulo N'Dyaye (48), and throughout the novel, his native Massambi serves him as a source of inspiration. In his constant struggle to subvert the discourse of his masters, he draws inspiration from the ancestors in Africa. For Brival, therefore, an authentic anticolonial discourse in the Caribbean originates with a recognition of the motherland.

Julien's cowardly attack on Macouba takes place after Julien discovers the place where his sister is living with the black man. Believing his victim to be dead, Julien fails to ward off the fatal bite that Macouba, as if suddenly invoking the powers of his African ancestors, inflicts on him. Macouba dies like the brave warrior he had been trained to be in his native land. For Brival, this episode signifies his hero's link with the past—a past in which Antilleans can take pride because it represents the spiritual link that is their history. In spite of the systematic deculturization imposed on the slaves in the Antilles, they did not completely lose a sense of belonging to the motherland in Africa. Brival thus implies that the re-writing of his people's history means going back to their ancestral roots in Africa and not starting his account of their history with the beginning of slavery.

Throughout the novel, Macouba's struggle resembles that of Dominique, whose life also reflects the systematic dehumanization and "chosification" of the slave. Taught to hate their own race, slaves were inculcated with a sense of inferiority for their whole race, but as Brival emphasizes, the slave was not a passive "Other." The revolt of the slaves, their attack on the plantation (which they burn down), and their killing of the slave master St. Julien reveal the concrete fashion in which they subvert the dominant discourse.

As in *Dominique Nègre Esclave*, the Christian religion is a prominent element of this discourse in *La Montagne d'Ebène*. In particular, the Christian message of humility is used to maintain the slaves in a perpetually subservient state. Yet the "prise de conscience" of the maroons counters the physical and psychological manipulations of the white békés. In his work on the myth of the Black in French society during the nineteenth and twentieth centuries, Fanoudh-Siefer mentions how the Bible was used to support the European argument that the black race descended from Ham, the cursed son of Abraham. Sainville's *Dominique Nègre Esclave* depicts how such myths inculcated black people with a sense of inferiority and transformed them into economic tools. They themselves often accept their inherent inferiority on the basis of these myths, as the case of one of Brival's characters illustrates:

> Yèyètte, elle-même, professait que sa race était perdue à jamais, victime de la malédiction de Cham dont leur parlait le père Jacob toutes les fois qu'il montait de St. Pierre pour catéchiser les esclaves des plantations avoisinantes. (11)

> [Yèyètte herself professed that her race was lost forever, victim of Ham's curse of which Jacob spoke to them every time he came up there from St. Pierre to give catechism lessons to the slaves in the neighboring plantations].

Brival's hero is the opposite of Yèyètte in this respect, for he successfully counters this attempt to deprive him of a sense of pride in his ancestors.

Fanoudh-Siefer also points out how the physical descriptions of black people in colonial literature emphasized their apparent ugliness in the eyes of Europeans. Constantly inculcated in slaves and in their descendants, the supposed physical ugliness of the black race is part of the process by means of which an inferior "Other" is created in the consciousness of black people in the Caribbean. As we see in the case of Yèyètte, the attempt to engender this inferiority complex among black slaves was often successful:

> [..] L'extrême laideur de ceux-ci (leur front proéminent à la manière des singes, leur nez écrasé aux narines béantes, leurs lèvres épaisses, leur crâne sec d'où levait une maigre tignasse hirsute et rugueuse, sans parler de l'affligeante couleur de leur peau!) ne suffisait-elle pas à les bannir de la race humaine? (11)
>
> [..] Was the extreme ugliness of the latter (their protruding forehead like that of monkeys, their flat nose with gaping nostrils, their thick lips, their dry skull from which stuck out thin coarse and shaggy hair) not enough to banish them from the human race?]

Yèyètte has interiorized her inferiority to such an extent that she sincerely believes in the inherent ugliness of her own people. For her and other black slaves like her, the articulation of a concrete counter-discourse will only become possible after they have rejected the false myths that have been foisted upon them by the white béké.

The problem that Fanon analyzes in his *Peau Noire Masques Blancs* is a contemporary one, but it has its roots in the history that inspired Sainville's and Brival's historical fiction. Yet why is Brival, writing in 1984, interested in producing the kind of historical fiction that Sainville was writing in 1948. To answer this question, one needs to recognize that the development of discursive processes in the era of slavery does not belong exclusively to the past. On the contrary, it continues to have a powerful impact on contemporary Antillean society. Brival is interested in historical fiction in the 1980s because he recognizes the need for Antilleans to constantly go back to their roots as they seek a viable sense of identity in a contemporary world where they are still living under French political, economic, and social domination. According to him, young Antilleans must be continually reminded of their history in a society where French control of the media and of the educational system accords a privileged status to the colonizer's false version of the past.

In *La Montagne d'Ebène*, the dehumanization of black people takes place in various ways. One of them is the intolerance of inter-racial marriage by the white béké. For example, Robert d'Auttincourt, a Bordeaux lawyer who marries a black lady from St. Dominique, is punished by being stripped of his license to practice law (10-11). Forbidding inter-racial marriages in itself inculcates a sense of

Conclusion

inferiority among black people, ultimately serving the same purpose as the promulgation of the Ham myth.

Another way of dehumanizing slaves was to treat them as breeding animals to be used at the will of the master to produce more labor for the sugar cane plantations. As Glissant noted, depriving slaves of their freedom to choose their own sexual partners was part of the pattern of "chosification." In *La Montagne d'Ebène,* this process is described in the following terms:

> Ces réunions' d'esclaves se déroulaient dans un hangar retiré, empestant, aux dires des femmes, l'odeur du pétun que l'on y faisait sécher d'ordinaire. Une fois les hommes et les femmes dévêtus et rassemblés par paires, le maître désignait lui-même les partenaires, sommés alors de s'accoupler—sous les yeux du maître, et parfois même de ceux de ses amis qu'il conviait à goûter ce spectacle peu ordinaire. (201)

> [These "meetings" of slaves took place in a remote shed, stinking, according to the women, of the smell of the petunia that was normally dried there. Once the men and women were undressed and assembled in pairs, the master himself chose the partners, who were then ordered to have sex in front of the master, and sometimes even of his friends whom he invited to have a taste of this extraordinary spectacle].

This passage speaks for itself. Brival's account is not gratuitous. Reduced to the level of animals, the black slaves are exploited as a source of voyeuristic amusement for the white béké. Brival's ideological stance emerges clearly in this passage which underscores the inhuman nature of the institution of slavery and suggests the physical as well as the psychological consequences that such treatment was bound to have on the slaves.

To complete his image of the colonizer-colonized relationship, Brival also evokes the mentality of the white béké vis-à-vis his "inferior Other." For the béké, the black slave has no rights. The slave owner St. Aubin even expresses disgust at seeing mulattoes fighting for their rights (40-41). In his eyes, even the products of white békés' lecherous philanderings are regarded as incapable of human dignity.

As in Sainville's *Dominique Nègre Esclave,* the inhuman treatment of slaves pervades *La Montagne d'Ebène.* For example, when Barthélemy visits his wife at another plantation without the permission of his master, he is punished by having his toes cut off. For the white béké, Barthélemy is no more than an economic implement, and he has no right to claim that the woman he has visited is his "wife" (59-60). Although Mathilde is a mulatress, she too is considered a member of the inferior black race. She is however, quite conscious of her ambiguous predicament:

> Mais elle tenait de sa mère l'essentiel: la pratique du culte de l'obi, la science des femmes, la connaissance des plantes et des racines, le goût de l'amour, et, surtout, la patience. (105)
>
> [But she inherited from her mother the essential; the practice of obi cult, the science of women, the knowledge of plants and roots, the taste of love and, especially, patience].

Mathilde has kept the African elements of her identity—her religion and her knowledge of medicinal herbs. The only thing she inherited from her white father was her light skin. Ironically, despite her blood relationship with white people, Mathilde identifies with the African origins that form her character and symbolize her recognition of the source of her being. By refusing to denounce her African origins, even though she has been exposed to her father's values, she is subverting the Euro-centric discourse of "Otherness."

Like the slaves in Sainville's *Dominique Nègre Esclave,* the maroons in Brival's *La Montagne d'Ebène* also subvert the Eurocentric discourse in other ways. Like Dominique, Macouba has love affairs that symbolically assert his identity as a revolted slave. He too makes love with the white master's daughter as a means of gaining revenge against the whites who have dehumanized his race. Initially, he had refused to lower his eyes in the presence of Mara, the master's daughter, and she was upset that the newly arrived slave from Africa stared at her with defiance. For this reason, she attempts to make him more subservient by inflicting physical pain on him. However, Macouba eventually breaks down the racial barriers and turns her hatred into genuine love. She is initiated into the male-female relationship for the first time when he makes love to her, and her letter to him reveals the extent to which she has fallen in love with him. The relationship between the two of them clearly reveals that he is more than an economic tool in the hands of the white béké. Capable of loving and evoking love in others, he is just as human as those who have persistently denied his humanity.

Julien, Mara's brother, epitomizes the white superiority complex. He cannot accept the fact that his sister has run away with Macouba, a maroon. However, her relationship with a black slave transformed her to the extent that she can call him (Macouba) "un des nôtres" [one of our people]. She now rejects the myths created by her own race and dreams of seeing her own son, Stephenson, grow up to participate in the movement for the abolition of slavery. In this context, he becomes a symbol of the Antilleans' hope that their history can be rewritten in a way that does not exclude their black heritage.

Although Macouba dies at the hands of Julien, his spirit lives on, for it has been incarnated in his son. But Stephenson is a mulatto. In symbolic terms, his mixed-race physical identity suggests the

Conclusion 181

"métissage culturel" that is a dominant reality of Antillean history. In Brival's quest for a viable cultural identity, he is not only interested in re-writing the role of the maroons in Antillean history, but also in underscoring the multidimensional racial element in that culture.

A significant difference between Brival's *La Montagne d'Ebène* and Glissant's historical fiction derives from Brival's refusal to ignore the Carib aspect of Antillean culture. In *La Montagne d'Ebène*, Mara visits the old Carib lady, Moina, to ask for medical help:

> Elle [Moina] était libre-couresse, comme les quelques rares survivants de sa race encore présents dans l'île, à qui la défaite et le massacre de leur peuple n'avaient pu imposer de subir les rigueurs de l'esclavage [...]. On disait la Caraïbe dotée de pouvoirs terrifiants, tel celui de faire revenir les morts pour les interroger à l'aide d'une calebasse creuse qu'elle s'appliquait contre l'oreille, ou celui, à distance, de faire passer la vie à trépas n'importe quelle créature humaine. (27)

> [She (Moina) was a free-runner, like the few survivors of her race still living on the island, whom the defeat and massacre of their people had prevented from slavery...It was said that the Carib had the gift of terrifying powers, such as that of being able to bring back the dead to interrogate them with the help of a hollow calabash which she applied on the ear, or the power to kill any human creature from far away].

Such beliefs did enter into the contemporary Antillean consciousness, and Brival's depiction of the old Carib woman draws attention to the historic genocide that was perpetuated on her people by Europeans. Indeed, the presence of such scenes in Brival's novel reveal that one cannot re-write the history of the Antilles without including the Carib element. In this sense, he goes further than other Antillean historical novelists like Glissant by adding an important dimension to the contemporary Antillean consciousness of and pride in an extraordinarily complex history.

In Brival's novel, the association between the maroons and the Caribs symbolizes the symbiotic nature of Antillean culture that evolved in a society dominated by colonial hegemonic discourse. However, although Mara solicits medical help from Moina, she does not regard the Carib woman as an equal and even kills her to protect her own status in society because Moina is the only one who knows about Mara's liaison with Macouba.

As in the historical novels of Sainville and Glissant, the authenticity of the historical background in *La Montagne d'Ebène* is reinforced by the use of real place names such as Martinique, Guadeloupe, Antigua, the Rue Cases-Nègres, the Côte de l'Or, and Bordeaux. He also uses the names of actual historical personalities such as Louis-Philippe. Thus, Brival creates an "illusion du réel" in the same way that Sainville and Glissant had done. Like them, he employs myths and true historical events to create a fictional universe that is structured around a desire to revalorize the image of the maroon in Antillean history.

La Montagne d'Ebène also has the same narrative structure as Sainville's *Dominique Nègre Esclave*. The omniscient narrator is diegetic, and Macouba the maroon (like Dominique) is the main character around whom all the action is centered. Brival uses interior monologue and letters to reveal the subjective consciousness of his characters. In one of these monologues Macouba reflects upon the plight of black people, victims of European colonial hegemony. At this point, he becomes Brival's spokesman for an ideologically committed anticolonialist position.

Brival's use of letters heightens the impression of historical verisimilitude in the novel, but it also raises questions about the "realism" of the narrative itself. For example, why does Mara write a letter to Macouba when she knows that Macouba is unlikely to ever read her letter? Within the context of Brival's fictional world, Mara's discourse is thus actually directed toward the reader, but if this is so, is the context of her letter dictated by the fact that she knows it will probably never reach its intended receiver, Macouba?

> Mon homme, écrivait Mara, comment te dire cette lettre que tu ne liras probablement jamais, sinon en m'imaginant que je le fais pour moi-même, pour cette autre partie de moi que tu es devenu. (103)

> [My man, Mara wrote, how do I address this letter to you that you will probably never read, if not by imagining that I write it for myself, for this part of myself that you have become].

As the contents of the letter show, Brival is using the letter as a device to reveal the inner feelings of Mara and to emphasize the psychological impact that her relationship with the black slave has had on her.

Another difficulty with Brival's use of letters occurs when Père Jacob writes to Bénédicte. The reader knows the contents of this letter before it reaches the person to whom it is addressed. Having witnessed the sealing of the letter when it was entrusted to a slave, readers realize that the slave (called a "négrillon") is the intermediary between the originator of the discourse and its intended audience. The slave therefore becomes the link that establishes the psychological realism of the historical events being narrated in the letter. The use of a technique borrowed from the epistolary novel enables readers to gain insight into the psyche of the characters involved in the panorama of Antillean history.

In seeking an authentic Antillean cultural identity, Brival, like Sainville and Glissant, revalorized the image of the maroon and attributed to him an important role in the abolition of slavery. Like the Negritude writers of the pre-independence period in Africa, Brival uses historical fiction to revive the debate over the question of cultural identity. He also adopts it to cast light upon the illusory freedom that Antilleans supposedly gained when their islands became "départements" of France. This juridical status implies that, politically and culturally, Antilleans are still under the control of metropolitan France. Yet emancipation from slavery will always be incomplete as long as the white béké continues to exercise the considerable economic, political, and discursive power that he inherited from the era of slavery.

In this re-writing of history through historical fiction as we have seen in the novels which have been discussed in this study, Negritude as a literary and cultural movement had a profound influence on some Black writers. The criticisms of Negritude as a definition of what could be called the "Black being" in philosophical terms are well known. But as Roger Toumson has asserted in his study on Antillean writers, the problems that this movement experienced are the type that every literary school goes through; and that is the relation between theory and practice. There are, according to Toumson, relationships of reciprocal and mutual interdependence between theory and practice (375). Certain black leaders, whether in the Caribbean or Africa, have used Negritude or African Personality to create the illusion of solidarity of the people against colonial or neo-colonial hegemony only to turn round and exploit their own people. When Papa Duvalier came to power in Haiti, he won the confidence of the rural Black population who had hitherto been excluded from active participation in the politics of their country. He did this by using his knowledge of voodoo to create the false impression that he identified with the people. He subsequently created one of the worst dictatorships in the hemisphere. This is a typical example of the divergence of practice from theory that the critics of Negritude have often used against its adepts.[1]

Negritude, as Toumson further demonstrates in his study, fed on the European theories of the time. This, one could say, is the reason why the movement and concept have been criticized for its universalizing theories:

> Le système spéculatif de la Négritude prend forme et consistance au confluent des courants alors dominants de la pensée philosophique et scientifique européenne (Toumson 375).
>
> [The speculative nature of Negritude takes form and becomes consistent at the confluence of dominant trends of European philosophical and scientific thoughts].

It is this tendency to adopt European concepts on the part of Senghor in particular that made him the target of most of the attack against Negritude. For example, when Senghor argued that emotion and feeling are African, and that they are at the heart of Negritude, the Ghanaian philosopher W. E. Abraham retorted by saying: "When Senghor says that the African is non-intellectual—that reason is Greek and feeling is African, that the African knows things with his nose—that's sheer nonsense! What does he think I have above my nose"? Abraham goes on to add that there is nothing particularly African about Senghor's poetry and that he is an "apologist of France speaking to Africa" (qtd. in Dathorne 1974, 308). Senghor sounded like an apologist of France because he used contemporary European theories, as Toumson has pertinently pointed out.

Negritude had a natural appeal to some francophone novelists as we have demonstrated in this book on historical fiction. In his study on black writers, Dathorne has argued that it was no accident that the creative attempt to invent a past (through Negritude as we see in Sainville) was the product of French West Indian colonials. They were people who were in alien land, had created no indigenous culture or new consciousness (Dathorne 1974, 308). It is this trauma of their immediate history being only that of slavery that motivates Glissant, Sainville, and other Caribbean writers to re-write history through historical fiction. The revalorization of the place of the maroon in this history becomes an obsession for them, because they see in this literary enterprise, an opportunity to influence the course of the history of black peoples and how this history is perceived in our contemporary world.

In a way, Negritude discourse ignored the cultural differences that exist between Africans and their descendants in the diaspora. Senghor at least tended to do so. He has been criticized for having developed a philosophical position modeled on European philosophy of universalism. However, the critics of Negritude have often, consciously or unconsciously, ignored the historical context within which this movement was born. During the late colonial period, it was necessary for colonized peoples to present a common front against European colonialist discourse. Irrespective of their countries of origin, colonized writers found themselves in the same predicament. In colonialist discourse, Africans were not regarded as different from their descendants in the diaspora. As Homi Bhabha has pointed out, however, the overall purpose of colonialist discourse was to reinforce the image of otherness in the colonial subject. Negritudist discourse was therefore a reaction to Europe's own concept of the Other—of the colonial subject. This point is crucial for an understanding of the historical novels that have been examined here, for they constitute a challenge to the notions of black people promulgated by Europeans throughout the colonial era. In essence, Negritude writers were reacting against the notions of history that had been manipulated by Europeans in defense of their own illusory sense of superiority. Within this context, Negritude writers were particularly concerned with rehabilitating the image of black people, who had been consistently marginalized in European accounts of history.

What this study has attempted to demonstrate is that African culture in the diaspora was an invention of slavery. Black Caribbeans, as Dathorne argues in her study, made the existing black and white cultures part of their being. The historical characters that Sainville and Glissant created are a product of this contact of cultures in the so-called New World. Dathorne remarks on the group affinity which created a synthesis among slaves and their descendants in the New World. This we witness in the activities of the maroons who become very symbolic characters for the historical novelist of the Caribbean. Dathorne also argues that ethnic groups became a race. "Negroization" takes place when there is a blending of the subject and the object. The disadvantage was that the "Negro" becomes a figment of the imagination because the larger group is almost invented by the dominant white group. The slave captain, Dathorne points out, refused to see African slaves as Yoruba or Ashanti and thus their "negroization" created a myth which became a misinterpretation of history and later a fact (1981, 5-8). It is this process of "negroization" that we witness in the treatment of slaves in the Caribbean novels that have been examined in this study. Sainville's novel in particular gives us a graphic painting of the process by which the slave was reduced to a non-being by public flogging and by copulation between male and female slaves as determined by the slave master's choice. The myth of the Negro develops in these dehumanizing encounters forged by the slave masters. The slave masters in Sainville and Glissant's novels saw their slaves only as blacks who confirmed their own stereotypes about the race.

An appeal to history is the crucial common denominator of all historical novels. In the African-Caribbean historical novel, the history associated with the dominant European discourse is undercut as a means of revalorizing the cultures and historical identities of colonized peoples. There are of course differences between the historical experiences of the Caribbean writers and their African counterparts. Africans were never physically removed from their motherland, whereas Antilleans had to grapple with a culture that had been forged from a variety of influences in a complex hegemonic situation. As committed writers, African and Caribbean historical novelists have similar ideological concerns, despite the fact that colonialist discourse persistently attempted to inculcate Antilleans with a sense of disdain for their African origins. In reality, the culture of these islands has been subjected to systematic creolization and acculturation. Historical novelists from this part of the world have attempted to create an awareness of precisely this fact among their readers.

What our reading of these fictional writings has illustrated can be supported by what White has demonstrated in his study on history and narrativity. In explaining Paul Ricœur's theory of narrative, discourse, and temporality, White argues that far from being an antithetical opposite of historical narrative, fictional narrative is its complement and ally in the universal human effort to reflect on the mystery of temporality. He thinks that narrative fiction permits historians to perceive clearly the metaphysical interest motivating their traditional effort to tell "what really happened" in the past in the form of a story (White 1987, 180). We would add then that the historical novelist uses this tool of narrative fiction to make a rapprochement with the historian in a way that makes fiction a sort of reflection of what really happened. After all, does White not argue that historical narrative itself may resemble fictional narratives?

Our reading of the historical novels from Africa reveals that the writers have been heavily influenced by traditional African oral narrative modes to different degrees. Some of them like Hazoumé, resorted to long ethnological diatribes which created what seemed like digressions that tended to obscure the possibility of a clear intrigue in the novel. As Koné explains, the traditional storyteller did not have to explain things in his narrative because the audience was of the same culture. However, the African novelist was conscious of his European reader whom he knew had certain prejudices about African rituals that are evoked in the novel (1985, 84). Malonga often addresses his reader directly in his novel; as if to justify what might lack verisimilitude in the eyes of his audience (reader).

This influence of oral tradition on the African writer partly explains why there is a lack of psychological development on the part of the characters in these novels. Koné has commented before in his studies that characters in *Doguicimi, Crépuscule des temps anciens* and *La Légende de M'Pfoumou Ma Mazono* are static like those of traditional heroic stories. The events in these novels tend to be episodic sometimes. But is it not also a "pitfall" of transforming what is oral narrative into a written form? We judge the novel by different criteria than we do for the African oral narrative. We need theories that take into cognizance the peculiarity of the African historical novel which has these two sources as the influence on the narrative technique as well as the ideological underpinnings.

The Caribbean writer is also inspired by oral tradition, but as already emphasized earlier, historical circumstances dictate the type of oral tradition that inspires their historical fiction. Vere Knight has commented in an article on the novel as history re-written that:

> Whereas the modern African writer could use heroic tradition, if not as a source of material at least as a "point de repère," the West Indian did not appear to have a tradition that he could use in the same way unless he adopted the same African tradition from which he was effectively separated by years and miles of alienation. Négritude counted among its many tasks that of reviving the heroic tradition which, in the case of the West Indians, really meant creating a heroic tradition. (64)

The maroon as a hero in Glissant's or Sainville's fiction represents in a way this creation of a heroic tradition in the French Antilles.

It is also worthy of note to emphasize that the African writer takes ideological initiative as an individual, an individual writer. The traditional narrator narrated in the name of the collectivity (Koné 1985, 1350). Yet, it should be added that the ideologically committed African writer writes as an individual, adopts an ideology as an individual, but with an urgent sense of responsiblity towards the African collectivity. Hazoumé, Boni and Malonga are inspired by Negritude which is an ideology of collectivity. Kourouma commits himself to expressing the voice of the oppressed people of the continent who are victims of totalitarian political systems.

The African-Caribbean historical novel can best be understood within the context of an Afro-centric approach. As Molefi Asante has argued, people engaged in theorizing about African peoples have often assumed their own "objectivity," which, in reality, is no more than the collective subjectivity of European culture (3). The same tendency can be observed in theories about people of African descent in the diaspora, and it can only be remedied by what Chinweizu has called a "decolonization of the mind." As Homi Bhabha has pointed out, there was not just the discourse of the colonizer; in addition, there has always been the discourse of the colonized—the dominated. This discourse constitutes a counter-discourse that has been recuperated in the African-Caribbean historical novel. In Boni's *Crépuscule des temps anciens*, the Bwa met French hegemonic discourse with a strong resistance against the invasion of their land. In Hazoumé's *Doguicimi*, Toffa and others resist French colonialist discourse with a discourse grounded in their own Dahomeyan (African) concept of the world. Toffa even points out that Europeans do not have the same belief systems and customs as the Dahomeyans. In Glissant's *Le Quatrième Siècle*, Sainville's *Dominique Nègre Esclave*, and Brival's *La Montagne d'Ebène*, the revolted slave becomes a hero in the culture— the symbol of revolt against European hegemonic discourse.

Chinweizu et al have warned in what they termed "an Afro-centric defense of the African novel" against an uncritical usage of canons of the nineteenth-century European novel upon African novels. We need to keep in mind both the tradition of African oral performance and the revolution in the techniques of the European novel (87). This study has demonstrated in many ways how the African historical novel has much in common with the classical European historical novel but also differs from it in many ways partly because of the influence of African oral tradition as well as the evolution of the historical novel itself. We can no longer apply only Euro-centric definitions of the historical novel in our reading of non Euro-American works.

The image of the African as a hero in historical fiction emerged in response to a felt need to re-write history from the perspective of the African. Written history as controlled by Europeans failed to accord black people their rightful place in their own history. African and Caribbean historical novelists sought to correct this anomaly. In the clash of discourses and counter-discourses that constitute the struggle for power in the contemporary world, it represents a powerful assertion of pride in a cultural identity that had previously been ignored and denigrated within the dominant Euro-centric discourse. In our questioning of Euro-centric discourse in an Afro-centric manner, we can use the theory of a Westerner, White, on historiography, to debunk the Western ethnocentric ideas that were the target of attack of Negritudist discourse that inspired some of the fiction that has been considered here. White argues that the possibility of representing the development of certain cultures in a specifically historical discourse is not sufficient grounds for regarding cultures whose development cannot be similarly represented, because of their failure to produce these kinds of records, as continuing to persist in the condition of pre-history. After all, he argues, the human species does not enter history in part. Also, the notion of the entrance into history of any part of the human species could not properly be conceived as a purely intramural operation, a transformation that certain cultures or societies undergo that is merely internal to themselves (White 1987, 55). It is this tendency to see other cultures only through the prism of Western modes of thought that inspired the sort of anti-colonial discourse that historical novelists like Glissant from the French-speaking Caribbean or Boni from Africa have produced.

Yet we need to ask the question as to why historical fiction did not become a popular genre among francophone African writers. This question invites a close examination of the evolution of writing in French in Africa. Negritude in Africa was expressed more in poetry than in fiction. Blair has expressed surprise that historical subjects have not been popular with African writers of fiction. National historical themes have been associated with literature of a strongly national bias, as exemplified by the patriotic aspects of nineteenth-century Romanticism (Blair 83). The theory she posits as to why the historical novel, unlike historical drama, has not been rooted in francophone African literature is very plausible. She suggests that

Conclusion

short tales of various types, including the historical legend, were an intrinsic part of the oral literature. They were part of a shared communal experience. In their desire to preserve a national identity, African writers could easily translate them into dramatic forms. Folktales, myths and fables form an important part of francophone African literature of pre-independence era because, according to her, some writers tried to reproduce the style and structure of griot chanting. The novel, on the other hand, Blair argues, was a foreign genre, studied and imitated originally by African writers in its late nineteenth and twentieth-century manifestations—French realist and naturalist models which had no indigenous associations with the life and cultural traditions of Africa (Blair 74). She also notes that when Africans adopted the novel form in the 1950s, they produced autobiographies and anti-colonial diatribes. We could conjecture that the anti-colonialist fiction produced in francophone Africa fulfilled in a way the function that historical novels would have served; revalorization of African culture in the face of European colonialist and racist discourse, and a re-awakening to instill a nationalist zeal.

However, it needs to be said that historical fiction as a mode of writing seems to be gaining grounds lately. In anglophone Africa, we witness this in the Ghanaian writer Ayi Kwei Armah's *Three Thousand Seasons*, and more recently in francophone black Africa with Ahmadou Kourouma's *Monnè, outrages et défis*, a novel about the history of the Mandingo people of West Africa. The historical constraints which dictated Hazoumé's position vis-à-vis the colonial master no longer exist, but there is a renewed interest (in a different form as manifest in post-colonial theories) in the way Negritudists rejected the imposition of Euro-American concepts of the world on other peoples. Historical fiction might be one of the most effective ways in which African writers can be critical both of this imposition of Euro-centric world-views as well as of dictatorial regimes in the continent. Ahmadou Kourouma's novel is a testimony of what francophone African writers have done with the legacy of historical fiction started by Paul Hazoumé. In a way, we can talk of "keeping the discourse [of Africanness] alive" (Kubayanda), for these writers' testimony is a passionate and powerful engagement with the history of their people. As for the French-speaking Caribbean, historical fiction has always been an important genre. Caribbean writers might react differently to the issue of the importance of Africa in their imaginative works; nonetheless history is a common denominator in their quest for a viable cultural identity. This book has attempted to illustrate how historical fiction as a genre has ideological significance for the African and the Afro-Caribbean writer. The study has underscored the narrative techniques which distinguish it from the classical European historical novel of the nineteenth-century. It has also identified characteristics which are common to the genre. We can no longer define historical fiction only in terms of what prevails in Europe. Oral tradition is one important influence on historical novels coming out of francophone Africa and the Caribbean, and the notion of what constitutes historical fiction must take into consideration all the elements identified in this study as characteristics of the genre.

NOTES

Preface

1. See Dan Izevbaye's review of Molefi Kete Asante's. *Kemet, Afrocentricity and Knowledge.* Trenton: Africa World Press, 1990. In *Research in African Literatures.* Spring, 23, 1 (1992): 203-207. See also Molefi Asante's rebuttal to the review in *Research in African Literatures.* Fall 23, 3 (1992): 152-155.

Introduction

1. Throughout the book, pages of articles or books are referred to in parenthesis. If the author has more than one text in the bibliography, the year of publication of the specific text is indicated too; otherwise only the page number is shown in parenthesis. If the reference does not specify page numbers but only the year of publication, it means the reference is to the whole text and not just a portion of it. For the primary texts which are the object of this study, only the page numbers are shown in parenthesis.

2. "Other" and "Otherness" are terms that define the relationship between the one who exercises power and the one who is the object of that power. In other words it refers to a relationship of dominator and dominated particularly in the colonial situation; a phenomenon in which one attempts to justify subjugation or superiority complex over others.

3. Dependency theory basically argues that some peoples are by nature unable to develop by themselves, so they need to be colonized by a superior race (European colonialists) to "civilize" them on how to progress economically and otherwise. Of course, this entails the exploitation of their resources which they are not capable of exploiting to the maximum. Also see Chancellor William's *The Destruction of Black Civilization.* Chicago: Third World Press, 1974.

4. In the French administrative system in Africa, those Africans (who turned out to be the new elite created through colonialism) who had French diplomas were considered to be more "civilized" because French education meant raising one's status and becoming more acceptable to the French because one was more assimilated.

5. Barbara Bush defines "maroon" as follows: "This term is derived from the Spanish *cimarrónes* meaning 'mountaineers', that is blacks who fled to the mountains from the plantations and established free communities." *Slave Women in Caribbean Society,* footnote (9). Mavis Campbell also writes in *The Maroons of Jamaica 1655-1796*;

"The word 'Maroon'—Marron to the French—has come to be used as a generic term to designate fugitive slaves from plantations in the New World, although the Iberians had their own designations. The etymology is uncertian, but consensus opinion would seem to accept the view that it derives from the Spanish word *cimarrón*, which originally referred to domestic cattle that had escaped to a wild existence. In the course of time, however, the term lost its faunal connotation to embrace runaway slaves almost exclusively. As *cimarrón* would seem to be a peculiarly New World term, first applied in Hispaniola, so also is its derivative, Maroon, when applied to runaway slaves. As far as Jamaica is concerned, the official documents, as well as early works on the island, did not make use of the term until well into the eighteenth century" (1-2).

6. René Depestre defines "béké" as "pieds-noirs ou colons blancs des Antilles" ["pieds-noirs" or white colonists of the Antilles]. *Bonjour et Adieu à la Négritude*; footnote (58). The béké today has inherited the power structure created by the béké of the era of slavery. Joseph Zobel's novel *La Rue Cases-Nègres* (of which there is a film version with English sub-titles) is partly about this phenomenon in the French Caribbean.

7. During a colloquium on his works at the University of Oklahoma in 1989, Glissant himself affirmed that he had been directly influenced by the "quimboiseur" in his own writing.

1
Paul Hazoumé: *Doguicimi*

1. All translations in the book are my own.

2. The argument here is that we need to understand how the author's personal life helps us understand the position he takes vis-à-vis French colonialism in Africa in his fictional creation. It is not always the case with all African writers, but in the case of Hazoumé, it certainly is a crucial factor.

3. This is not meant to suggest that African writers did not know their own languages well, but rather that they were more used to reading and writing in French, the official language used in formal education. It should not be surprising that Negritude was born outside the African continent. The need to redefine oneself and to defend one's culture becomes more crucial when one is removed from one's culture and made to experience some of the racism of the colonials in the metropole. The hypocrisy of the whole enterprise of colonialism

becomes a lived experience for these black students who find themselves in France.

2
Nazi Boni: *Crépuscule des temps anciens*

1. 1960 was the year that most francophone countries of sub-Saharan Africa gained their independence from France. Though *Crépuscule des temps anciens* was published in 1962, that is two years later, the novel must have been in gestation before 1962 when these countries were fighting for independence.

2. I am not suggesting here that Boni's myth was influenced by Christian mythology (there is no evidence to that effect), but simply that coincidently there is a similarity in the way both societies portray and perceive the role of women in their creation myths.

3
Jean Malonga: *La Légende de M'Pfoumou Ma Mazono*

1. It is not to suggest that this sort of criticism against Negritudists is misplaced, but rather that we cannot ignore the general lack of consciousness of gender issues on the part of the Western educated so-called African "évolué" writer of the time.

I take issue with the position taken by some Africanists that motherhood (in Africa) should not be glorified. We certainly do not have the same concept of what motherhood is. It is a perversion to see motherhood in Africa as nothing but the production of children for a husband's family! Camara Laye's poem "A ma mère" in his *L'Enfant Noir* evokes what a mother means to her children and her society. It is not just *merely* a glorification of her womanhood.

I discovered Irène Assiba d'Almeida's book only after I had finished writing this manuscript. She writes on gender relations in the African context. *Francophone African Women Writers: Destroying the Emptiness of Silence.* Gainesville: University Press of Florida, 1994.

4
Ahmadou Kourouma: *Monnè, outrages et défis*

1. I have used the term "francophone African writers" throughout in this book even though I am aware of all the connotations that it carries. I use it only to mean the obvious: writers from former French colonies in Africa who write their fiction in French.

5
Léonard Sainville: *Dominique Nègre Esclave*

1. "Départementalisation" meant that the Caribbean islands under French colonial rule would become overseas territories of France instead of becoming autonomous, independent states.

2. "petite bande": At an early age slave children were expected to work. The term refers to the group of children made to work in their age groups.

3. "Voyeur" means that the slave master had the power of surveillance over the life of his slaves. He watched all their activities daily to ensure that the slaves did not become a threat to his status quo.

4. Dominique has many of the characteristics of the "pícaro" as we know him in Spanish literature (e.g., *El Lazarillo de Tormes*). But unlike the typical pícaro, he does not accept his situation. Whereas the pícaro in Spanish literature accepts his or her status quo, Dominique does not. He is not just satisfied with staying alive and getting by like the typical picaresque hero. The use of the term suggests a modified form of the genre. It is a common trend that European classical genres take on modified forms in other contexts. The Cameroonian writer Ferdinand Oyono also uses a modifed form of the picaresque hero in his novel *Voyage à New York*.

5. The issue of how much the Christian religion was used to subjugate slaves has been well documented. A Papal Bull of Pope Nicolas V legitimated in 1450 the trade of peoples considered "pagan" and "other enemies of Christ" and recommended that they be "subjected to perpetual slavery." It needs to be emphasized though, that the reader should bear in mind Sainville's own Marxist tendencies. This is what Jack Corzani stresses in *La Littérature des Antilles-Guyane Francaises*, Tome VI, 92. Jean-Bertrand Aristide, elected president of Haiti by popular vote, deposed by a military junta in 1991 and re-instated as a result of a United States military intervention in the island in 1994, clashed with the Catholic church over his "liberation theology" which he used in his work as priest and as someone actively involved politically in fighting for the downtrodden. In Martinique and Guadeloupe, the complex inculcated in children at school seeks to portray Christianity as the religion which is supposed to be superior to what comes from their African origins. This is what in my view works against a total freedom—learning an objective truth about other religions. See Jean-Bertrand Aristide.

"The Church in Haiti: Land of Resistance," *Caribbean Quartely* 37, 1 (1991): 108-113.

6. Roger Toumsom writes: "Azaïs fut mêlé au soulèvement en masse au cours duquel, vers 1657, sous l'administration du Gouverneur Houël, des esclaves égorgèrent leurs maîtres blancs. Quelques-uns parvinrent à s'enfuir de la Guadeloupe et à aborder en Martinique où ils se joignirent aux marrons de l'intérieur. Dans *Dominique Nègre Esclave*, Léonard Sainville respecte dans l'ensemble ce canevas historiographique puisque l'action du roman se déroule sur les deux îles à la fois." (340)

[Azaïs was involved in the mass uprising in which, around 1657, under the administration of Governor Houël, some slaves slaughtered their White masters. Some of them succeeded in escaping from Guadeloupe to Martinique where they joined the maroons from the inland. In *Dominique Nègre Esclave*, Léonard Sainville respects on the whole this historiographic framework since the action of the novel takes place on both islands at the same time].

6
Edouard Glissant: *Le Quatrième Siècle*

1. See Piska Degras' beautiful article on the symbolic and metaphorical function of name and naming in the Caribbean. "Name of the Fathers, History of the Name: Odono as Memory." *World Literature Today* 63 (1989): 613-619.

Conclusion

1. This is an interview granted by the Martiniquan Aimé Césaire as well as the Haitians Jean Metellus and René Depestre to Radio France d'Outre Mer à Fort-de-France on January 27th 1986 on the overthrow of the Duvalier regime that year. These are only extracts of what Césaire and Depestre said in the interview which I transcribed:

Césaire: "Duvalier est devenu un très grand spécialiste du vaudou et c'est de tout cela qu'il a fait arme politique redoutable car il est un grand connaisseur du peuple haïtien...Les gens de la campagne ne savaient même pas très bien qui, qui était le président..Ils vivaient dans les montagnes, et la politique c'était le fait des hommes des villes. Mais François Duvalier, parce que connaissant le vaudou, parce que connaissant la paysannerie a lui le premier introduit la paysannerie de la politique haïtienne et hélas, il l'a introduite sur sa pire forme...Il a introduit la forme du "Ton-Ton Macoutisme". Le S.S allemand est devenu un Ton-Ton Macout".

[Duvalier became a very big specialist of voodoo and it is from all this that he created a formidable political weapon, for he is very knowledgeable about the Haitian people. The country-side dwellers did not even know very well who, who was the president. They lived in the mountains and politics was for the city dwellers. But François Duvalier, because he knew voodoo, because he knew the peasants, was the first to introduce the peasantry of Haitian politics and unfortunately he introduced it in its worst form. He introduced the form of "Ton-Ton Macoutism". The German S.S. became a Ton-Ton Macout].

René Depestre: "Il y a d'une part, c'était ce que j'ai appelé personnellement la Négritude totalitaire. Duvalier essayait de constituer une mythologie...ce qu'il appelle lui-même le 'Duvalierisme intégral'... C'est une sorte de retour de la colonisation sous des formes indigènes et Duvalier en quelque sorte aura été le dernier colon d'Haïti, si on peut dire...Duvalier a pu utiliser cet élément puisque dans toute l'histoire d'Haïti, il y a eu une, une lutte de classes, une lutte acharnée d'une part entre un patriciat mulâtre et un patriciat noir. Le pouvoir de Duvalier a été un pouvoir qui a exploité cette composante de la lutte des classes en Haïti; cette composante de, de l'histoire de notre pays pour dominer le peuple haïtien".

[On the one hand there is what I have personally called totalitarian Negritude. Duvalier tried to create a mythology... what he himself calls "total Duvalierism." It is a kind of return of colonization in indigenous forms and Duvalier in a way, will be the last colonist of Haiti, if one can say so. Duvalier has been able to use this element since in all the history of Haiti, there has been a, a class struggle, a bitter struggle on the one hand between a mulatto patriarchy and a black patriarchy. Duvalier's power has been a power that exploited this factor in the class struggle in Haiti; this factor of, of the history of our country to dominate the Haitian people.]

Maryse Condé made an important commentary on Negritude in an article. "Négritude Césairienne, Négritude Senghorienne". *Revue de Littérature Comparée*. 48 (1974): 409-419. She argues succinctly to debunk the concept, giving examples of how Negritudists have ignored the ignominies committed by African kings for example and how they collaborated with Europeans in the slave trade. Yet, we should not ignore the techniques used by Europeans to create African collaborators; using the divide and rule tactics and enticing one ethnic group against another. Read among others, a *European* authority on African slave trade, Basil Davidson. *The African Slave Trade*. Boston, Toronto: Little Brown & Co, 1980 (revised and expanded edition).

Bibliography

Primary Sources

Boni, Nazi. *Crépuscule des temps anciens.* Paris: Présence Africaine, 1962.

Brival, Roland. *La Montagne d'ébène.* Paris: Jean-Claude Lattès, 1984.

Couchoro, Felix. *L'Esclave.* Paris: Editions de La Dépêche Africaine, 1929.

Glissant, Edouard. *Le Quatrième Siècle.* Paris: Seuil, 1964.

Hazoumé, Paul. *Doguicimi.* 1938. Paris: Maisonneuve et Larose, 1978.

Ikellé-Matiba, Jean. *Cette Afrique-là!* Paris: Présence Africaine, 1963.

Kourouma, Ahmadou. *Monnè, outrages et défis.* Paris: Seuil, 1990.

Malonga, Jean. *La Légende de M'Pfoumou Ma Mazono.* Paris: Présence Africaine, 1954.

Sainville, Léonard. *Dominique Nègre Esclave.* 1951. Paris: Présence Africaine, 1978.

Secondary Sources

Achebe, Chinua. *Things Fall Apart.* New York: Astor-Honor, 1959.

Achiriga, Jingiri. *La révolte des romanciers noirs.* Sherbrooke: Naaman, 1973.

Adande, Alexandre Sènou. "Paul Hazoumé: Ecrivain et chercheur." *Présence Africaine* 114 (1980): 197-203.

Adotevi, Stanislas. *Négritude et négrologues.* Paris: Union Générale d'Editions, 1972.

Asante, Molefi Kete. *The Afrocentric Idea.* Philadelphia: Temple University Press, 1987.

Aschcroft Bill, Griffiths Gareth, Tiffin Helen. *The Empire Writes Back: Theory and Practice in Post-Colonial Literatures:* London, New York: Routledge, 1989.

Atangana, Nicolas. "La femme africaine dans la société." *Présence Africaine* 13 (1957): 136-138.

Balandier, Georges. *Ambiguous Africa: Cultures in Collision.* New York: Pantheon Books, 1966.

Barthes, Roland, et al. *Littérature et réalité.* Paris: Seuil, 1982.

___. *Mythologies.* Trans. Annette Lavers. New York: Hill & Wang: 1972.

Bhabha, Homi. "The Other Question: Difference, Discrimination and the Discourse of Colonisation" in Francis Baker, ed. *Literature, Politics and Theory: Papers from the Essex Conference 1976-1984.* London, New York: Methuen, 1986. 148-172.

Bjornson, Richard. *The African Quest for Freedom and Identity: Cameroonian Writing and the National Experience.* Bloomington, Indianapolis: Indiana University Press, 1991.

___. "Introduction." Paul Hazoumé. *Doguicimi: The First Dahomean Novel (1937).* Trans. Richard Bjornson. Washington, D.C: Three Continents Press, 1990. xvii-xliii.

Blair, S. Dorothy. *African Literature in French: A History of Creative Writing in French from West and Equatorial Africa.* Cambridge: Cambridge University Press, 1976.

Blerald, Alain. *Négritude et politique aux Antilles.* Paris: Editions Caribéennes, 1981.

Boahen, Adu. *African perspectives on colonialism.* Baltimore: Johns Hopkins University Press, 1987.

Boni, Nazi. *Histoire synthétique de l'Afrique résistante: Les réactions des peuples africains face aux influences extérieures.* Paris: Présence Africaine, 1971.

Bush, Barbara. *Slave Women in Caribbean Society: 1650-1838.* Kingston: Heineman, 1990.

Cabral, Amilcar. *Return to source: Selected speeches of Amilcar Cabral.* ed. Africa Information Service. New York: Monthly Review Press, 1973.

Cailler, Bernadette. *Conquérant de la nuit nue: Edouard Glissant et l'H(h)istoire antillaise.* Tubingen: Narr, 1988.

Campbell, Mavis C. *The Maroons of Jamaica: 1655-1796.* Trenton: Africa World Press, 1990.

Case, Frederick Ivor. "Edouard Glissant and the Poetics of Cultural Marginalization." *World Literature Today* 63 (1989): 593-598.

___. *The Crisis of Identity: Studies in the Guadeloupean and Martiniquan Novel.* Sherbrooke: Naaman, 1985.

Caudwell, Christopher. *Studies and Further Studies in a Dying Culture.* New York, London: Monthly Review Press, 1972.

Clark, Beatrice Smith. "IME Revisited: Lectures by Edouard Glissant on Socio-Cultural Realities in the Francophone Antilles." *World Literature Today* 63 (1989): 599-605.

Césaire, Aimé. *Cahier d'un retour au pays natal.* 1947. Paris: Présence Africaine, 1983.

___. *Discours sur le colonialisme.* 4è édition. Paris: Présence Africaine, 1955.

Chévrier, Jacques. *Littérature Nègre: Afrique, Antilles, Madagascar.* Paris: Collin, 1974.

Chréacháin, Fírinne ní. "Precolonial Africa, or: Of Men and Gods According to Kourouma: A Critique of the Négritude Position." *Contemporary French Civilization.* 14.2 (1990): 227-244.

Condé, Maryse. *Civilisation du Bossale: Réflexions sur la littérature orale de la Guadeloupe et de la Martinique.* Paris: L'Harmattan, 1978.

Corzani, Jack. *La Littérature des Antilles-Guyane Françaises.* Fort-de-France: Désormeaux, 1980.

___. "Guadeloupe et Martinique: La Difficile voie de la Négritude et de l'Antillanité." *Présence Africaine* 76 (1970): 16-42.

___. *Littérature antillaise (prose)*. vol. 2. of *Encyclopédie antillaise*. Fort-de-France: Desormeaux, 1971.

Corzani, Jack, Ricard, Alain. eds. *Littératures africaines et enseignement*. Actes du Colloque International de l'Université de Bordeaux III, 15-17 March 1984. Bordeaux: Presse Universitare de Bordeaux, 1985.

Curtin, Philip D. ed. *Africa and the West: Intellectual Responses to European Culture*. Madison: University of Wisconsin Press, 1972.

Dathorne, O. R. *The Black Mind: A History of African Literature*. Minneapolis: University of Minnesota Press, 1974.

Davidson, Basil. *Les Africains: Introduction à l'histoire d'une culture*. Paris: Seuil, 1971.

Decraene, Philippe. "Paul Hazoumé: Doyen des écrivains dahoméens." *L'Afrique Littéraire et Artistique* 23 (1972): 11-12.

Degras, Priska. "Name of the Fathers, History of the Name: Odono as Memory." *World Literature Today* 63 (1989): 613-619.

Delafosse, Maurice. *Les Noirs de l'Afrique*. Paris: Payot, 1941.

Demaison, André. *La vie des Noirs d'Afrique*. Paris: Bourrelier et Cie, 1936.

Depestre, René. *Bonjour et adieu à la Négritude*. Paris: Laffont, 1980.

___. "Les Métamorphoses de la Négritude en Amérique". *Présence Africaine* 75 (1970): 19-33.

Diop, Cheikh Anta. *L'Unité Culturelle de l'Afrique Noire*. Paris: Présence Africaine, 1959.

Djivo, Joseph Adrien. *Guézo: La rénovation du Dahomey*. Dakar, Abidjan: N.E.A., 1977.

Du Bois, William E. Burghardt. *The Souls of Black Folk: Essays and Sketches*. Chicago: A.C. McClurg & Co., 1903.

Duchet, Claude. "Discours social et texte italique dans Madame Bovary." In Michael Issacharoff. ed. *Langages de Flaubert*. Actes du Colloque de London-Canada. Paris: Minard, 1976. 143-163.

Erickson, John. *Nommo: African Fiction in French South of the Sahara.* York, S.C: French Literature Publications Co., 1979.

Fabre, Michel. *Black American Writers in France, 1840-1980: From Harlem to Paris.* Urbana, Chicago: University of Illinois Press, 1991.

Fanoudh-Siefer, Léon. *Le mythe du nègre et de l'Afrique noire dans la littérature française: De 1800 à la 2ème Guerre Mondiale.* Paris: Librairie C. Klincksieck, 1968.

Fanon, Frantz. *Peau Noire, Masques Blancs.* Paris: Seuil, 1952.

___. *Les Damnés de la terre.* Paris: Maspero, 1974.

Foucault, Michel. *Surveiller et punir: Naissance de la prison.* Paris: Gallimard, 1975.

Frobenius, Léo. *Histoire de la civilisation africaine.* Paris: Gallimard, 1952.

Genette, Gérard. *Narrative Discourse: An Essay in Method.* Ithaca: Cornell University Press, 1980.

Geno, Thomas, Julow, Roy, et al. *Littératures ultramarines de langue française: Génèse et jeunesse.* Actes du Colloque de l'Université du Vermont. Sherbrooke: Naaman, 1974.

Glissant, Edouard. *Le Discours Antillais.* Paris: Seuil, 1981.

___. *L'Intention poétique.* Paris: Seuil, 1969.

___. "La Poétique d'Edouard Glissant." *Antilla* 416 (1991): 28-32.

Goldmann, Lucien. *Pour une sociologie du roman.* Paris: Gallimard, 1964.

Guérin, Daniel. *Les Antilles décolonisées.* Paris: Présence Africaine, 1956.

Haley, Alex. *Roots: The Saga of an American Family.* Garden City: Doubleday, 1976.

Hamon, Philippe. "Qu'est-ce qu'une description?" *Poétique* 12 (1972): 465-485.

___. "Un discours contraint." *Poétique* 16 (1973): 411-445.

Hampaté Ba, Amadou. *Aspects de la civilisation africaine.* Paris: Présence Africaine, 1972.

Hardy, Georges. *Histoire sociale de la civilisation française.* Paris: Larose, 1953.

Herskovits, Melville J. *L'Héritage du Noir: Mythe et réalité.* Paris: Présence Africaine, 1958.

Hountondji, Paulin. *African Philosophy: Myth and Reality.* Bloomington: Indiana University Press, 1983.

Huannou, Adrien, Robert Mane. eds. *"Doguicimi" de Paul Hazoumé.* Paris: L'Harmattan, 1987.

Huannou, Adrien. "Hommage à un grand écrivain: Paul Hazoumé." *Présence Africaine.* 114 (1980): 204-208.

___. "Paul Hazoumé, romancier." *Présence Africaine.* 105-106 (1978): 203-215.

___. "Réflexion sur l'œuvre littéraire de Paul Hazoumé." *Culture Française.* (1982): 37-43.

Hulme, Peter. *Colonial Encounters: Europe and the Native Caribbean: 1492-1797.* London, New York: Methuen, 1986.

Irele, Abiola. *The African experience in literature and ideology.* London: Heinemann, 1981.

___. "Narrative, History, and the African Imagination". *Narrative.* 1.2 (1993): 156-172.

Jahn, Janheinz. *Muntu l'homme noir et la culture néo-africaine.* Paris: Seuil, 1961.

JanMohammed, Abdul R. "The Economy of Manichean Allegory: The Function of Racial Difference in Colonialist Literature." *Critical Inquiry.* 12.1 (1985): 59-87.

___. *Manichean Aesthetics: The Politics of Literature in Colonial Africa*. Amherst: University of Massachusetts Press, 1983.

Jameson, Frederic. *The Political Unconscious: Narrative as Socially Symbolic Act*. Ithaca: Cornell University Press, 1981.

Jefferson, Ann, David Robey. *Modern Literary Theory: A Comparative Introduction*. Ottawa: Barnes & Noble, 1974.

Joppa, Francis A. *L'Engagement des écrivains africains noirs de langue française: Du Témoignage au dépassement*. Sherbrooke: Naaman, 1982.

Julien, Eileen. *African Novels and the Question of Orality*. Bloomington, Indianapolis: Indiana University Press, 1992.

July, Robert W. *An African Voice: The Role of the Humanities in African Independence*. Durham: Duke University Press, 1987.

Kemedjio, Cilas. "Rape of Bodies, Rape of Souls: From the Surgeon to the Psychiatrist, From Slave Trade to the Slavery of Comfort in the Work of Edouard Glissant." *Research in African Literatures*. 25.2 (1994): 51-79.

Kenyatta, Jomo. *Au pied du mont Kenya*. Paris: Maspero, 1973.

Kesteloot, Lylian. *Les Écrivains noirs de langue française: Naissance d'une littérature*. Université Libre de Bruxelles: Institut de Sociologie, 1963.

Kimoni, Ijay. *Destin de la littérature négro-africaine*. Sherbrooke: Naaman, 1975.

Ki-Zerbo, Joseph. *Histoire de l'Afrique Noire: D'Hier à demain*. Paris: Hatier, 1972.

Knight, W. Vere. "Edouard Glissant: The Novel as History Rewritten." *Black Images* 3.1 (1974): 64-79.

Kubayanda, Josaphat B. "On Colonial/Imperial Discourse and Contemporary Critical Theory." University of Maryland 1992 Lecture Series. Working Paper no. 10.

___. "The Phenomenon of Recognition: The African Ideal in the Caribbean Text." *Journal of Caribbean Studies*. 8.3 (1991-1992): 175-185.

___. *The Poet's Africa: Africanness in the Poetry of Nicolás Guillén and Aimé Césaire*. New York: Greenwood Press, 1990.

Leiris, Michel. *Contacts de civilisations en Martinique et en Guadeloupe*. Paris: UNESCO, 1955.

Lirus, Julie. *Identité Antillaise*. Paris, Editions Caribéennes, 1979.

Lukács, Georg. *The Historical Novel*. London: Merlin Press, 1962.

Mbiti, John. "Man in African Religion". In Mowoe, Isaac and Richard Bjornson. eds. *Africa and the West: The Legacies of Empire*. New York, Westport: Greenwood, 1986. 55-67.

Melone, Thomas. *De la Négritude dans la littérature négro-africaine*. Paris: Présence Africaine, 1962.

Memmi, Albert. *Portrait du colonisé précédé du portrait du colonisateur*. Paris: Payot, 1973.

Menil, René. *Tracées: Identité, Négritude, Esthétique aux Antilles*. Paris: Robert Laffont, 1981.

Midiohouan, Guy Ossito. *L'idéologie dans la littérature négro-africaine d'expression française*. Paris: L'Harmattan, 1986.

Miller, Christopher. *Theories of Africans: Francophone literature and Anthropology in Africa*. Chicago: University of Chicago Press, 1990.

Ndengue, J.M. Abanda. *De la Négritude au Négrisme*. Yaoundé: CLE, 1970.

N'Diaye, Jean-Piere. *Elites Africaines et culture occidentale: Assimilation ou résistance*. Paris: Présence Africaine, 1969.

Ngugi, Wa Thiong'o. *Decolonizing the African Mind: The Politics of Language in African Literature*. Nairobi, London: Heinemann, 1987.

___. *Homecoming: Essays on African and Caribbean Literature, Culture and Politics*. London: Heinemann, 1978.

Nkashama, P. Ngandu. *La Littérature africaine écrite en langue française*: Issy-les-Moulineaux. St. Paul, 1979.

Nkrumah, Kwame. *Consciencism: Philosophy and Ideology for Decolonization.* London: Panaf Books, 1970.

Nnaemeka, Obioma. "Feminism, Rebellious Women and Cultural Boundaries: Reading Flora Nwapa and Her Compatriots." *Research in African Literatures* 26:2 (1995): 80-113.

Ntonfo, André. *L'Homme et l'identité dans le roman des Antilles et Guyanne Françaises.* Sherbrooke: Naaman, 1982.

Ormerod, Beverly. *An Introduction to the French Caribbean Novel.* London, Portsmouth: Heinemann, 1985.

Ouologuem, Yambo. *Le devoir de violence.* Paris: Seuil, 1968.

Pageard, Robert. *Littérature négro-africaine.* Paris: Le Livre Africain, 1966.

Pluchon, Pierre. *Histoire des Antilles et de la Guyanne: Martinique, Guadeloupe, Haïti, Guyanne.* Toulouse: Payot, 1982.

Racine, Daniel. "The Antilleanity of Edouard Glissant." *World Literature Today* 63 (1989): 620-625.

Radford, Daniel. *Edouard Glissant.* Paris: Seghers, 1982.

Roget, Wilbert J. "Land and Myth in the Writings of Edouard Glissant." *World Literature Today* 63 (1989): 626-631.

Ricard, Alain. *Félix Couchoro 1900-1968: Naissance du roman africain.* Paris: Présence Africaine, 1988.

Ricœur, Paul. *Histoire et Vérité.* Paris: Seuil, 1955.

Said, Edward. *Orientalism.* New York: Pantheon Books, 1978.

Sainville, Léonard. "La condition des Noirs dans les Antilles Françaises de 1800 à 1850." Thèse de Doctorat d'État. Université de Paris-Sorbonne, 1970.

Salami, Sabit. "L'Esclave: Roman de Félix Couchoro." In Ambroise Kom. ed. *Dictionnaire des Oeuvres Littéraires Négro-Africaines de Langue Française: Des Origines à 1978.* Sherbrooke: Naaman, 225-226.

Sartre, Jean-Paul. *Situations III*. Paris: Gallimard, 1949.

Senghor, L. Sedar. *Liberté 3: Négritude et Civilisation de l'Universel*. Paris: Seuil, 1977.

Sheppard, Tresidder. *The Art and Practice of Historical Fiction*. London: Humphrey Toulmin, 1930.

Silenieks, Juris. "Introduction." In Edouard Glissant. *Monsieur Toussaint*. Trans. Joseph Foster and Barbara Franklin. Washington D.C.: Three Continents Press, 1981. 5-15.

Soyinka, Wole. *Myth, Literature and the African World*. Cambridge: Cambridge University Press, 1976.

Suret-Canale, Jean. "Preface". In Nazi Boni. *Histoire synthétique de l'Afrique résistante: Les réactions des peuples africains face aux influences extérieures*. Paris: Présence Africaine, 1971. 1-13.

Todorov, Tzvetan. *La Conquête de l'Amérique: La question de l'Autre*. Paris: Seuil, 1982.

___. *Nous et les autres: la réflexion française sur la diversité humaine*. Paris: Seuil, 1989.

Toumson, Roger. *La Transgression des Couleurs: Littérature et langage des Antilles (XVIIIe, XIXe, XXe siècles)*. Paris: Editions Caribéennes, 1989.

Towa, Marcien. *Essai sur la problématique philosophique dans l'Afrique actuelle*. Yaoundé: CLE, 1971.

___. *Léopold Sédar Senghor: Négritude ou servitude?* Yaoundé: CLE, 1971.

Veynes, Paul. *Comment on écrit l'Histoire*. Paris: Seuil, 1971.

Veynes, Paul. "Histoire". In *Encyclopoedia Universalis France*. 1970, 8: 423-424.

Wauthier, Claude. *L'Afrique des Africains: Inventaire de la Négritude*. Paris: Seuil, 1964.

Webb, Barbara J. *Myth and History in Caribbean Fiction: Alejo Carpentier, Wilson Harris, and Edouard Glissant.* Amherst: The University of Massachusetts Press, 1992.

White, Hayden. *The Content of the Form: Narrative Discourse and Historical Representation.* Baltimore: Johns Hopkins University Press, 1987.

___. *Metahistory: The Historical Imagination in Nineteenth-Century Europe.* Baltimore: Johns Hopkins University Press, 1973.

___. *Tropics of Discourse: Essays in Cultural Criticism.* Baltimore: Johns Hopkins University Press, 1978.

Williams, Chancellor. *The Destruction of Black Civilization.* Chicago: Third World Press, 1974.

Wynter, Sylvia. "Beyond the World of Man: Glissant and the New Discourse of the Antilles." *World Literature Today* 63 (1989): 637-647.

INDEX

Abraham, W.E., 184
Achebe, Chinua, 27, 84
Adande, Alexandre, 34, 36
Africans the, 92
African Personality, 183
Afro-American, 6
Afro-Antillean, 7, 124
Afro-Caribbean, xi, 6, 26
Afro-centric, xi, xii, 187, 188
Amerindian, 26
anciens combattants, 60, 61
Antillano-Guyanese, 124
Antilleanité, 16, 26
Antilleanity, 27, 165
Armah, Ayi Kwei, 189
Aristide, Jean-Bertrand, 194
Asante, Molefi Kete, 187, 191
Aschcroft, Bill, 167
Atangana, Nicholas, 71
Azikewe, Nnamdi, 34

Bachelard, Gaston, 10
Balzac, Honoré de, 28
Banjo, 6
Baker, Francis, 4
Blandier, George, 10
Barthes, Roland, 14, 15
béké, 23, 126, 128-131, 133, 134, 137, 138, 140-142, 144, 150, 151, 153, 155, 157, 160, 165, 177-180, 183, 192
Bennet, Arnold, 1
Bhabha, Homi, 23, 38, 63, 64, 184, 187
Bjornson, Richard, 30, 33, 45
Blair, Dorothy, 4, 52, 96, 98, 188, 189
Boahen, Adu, 21, 22
Boni, Nazi, 16, 19-23, 28, 30, 57, 59, 60, 62-66, 68-72, 74-77, 80, 82, 84, 101, 104, 105, 108, 144, 145, 165, 167-169, 171-174, 179, 187, 188, 193

bon sauvage, 151
Bréton, André, 7, 10
Briault, Maurice Réverend, 14
Brival, Roland, 29, 30, 131, 175-178, 180-183
Burkina Faso, 58, 80
Bush, Barbara, 140, 191

Cabral, Amilcar, 77
Campbell, Mavis, 191
Cailler, Bernadette, 151
Camus, Albert, 10, 53
Case, Frédéric, 159, 162
Césaire, Aimé, xi, 6, 7, 10, 20, 24, 33, 34, 107, 109, 123, 126, 127, 140, 153, 195
Chevrier, Jacques, 55
Chréacháin, Fírinne nf, 101
Chinweizu, 187
cimarrón, 191, 192
code noir, 125
Condé, Maryse, 140, 141, 196
Corzani, Jack, 166, 167, 194
Côte de l'Or
Couchoro, Felix, 30, 170-172
Cuba, 7
cultural métissage (métissage culturel), 144, 149, 181

Damas, Léon-Gotran, 6, 7, 33
Dark Continent, 9, 19
Dathorne. O. R., 7, 184, 185
Davidson, Basil, 197
Decraene, Philipe, 34
de Graft Johnson, Charles, 34
Degras, Priska, 195
Delafosse, Maurice, 9, 14
de Lafayette, Madame, 17
Démaison, André, 61
Depestre, René, 136, 140, 156, 157, 192, 195, 196
départementalisation, 194
Département d'Outre-Mer, 124

de Tocqueville, Alexis, 134, 135
Diagne, Blaise, 5
Diallo, Bakary, 35
Diop, Alioune, 10
Diop, Anta, 21, 34
Dubois, W.E.B., 5
Duchet, Claude, 164
Duvalier, François, 183, 195, 196
Djivo, Joseph, 43

Erickson, John, 41, 52
L'Etudiant Noir, 7
évolué, 16, 18, 19, 36, 53, 54, 172, 193

Fabre, Michel, 6
Fanon, Frantz, xi, 25, 55, 107, 142
Fanoudh-Siefer, Léon, 9-11, 13-15, 177, 178
Flaubert, Gustave, 4, 118
Foucault, Michel, 57, 125, 126, 130
French Caribbean, 24, 130, 143, 189, 192
French West Africa, 184
Frobenius, Leo, 9
Front Populaire, 8

Glissant, Edouard, xi, 12, 16, 24-28, 30, 123, 124, 135, 136, 147, 149-162, 164-169, 174, 175, 179, 181-183, 185, 187, 188, 192
Gobineau, Joseph Arthur, 134
Gold Coast, 34
Goldmann, Lucien, 30, 31
Griaule, Marcel, 10
griot, 104-106, 114
Guérin, Daniel, 152

Haiti, 7, 140, 142, 183, 194, 196
Harley, Alex, 31

Hardy, George, 36, 37
Harlem Renaissance (American Negro-Renaissance) 5-7
Hampaté, Bâ Amadou, 70
Hayford, Caseley, 34
Hazoumé, Paul, xi, 10, 16-19, 22, 28, 33-35, 37-55, 59, 61, 62, 64, 68-72, 77, 95, 98, 101, 103, 144, 145, 165, 167-172, 186, 187, 189, 192
Hugo, Victor, 4
Hughes, Langston, 5
Huannou, Adrien, 33, 46, 50, 171
Hulme, Peter, 19, 20, 24

Ikellé-Matiba, Jean, 30, 173-175
indigénisme, 7
Irele, Abiola, 121
Izevbaye, Dan, 191

Jamaica, 192
JanMohammed, Abdul, 38
Jameson, Frederic, 26
Jones, Edward, 7
Julien, Eileen, 122
July, Robert, 33

Kemedjio, Cilas, 151
Kenyatta, Jomo, 5
Kesteloot, Lylian, 6, 10, 33, 55
Ki-Zerbo, Joseph, 60
Koné, Ahmadou, 97, 98, 104, 120, 121, 186, 187
Kourouma, Ahmadou, 16, 23, 28, 31, 55, 101-105, 107-118, 120-122, 167-169, 173, 174, 187, 189, 194
Knight, Vere, 186
Kubayanda Joseph, 166, 189

La Bruyère, Jean de, 134
La Fontaine, Jean de, 134
Laye, Camara, 193

Légitime Défense, 7
Leiris, Michel, 10
Lévy-Bruhl, Lucien, 9, 12-14
liberation theology, 194
Lugard, Lord, 10, 11
Lukács, George, 3, 4, 27, 169

magical realism (marvelous realism), 65, 86, 88
Malidoma, Somé Patrice, 189
malinké/mandingo, 101-105, 109, 115-117, 189
Malonga, Jean, 16, 23, 28, 30, 79-82, 84, 86, 87, 90-92, 95-98, 101, 168, 186, 187, 193
Manessy, George, 20, 21
maroon (marron), 23, 24, 26, 124, 125, 130, 143, 145, 147, 149, 150, 153, 154, 157, 159, 160, 169, 175, 187, 191, 192, 195
marxist (marxism), 124, 139, 143, 194
Mazrui, Ali, 92
Mbiti, Jean, 67, 68
McKay, Claude, 5, 6
Metellus, Jean, 195
Memmi, Albert, xi, 35, 106
Menil, René, 147
Midiohouan, Guy Ossito, 35, 36
Miller, Christopher, 34, 35, 54
mise-en-abyme, 30, 174
mission civilisatrice, 55, 69
Monod, Théodore, 10
Montesquieu, Charles de Secondat, 25

nègre bossale, 140
Negritude (Negritudist), xi, xii, 1, 4-9, 11, 12, 14, 16, 17, 22, 27, 28, 30, 33-35, 46, 52-54, 57, 60, 64, 67, 69-71, 77, 79, 80, 93, 101, 102, 122, 123, 131, 142, 149, 161, 166, 170, 171, 175, 183, 185, 187-189, 192, 193, 196
negroization, 185
New World, 141, 185, 192
Nield, Jonathan, 1, 168
Nkrumah, Kwame, 5
Noirs de l'Afrique les, 9
Ntonfo, André, 150, 151, 157
Nyobe, Ruben Um, 174

Ogundipe-Leslie, Molara, 17
Okpewo, Isidore, 79
Ormerod, Beverly, 135
Oyono, Ferdinand, 194
Ouologuem, Yambo, 121

Pascal, Blaise, 134
picaresque (pícaro), 23, 130, 138, 194
pied-noir, 192
Présence Africaine, 10, 34
Price-Mars, Dr., 34
Puerto Rico, 7

quimboiseur, 152, 155, 158, 192

Rabelais, François de, 14
Rabemananjara, Jacques, 34
Racine, Daniel, 165
realism, 182
Renan, Ernest, 134
Revue du Monde Noir, 6
Ricœur, Paul, 186
Roget, Wilbert, 161
Romanticism, 188

Said, Edward, xi, 20, 23, 35, 38
Sainville, Léonard, xi, 6, 16, 23, 24, 26, 28-30, 123-125, 127, 129-131, 133-135, 137-139, 141-146, 149, 152-155, 158, 165-169, 174-182, 184, 185, 187, 194, 195

Salami, Sabit, 170
Sartre, Jean-Paul, 10, 27, 53, 61, 117, 123
Schœlcher, Victor, 8, 24, 26, 27, 169
Senghor, Léopold, xi, 6, 7, 9, 10, 15, 16, 25, 33, 34, 93, 172, 174, 184, 196
Scott Walter, 1-4, 28, 168, 169
Sheppard, Alfred, 1-3, 167
Silenieks, Juris, 26
Souls of Black Folk the, 5
Strauss, Claude-Levi, 53
style indirect libre, 162, 164
Suret-Canale, J, 58

Taine, Hippolyte, 134
tirailleur, 107
Todorov, Tzvetan, 134, 135
ton-ton macout, 196
Toumson, Roger, 7, 8, 27, 145, 147, 183, 184, 195

Upper Volta, 19, 58

Veynes, Paul, 2, 3, 101, 120, 144, 169
Vigny, Alfred de, 4, 168
voodo, 140, 196
Voltaire, François Marie Arouet, 25
voyeur, 136, 194

Wa Thiongo, Ngugi, 77
Wauthier, Claude, 34
Webb, Barbara, 26, 152
West Indies, 161
White, Hayden, 53-55, 121, 186, 188
William, Chancellor, 191
Wright, Richard, 10, 34

Zabus, Chantal, 73
Zobel, Joseph, 192

FRANCOPHONE CULTURES & LITERATURES

General Editors: Michael G. Paulson & Tamara Alvarez-Detrell

This series will include studies about the literature, culture, and civilization of all French-speaking countries except France, i.e. studies on the Francophone areas in Africa, the French-speaking islands in the Caribbean, as well as studies that deal with the French aspects in Canada. Cross-cultural studies between these geographic areas are also encouraged. The book-length manuscripts may be written in either English or French.

Authors wishing to have works considered for this series should send a one page synopsis to:

>Dr. Michael G. Paulson
>Department of Foreign Languages
>Kutztown University
>Kutztown, PA 19530